THE POLITICAL PSYCHOLO(
OF WOMEN IN U.S. POLITIC

This book is a fascinating exploration of cutting edge research on the many ways that gender influences political participation and preferences—it's a must read for anyone with an interest in the intersection of gender and politics.

Linda J. Skitka, Social and Political Psychologist,
University of Illinois at Chicago, USA

The Political Psychology of Women in U.S. Politics is a comprehensive resource for students, researchers, and practitioners interested in women and politics. Highly original and drawing from the best available research in psychology and political science, this book is designed to summarize and extend interdisciplinary research that addresses how and why men and women differ as citizens, as political candidates, and as officeholders. The chapters in this volume are focused on differences in the political behavior and perceptions of men and women, yet the chapters also speak to broader topics within American politics—including political socialization, opinion formation, candidate emergence, and voting behavior. Broadly, this volume addresses the causes and consequences of women's under-representation in American government.

This book is the ideal resource for students and researchers of all levels interested in understanding the unique political experiences of diverse women, and the importance of rectifying the problem of gender disparities in American politics.

Angela L. Bos is Associate Professor of Political Science at the College of Wooster. Her teaching and research in U.S. politics is focused in the areas of women and politics, political psychology, media and politics, political parties and elections, and research methods.

Monica C. Schneider is Associate Professor of Political Science at Miami University in Oxford, Ohio. She studies gender and racial stereotypes in American politics, and the gender gap in ambition. She is also passionate about the advancement of women in the academy and improving outcomes for undergraduates.

Routledge Studies in Political Psychology—4
Edited by Howard Lavine
University of Minnesota

Advisory Board: Ted Brader, University of Michigan; Eugene Borgida, University of Minnesota; Marc Ross, Bryn Mawr College and Linda Skitka, University of Illinois, Chicago

Routledge Studies in Political Psychology was developed to publish books representing the widest range of theoretical, methodological and epistemological approaches in political psychology. The series is intended to expand awareness of the creative application of psychological theory within the domain of politics and foster deeper appreciation of the psychological roots of political behavior.

THE POLITICAL PSYCHOLOGY OF WOMEN IN U.S. POLITICS

*Edited by Angela L. Bos
and Monica C. Schneider*

Routledge
Taylor & Francis Group

NEW YORK AND LONDON

First published 2017
by Routledge
711 Third Avenue, New York, NY 10017

and by Routledge
2 Park Square, Milton Park, Abingdon, Oxon, OX14 4RN

Routledge is an imprint of the Taylor & Francis Group, an informa business

© 2017 Taylor & Francis

The right of Angela L. Bos and Monica C. Schneider to be identified as
the authors of the editorial material, and of the authors for their individual
chapters, has been asserted in accordance with sections 77 and 78 of the
Copyright, Designs and Patents Act 1988.

Library of Congress Cataloging in Publication Data
A catalog record for this book has been requested

ISBN: 978-1-138-68323-5 (hbk)
ISBN: 978-1-138-68324-2 (pbk)
ISBN: 978–1-315-54468-7 (ebk)

Typeset in Bembo
by Apex CoVantage, LLC

CONTENTS

Gender Gaps in Public Opinion, Public Policy, and Political Action

PART II
Women as Candidates

Gender and Political Ambition

Gender Stereotypes and Group Identity

PART III
Women in Political Leadership

FIGURES

We began our own collaboration when we started graduate school in 2001, working together on many projects ranging from the personal to the intellectual. Our most treasured projects, however, are our four children, Liam, Harrison, Naomi, and Mitchell. We dedicate this book to their futures, which we hope will be more hospitable to women's political engagement.

CONTRIBUTORS

Editors

Angela L. Bos is Associate Professor and Chair of Political Science at the College of Wooster. Her teaching and research in U.S. politics is focused in the areas of women and politics, political psychology, media and politics, political parties and elections, and research methods. Her articles have been published in journals such as *Political Psychology, Political Communication, PS: Political Science and Politics, Politics and Gender,* and the *Journal of Applied Social Psychology.* Together with Monica Schneider, she has organized two mentoring conferences entitled *New Research on Gender and Political Psychology,* the first of which received funding from the NSF.

Monica C. Schneider is an Associate Professor of Political Science at Miami University in Oxford, Ohio. She studies gender and racial stereotypes in American politics, and the gender gap in ambition. She is also passionate about the advancement of women in the academy and improving outcomes for undergraduates. Her research has been published in many journals, including *Political Psychology, American Politics Research, Journal of Women, Politics, and Policy, Journal of Politics, Groups, and Identities,* and *Psychology of Women Quarterly.*

Contributors

Nichole M. Bauer is an Assistant Professor of Political Science at the University of Alabama. Her research investigates how feminine stereotypes affect evaluations of female politicians. Her research is published in *Political Behavior, Political Psychology,* and *Politics, Groups, and Identities* among other outlets.

Christina E. Bejarano is Associate Professor of Political Science at the University of Kansas. Her research examines the conditions under which racial/ethnic minorities and women successfully compete for U.S. electoral office, which is reflected in her book *The Latina Advantage: Gender, Race, and Political Success* (from University of Texas Press). She also studies how racial/ethnic minorities and women can influence the current electoral environment, which is reflected in her book *The Latino Gender Gap in U.S. Politics* (Routledge).

Britney G Brinkman is Associate Professor of Counseling Psychology at Chatham University. She is the author of *Detection and Prevention of Identity-Based Bullying: Social Justice Perspectives* (Routledge) and has published research about media literacy, prejudice reduction, and doing social justice work with girls.

Heather E. Bullock is Professor of Psychology and Director of the Blum Center for Poverty, Social Enterprise, and Participatory Governance at the University of California, Santa Cruz. Her research focuses on women's experiences of poverty, intersections of classism, sexism, and racism, and attitudes toward anti-poverty policies. She is author of *Women and Poverty: Psychology, Public Policy, and Social Justice* and co-author of *Psychology and Economic Injustice: Personal, Professional, and Political Intersections* (with B. Lott).

Rachel Calogero is Associate Professor of Psychology at the University of Kent, Canterbury, England. She is senior editor of *Self-Objectification in Women: Causes, Consequences, and Counteractions* from the American Psychological Association. Her research on self-objectification and collective action has appeared in many journals including the *Journal of Personality and Social Psychology* and *Psychological Science*.

Susan J. Carroll is Professor of Political Science at Rutgers University and Senior Scholar at the Center for American Women and Politics (CAWP) of the Eagleton Institute of Politics. She has published or edited five books, most recently *More Women Can Run: Gender and Pathways to the State Legislatures* (Oxford University Press 2013, with Kira Sanbonmatsu) and *Gender and Elections: Shaping the Future of American Politics* (Third Edition, Cambridge University Press 2014, with Richard L. Fox), along with numerous journal articles and book chapters focusing on women candidates, voters, elected officials, and political appointees in the United States. Her current research focuses on the politics of the gender gap in voting and women's representation in Congress.

Grace Deason is an Assistant Professor of Psychology at the University of Wisconsin—La Crosse. She is currently working on several research projects that examine stereotypes of mothers and the impact of motherhood in American politics. Her recent work has appeared in *Journal of Personality and Social Psychology*, *Basic and Applied Social Psychology*, and *Public Opinion Quarterly*.

Brian Frederick is Associate Professor and Chair of Political Science at Bridgewater State University. His research focuses on the U.S. Congress, women and politics, campaigns and elections and political psychology. His research has appeared in journals such as *Political Behavior*, *Public Opinion Quarterly*, *State Politics and Policy Quarterly*, and *American Politics Research*.

Jill Greenlee is an Associate Professor of Politics and Women's, Gender and Sexuality Studies at Brandeis University. Greenlee's current scholarship investigates the relationships between major life-cycle events, such as becoming a parent, and the political attitudes and behaviors of ordinary citizens. Greenlee has published work in journals such as *Political Psychology*, *Politics and Gender*, and *Politics, Groups and Identities*.

Shannon Jenkins is Associate Professor and Chair of Political Science at University of Massachusetts Dartmouth. Her research focuses on American public policy and state and local politics. Her research has appeared in journals such as *Legislative Studies Quarterly* and *Political Research Quarterly*. She is the author of *The Context of Legislating: Constraints on the Legislative Process in the United States* (Routledge).

Kristin Kanthak is Associate Professor of Political Science at the University of Pittsburgh. Much of her work considers gender-based election aversion and its consequences for effective representation. Her work has been published in the *American Political Science Review*, *American Journal of Political Science*, *British Journal of Political Science*, and other outlets. She is co-editor of *State Politics and Policy Quarterly*.

Carrie Langner is an Associate Professor of Psychology at California Polytechnic State University—San Luis Obispo. She investigates social hierarchy, collective identity, and political activism. Professor Langner's work has been published in journals such as the *Journal of Personality and Social Psychology*, the *Journal of Experimental Social Psychology*, and *Politics, Groups and Identities*.

Mary-Kate Lizotte is an Associate Professor of Political Science at Augusta University. Her main area of research on gender differences in public opinion, voting, and party identification has appeared in various journals and edited volumes.

Kjersten Nelson is Associate Professor of Political Science at North Dakota State University. Her research focuses on the effects of gender and the courts out-vote men (Center for American Women and Politics 2015) and win elections for political office at the same rate as their male counterparts, even if they run at much lower numbers (Seltzer, Newman, and Leighton 1997). Hillary Clinton, at a campaign rally in D.C. at the conclusion of her 2008 campaign, referred to the historic number of votes she received, noting that her campaign created "about eighteen million cracks" in the "highest, hardest glass ceiling" (June 7, 2008). Thus many scholars conclude that, to the extent that women *want* to be involved in politics, they will be successful, since the major legal and social barriers, such as media bias and the outright refusal to vote for a woman, have been removed (e.g., Brooks 2013; Dolan 2014; Hayes and Lawless 2015; Lawless and Fox 2005).

While there have been gains for women in politics, however, numerous political "gaps" between men and women persist. Women are less engaged in politics relative to men, reporting lower levels of interest in politics, political knowledge, participation in areas such as donating money and volunteering time, and ambition to seek political office and careers (Burns, Schlozman, and Verba 2001; Lawless and Fox 2005; O'Connor and Yanus 2009). Women differ from men with regard to political attitudes; for example, compared to men, women are more likely to support maintained or increased government spending and are less likely to support the military's use of force (e.g., Norrander 2008). In every presidential election since 1980, women were far more likely to support Democratic candidates, compared to Republican candidates (Center for American Women and Politics 2014b).

A psychological—as opposed to a structural or economic—approach represents a promising way to better understand these gaps; the field of psychology is rich with explanations for why people have attitudes and behave the way that they do. The stakes are high in understanding attitudinal and behavioral gaps between men and women because the political consequences for women are dramatic: Despite gains, women are descriptively underrepresented at every level of elected office and in non-elective positions (Center for American Women and Politics 2014a; EEOC 2013). In particular, only 19.3 and 20 percent of the U.S. House and Senate, respectively, are currently composed of women (Center for American Women and Politics 2016b; Center for American Women and Politics 2016c), and 24.5 percent of state legislatures (Center for American Women and Politics 2016a). Simply put, these inequalities reflect women's disadvantage in terms of both the resources and the influence necessary to affect their government.

The chapters in this book address how gender shapes political experience. The interdisciplinary approach of this book—specifically the integration of political science and psychology—has unique strengths that can best explain the attitudinal and behavioral gaps between men and women that result in women's lack of influence in the political process. A well-executed interdisciplinary approach draws on the strengths of multiple disciplines. Using small-N experimental methods, as psychologists do, combined with large observational studies used by political scientists, triangulates findings (Kinder and Palfrey 1993).

Generally, political science values research designs that account for macro-level social and political context through control variables, and analyze data from representative samples to enhance external validity. In contrast, psychology's emphasis falls on precision in understanding individual-level causal mechanisms, and establishing cause-and-effect, to maximize internal validity (Borgida, Federico, and Sullivan 2009). Substantively, political science offers normative grounding as to why we should care about issues of gender equality and representation in a democracy, while psychology offers well-developed theories, such as those related to human cognition, emotion, and motivation, to explain attitudes and human behavior and which can be applied to politics. This volume illustrates the combinations of these two approaches.

Consider a substantive example: The gender gap in political attitudes and its relationship with voting behavior. The goal for political scientists has been to identify robust gender differences in attitudes over time in representative samples (e.g., Norrander 2008), and to demonstrate whether gaps persist when controlling for important political variables such as party identification (Kaufmann and Petrocik 1999). In one study, authors conducted regression analyses of large-N observational studies to test different explanations for the origin of the gender gap, such as feminism, socioeconomic status, value differences, and women's autonomy (Howell and Day 2000). In a study from psychology, researchers manipulated the issue positions of a fictitious candidate, ascribing issue positions where a gender gap does or does not exist, to demonstrate a causal link between the gender gap in individual issue positions and voting behavior (Eagly et al. 2003). This example illustrates psychology's tendency to use experimental research to focus on identifying causal mechanisms.

While neither field offers a definitive understanding of the origins or consequences of gender gaps in attitudes, we believe more can be gleaned from an integrative approach. In Chapter 4 of this volume, for example, Mary-Kate Lizotte draws from psychology's Social Role Theory, which offers precise explanations for women's and men's behavior, and tests its explanatory power in explaining gender gaps in issue attitudes using a nationally representative American National Election Studies sample. By drawing from the best features of both disciplines, this approach and those like it can help us understand the pervasive role that gender plays in shaping political experiences.

Overview of the Political Psychology of Women in U.S. Politics

By integrating approaches, this volume offers a set of chapters designed to break new ground. This volume is not intended to be an exhaustive collection but a sampling of existing research and its extension through innovative approaches, the meticulous application of psychological theories, and, in many cases, new data sets or analyses. The chapters also speak to broad themes within the study of

American political behavior—including political socialization, opinion formation, candidate emergence, voting behavior, candidate evaluations, and elite decision-making. However, unlike other approaches to these questions, each chapter applies psychological theory to advance a scholarly understanding of the ways in which the political experiences of women continue to be gendered, causing significant differences in the behaviors and preferences of men and women. We conceptualized the volume to address three different classifications of women, summarized here: women as citizens, women as candidates, and women as officeholders.

Women as Citizens

We begin with the process of political socialization. Zoe Oxley goes beyond traditional models of party identification acquisition, which examine the causal relationship between the party identification of parents and children (e.g., Jennings and Niemi 1968), to investigate how gender affects socialization and whether children are more likely to share the party identification of their mother or father. Using data from the 1990s and 2010s, she uses social learning theory to predict that mothers, especially those who have a large role in child-rearing, will be more likely than fathers to transmit party identification to their children. She finds evidence for this hypothesis, and, moreover, that children are more likely to be influenced by the parent with whom they share a gender identity. Thus, the transfer of party identification is gendered because it depends upon the gender identity of both parents and children.

We know that the teenage years are formative in political development, particularly in an era where many youth are disillusioned with politics (Lawless and Fox 2015). In Chapter 3, Britney Brinkman problematizes traditionally narrow definitions of activism that exclude activities in which adolescent girls engage. In this way, she asks readers to rethink the stereotype that adolescent girls do not participate in politics. Moreover, she finds that a set of lectures and activities, the Girls, Activism and Social Change Program, developed the social capital and skills of adolescent girls and increased their engagement in activism. These findings suggest avenues for increasing girls' activism.

The work on socialization to politics sets the stage for understanding gender gaps in adult political attitudes and engagement. In Chapter 4, Mary-Kate Lizotte's findings from original data analyses illustrate how gender differences in policy attitudes are partially explained by women's roles as mothers. Lizotte reviews the many well-documented gender differences in public policy attitudes (e.g., women are less likely than men to support the use of force) and social science explanations for them. She pushes the research forward by drawing from psychological theory, specifically Social Role Theory (SRT), to explain gender differences in policy attitudes. SRT provides a framework for understanding how the intersecting and overlapping roles of men and women, specifically parenthood and gender identity, affect attitudes towards government spending and services.

In Chapter 5, Heather Bullock and Harmony Reppond demonstrate the ways that redistributive programs in the U.S. are gendered, as women are disadvantaged relative to men. The authors review explanations for differences in support for redistributive policies (e.g., intergroup stereotypes, self-interest, and ideology), arguing that no single explanation can fully account for these divergences. They focus on how beliefs such as individualism underlie "hierarchy-enhancing" beliefs (e.g., system justification, belief in a just world, and social dominance orientation) and motivate citizens to keep things the way they are with respect to income inequality. Members of subordinate groups often support these hierarchy-enhancing beliefs, which partially explains women's reluctance to fully support redistributive policies.

Moving from gender gaps in political attitudes to gender gaps in engagement, in Chapter 6, Rachel Calogero offers a new explanation for women's depressed political engagement: The deeply-entrenched beauty socialization and sexual objectification women regularly encounter in westernized societies. In particular, Calogero presents empirical evidence that self-objectification (a self-perspective that reflects internalized objectification) depresses women's motivation to participate in changing the political and social systems that treat them unfairly. This chapter highlights sexual and self-objectification as key sociocultural and psychological factors that impact women's political consciousness and activism. In conclusion, Calogero considers the wider implications of learning to view and value oneself predominantly through an appearance-focused lens on compliance with traditional gender roles and gender social change.

While multiple chapters in this volume discuss how intersectional roles influence women's political attitudes and experiences, Christina Bejarano, in Chapter 7, synthesizes what we know about intersecting identities using the psychological literature on social identity and identity consciousness, while laying out a clear path for future empirical work to pay closer attention to how gender intersects with identities such as race, ethnicity, and sexual orientation. Bejarano pushes past the idea of an "either-or" model where voters and candidates might choose one of their identities as the lens through which to evaluate politics. Rather, she considers the interaction of multiple identities as truly intersectional, creating their own sense of group consciousness, their own stereotypes, and their own unique effects on political outcomes. This chapter neatly lays out the complications of studying the multiple identities of voters *and* of candidates and the ways that those identities interact. This chapter also serves as a bridge from discussing women as citizens to women as candidates.

Women as Political Candidates

Political candidates must take the first step of deciding to run for political office. Thus, Chapters 8 and 9 posit contrasting psychological approaches for explaining women's political ambition. Kristin Kanthak synthesizes theories from economics, such as cost-benefit analyses, and theories from psychology, particularly work on

————. 2016a. *Women in State Legislatures 2016*. New Brunswick, NJ: Eagleton Institute of Politics, Rutgers University. http://cawp.rutgers.edu/women-state-legislature-2016.

————. 2016b. *Women in the U.S. House 2016*. New Brunswick, NJ: Eagleton Institute of Politics, Rutgers University. http://cawp.rutgers.edu/women-us-house-representatives-2016.

————. 2016c. *Women in the U.S. Senate*. New Brunswick, NJ: Eagleton Institute of Politics, Rutgers University. http://cawp.rutgers.edu/women-us-house-representatives-2016.

Chozick, Amy. 2016. "Hillary Clinton Raises Her Voice, and a Debate over Speech and Sexism Rages—The New York Times." *New York Times*, February 4. http://www.nytimes.com/2016/02/05/us/politics/hillary-clinton-speeches-sexism.html.

Dolan, Kathleen A. 2014. *When Does Gender Matter? Women Candidates and Gender Stereotypes in American Elections*. New York: Oxford University Press.

Eagly, Alice H., Amanda B. Diekman, Monica C. Schneider, and Patrick Kulesa. 2003. "Experimental Tests of an Attitudinal Theory of the Gender Gap in Voting." *Personality and Social Psychology Bulletin* 29 (10): 1245–1258.

EEOC. 2013. "Job Patterns for Minorities and Women in State and Local Governments." EEO-4. www.eeoc.gov/eeoc/statistics/employment/jobpat-eeo4/2013/.

Hayes, Danny, and Jennifer L. Lawless. 2015. "A Non-Gendered Lens? Media, Voters, and Female Candidates in Contemporary Congressional Elections." *Perspectives on Politics* 13 (1): 95–118.

Howell, Susan E., and Christine L. Day. 2000. "Complexities of the Gender Gap." *Journal of Politics* 62: 858–874.

Huddy, Leonie, and Nayda Terkildsen. 1993. "Gender Stereotypes and the Perception of Male and Female Candidates." *American Journal of Political Science* 37 (1): 119–147.

Jennings, M. Kent, and Richard G. Niemi. 1968. "The Transmission of Political Values from Parent to Child." *American Political Science Review* 62 (1): 169–184.

Kaufmann, Karen M., and John R. Petrocik. 1999. "The Changing Politics of American Men: Understanding the Sources of the Gender Gap." *American Journal of Political Science* 43 (3): 864–887.

Kinder, Donald R., and Thomas R. Palfrey. 1993. "On Behalf of an Experimental Political Science." In *Experimental Foundations of Political Science*, edited by Donald R. Kinder and Thomas R. Palfrey, 1–39. Michigan Studies in Political Analysis. Ann Arbor: University of Michigan Press.

Lawless, Jennifer L., and Richard L. Fox. 2005. *It Takes a Candidate: Why Women Don't Run for Office*. New York: Cambridge University Press.

Lawless, Jennifer L., and Richard Logan Fox. 2015. *Running from Office: Why Young Americans Are Turned off to Politics*. New York: Oxford University Press.

McConnaughy, Corrine. 2016. "Do Gendered Comments Help or Hurt Hillary Clinton?" *The Washington Post*, March 17. https://www.washingtonpost.com/news/monkey-cage/wp/2016/03/17/heres-how-it-helps-hillary-clinton-when-male-pundits-tell-her-to-stop-shouting-and-smile/.

Norrander, Barbara. 2008. "The History of the Gender Gap." In *Voting the Gender Gap*, edited by Lois Duke Whitaker and Barbara Norrander, 9–32. Urbana: University of Illinois Press.

O'Connor, Karen, and Alixandra B. Yanus. 2009. "The Chilly Climate Continues: Defrosting the Gender Divide in Political Science and Politics." *Journal of Political Science Education* 5 (2): 108–118.

Sapiro, Virginia. 1981. "If U.S. Senator Baker Were a Woman: An Experimental Study of Candidate Image." *Political Psychology* 3 (April): 61–83.

Schneider, Monica C., and Angela L. Bos. 2014. "Measuring Stereotypes of Female Politicians." *Political Psychology* 35 (2): 245–266.

Seltzer, Richard A., Jody Newman, and Melissa Voorhees Leighton. 1997. *Sex as a Political Variable: Women as Candidates and Voters in U.S. Elections.* Boulder, CO: Lynne Rienner Publishers.

PART I

Women as Citizens

Gender Socialization

2

GENDER AND THE SOCIALIZATION OF PARTY IDENTIFICATION[1]

Zoe M. Oxley

"Hey son, how was your day?" asks Dre Johnson Sr. "Great," says 14-year-old Junior, "I joined the Young Republicans club at school." Dre later shares this news with his wife, Rainbow: "Bow, we have a problem. Junior is a Republican." A long and humorous conversation ensues with Bow trying to make sense of what Dre told her. "So he wants to shop at Banana Republic" is followed by "A notary public? That's a noble profession." When Bow finally realizes what her husband meant, shock and outrage flow. "No, no, no, we don't do that, Dre. We are compassionate liberals who believe in tolerance, acceptance. . . . When did he start believing that immigrants should go back across the border, that evolution doesn't exist?" (ABC 2015).

That fictional scene took place in the kitchen of the African American Johnson family, on the ABC sitcom *black-ish*. It was reminiscent of a 1980s NBC sitcom, *Family Ties*. That show revolved around Alex P. Keaton, the teenaged son of Steven and Elyse Keaton, White political liberals who had served in the Peace Corps and protested the Vietnam War. In contrast, Alex was most assuredly a conservative, Reagan-loving, Republican. He wore a tie and carried a briefcase. Alex's and his parents' different worldviews provided a constant source of tension on *Family Ties* (Saenz 2016; Stewart 2007). Such scenarios certainly make for entertaining television, but are the intergenerational differences of the Johnson and Keaton families typical of actual American families? Not especially. In this chapter, I review past research that has examined political socialization within families. One clear conclusion is that parents and children often share core political orientations, such as partisanship. Whether explicitly or not, parents generally transmit their party identification successfully to their children.

This chapter extends the socialization literature by asking two specific questions about the transmission of partisanship: Are children more likely to share the party identification of their mother or their father? Have mother–child and father–child partisan similarity changed over time? To answer these questions, I draw upon social learning theory. This theoretical perspective highlights cue-giving, suggesting that children follow the partisan cues of their parents, most notably the parent to whom they feel most close and with whom they spend the most time. Understanding the transmission of partisanship within families, especially any overtime patterns, will thus require that we consider the changing habits of mothers and fathers vis-à-vis work outside the home and time spent parenting. Furthermore, family dynamics are not immune to broader changes in the political environment. Over recent decades, views toward women and politics have been liberalizing. Fewer Americans today believe that politics is purely a man's domain and women have increased their role and authority as political actors (Burns et al. 2016). I discuss these changes in gender roles more fully, tying them to socialization dynamics within families. I then compare mother–child versus father–child partisan similarity.

Political Socialization of Party Identification

Of the many political attitudes held by Americans, perhaps the most important is party identification. Beginning with the 1960 publication of *The American Voter*, the dominant view among scholars is that partisanship is "a psychological identification, which can persist without legal recognition or evidence of formal membership and even without a consistent record of party support" (Campbell et al. 1960, 121). In the American context, party identification is thus a self-classification, reflecting whether one considers herself to be a Republican or a Democrat, a member of a different political party, or politically independent. Party affiliation is a core political attitude. It strongly influences the democratically important act of voting, for instance. People's opinions toward specific policy issues are also related to their partisanship. Across a range of domestic and foreign policy issues, Democrats and Republicans stake out different positions (Levendusky 2009). Finally, party identification acts as a filter that influences the interpretation of new information (Leeper and Slothuus 2014).

Given its centrality to American public opinion, scholars have long been interested in where partisan identification originates. The process by which people develop political attitudes is known as political socialization. Such socialization begins in childhood, although as children enter adolescence, their connections with politics expand and deepen. As Britney Brinkman illustrates in her chapter in this volume, civic engagement and political activism begin during this life stage. Furthermore, partisanship and opinions toward key issues start to form. The primary agents of socialization are family, schools, peers, and the news media. Among these, parents play the central socializing role for most children (Beck 1977; Kinder 2006; Stoker and Bass 2011). As put by two socialization researchers, "Whether the child is conscious or unaware of the impact, whether the process is role-modelling or overt transmission, whether the values are political and directly usable or 'nonpolitical' but transferable, and whether what is passed on lies in the cognitive or affective realm, it has been argued that the family is of paramount importance" (Jennings and Niemi 1968, 169).

An important source of our understanding of political socialization in the United States is the Youth-Parent Socialization Study, a research project began by Kent Jennings and Richard Niemi in 1965. That year, Jennings and Niemi conducted a nationally representative survey of high school seniors. Parents of these seniors were also surveyed. The original sample of high school students was then reinterviewed three more times, in 1973, 1982, and 1997. Furthermore, in 1997, children of the 1965 high school seniors were also interviewed. In all, their data span three generations, with two separate sets of parent-child interviews (1965 and 1997), making this study well suited for examining socialization in different time periods.[2] Finally, it should be noted that our knowledge of parent-to-child transmission of partisanship, from this and other studies examined in this chapter, pertains only to children of heterosexual parents.

Several findings from this study are noteworthy. First, when parents share the same party identification, transmission of this affiliation to children is quite successful. In both 1965 and 1997, approximately 75 percent of the high school seniors reported the same identification as their parents (Jennings and Langton 1969; Jennings and Niemi 1974; Jennings, Stoker, and Bowers 2009). Second, transmission of attitudes from parents to their offspring varies across attitudes, with parent–child agreement being higher for party identification than for other political orientations, such as issue opinions, opinions toward social groups, and political trust (Jennings and Niemi 1968; Jennings, Stoker, and Bowers 2009).

Finally, as adolescents age into their twenties, there can be movement away from their parents' party identification. In 1973, for example, when members of the class of 1965 were in their mid-twenties, parent–child partisan agreement was lower than when those twenty-somethings had been in their teens (Beck and Jennings 1991; Jennings and Niemi 1981; see also Jennings, Stoker, and Bowers 2009). These results are in line with the impressionable years model of socialization, which highlights that political attitudes fluctuate for many people while they are in late adolescence or early adulthood. During these years, life circumstances change and friendships and experiences are new, often triggering changes in one's political orientations (Dinas 2013; Kinder 2006). As people leave the impressionable years, their political attitudes typically fluctuate less (Jennings and Markus 1984; Stoker and Jennings 2008).

To explain these various patterns of political socialization, Jennings and his colleagues turned to social learning theory, most especially observational learning. This approach understands learning as a "process in which a person patterns his thoughts, feelings, or actions after another person who serves as a model" (Bandura 1969, 214; see also Bandura 1986). Much intergenerational learning, including political learning, results from children observing and taking cues from their parents. Parents are especially influential models because of the amount of time children spend with their parents (especially in comparison to other socialization agents) and because of the warmth children tend to feel toward their parents. Social learning approaches also help us to understand why parental transmission of partisanship is higher among homogeneous partisan compared to heterogeneous partisan parents. When parents agree, partisan signals in the household are consistent rather than conflicting. Furthermore, social learning theory can also explain why parent–adolescent partisan agreement is higher in households that are more politicized. When parents are more politically engaged and more likely to discuss politics at home, cues as to their political attitudes are disseminated to the children. In contrast, "low levels of parent politicization should leave the child either bereft or relatively open to influence from other socialization agents" (Jennings, Stoker, and Bowers 2009, 787). Finally, theories of social learning suggest that child–parent similarity should be highest among attitudes that are especially salient and likely to be reinforced repeatedly, conditions that are more often satisfied for partisanship than other attitudes (Jennings and Niemi 1974, 1981).

Gender and the Socialization of Partisanship

Most socialization research considers parents jointly, as a single unit, pitting parental influence against other socialization agents or exploring variation in parent–child agreement across attitudes. Far less studied has been whether fathers and mothers have differential influence on the political views of their children. Two 1950s surveys concluded that young adults were slightly more likely— approximately two percentage points—to share their mothers' than their fathers' partisanship (Maccoby, Matthews, and Morton 1954; Nogee and Levin 1958). Similar results emerged from a survey of adults who had been adolescents in an even earlier decade. These adults demonstrated more similarity with their mothers than fathers, most especially when the mother claimed a party identification. In families where the father was partisan and the mother independent, the father–offspring relationship was stronger than that between mothers and their offspring (Beck and Jennings 1975).

While suggestive, these studies are somewhat limited because respondents were asked to recall the party affiliations of their parents. Such items are less reliable than are direct assessments of one's own partisanship. In the obvious case, a person might not be certain of the partisanship of his or her parents, but will proffer a guess. These guesses might in the end be accurate, but they are guesses nonetheless. Furthermore, in explorations of socialization during adolescence, it is ideal to know the parents' partisanship when the child was an adolescent. The further removed people are from this period of life, the less reliable are assessments of what their parents' party affiliations had been when they were growing up. In contrast, ideal is collecting measures of party identification from adolescents and their parents separately. This, of course, is precisely what Jennings and Niemi did in 1965.

The Jennings and Niemi data confirmed the earlier results that mothers were somewhat more successful at transmitting party identification than were fathers, and extended those findings. First, in homes where the parents possessed different party affiliations, children were slightly more likely to adopt their mother's than their father's party (40 percent of offspring agreed with mother, 35 percent with father and 25 percent with neither; Jennings and Niemi 1974). Second, defections away from a parent's party were more likely for fathers than mothers. This was the case whether one of the parents was independent or whether both parents were partisan, albeit identifying with different parties (Jennings and Langton 1969). Third, same-sex transmission patterns emerged. In households with heterogeneous partisan parents, whereas 40 percent of children overall shared their mother's partisanship, 47 percent of daughters did (compared to 33 percent of sons). Similarly, sons were more likely to possess the same party affiliation as their fathers than were daughters (39 percent versus 30 percent; Jennings and Langton 1969; Jennings and Niemi 1974). This pattern was not due to daughters feeling closer to mothers and sons closer to fathers, as both daughters and sons felt closer to their mothers than their fathers. Instead, a different aspect of social learning seems the more likely cause: which parent a child turns to for cues. Sons are more likely to model their fathers' and daughters their mothers' attitudes and behaviors, in political and nonpolitical domains (Campbell 1969; Jennings and Niemi 1974). Jennings and Langton (1969, 331) also turned to psychoanalytic theory to explain same-sex transmission of partisanship, noting that both "theory and clinical work reveal that the normal resolution of Oedipal tendencies prohibits strong cross-sex identification."

These findings, especially that mothers were more successful at transmitting party identification than were fathers, upended conventional wisdom. Politics was viewed as a man's world, after all, and if any parent were to be more politically engaged, it was thought to be the father. Additionally, children of that era, even those as young as age 10, were more likely to select their fathers than their mothers when asked which parent would best provide political advice (Greenstein 1961). Yet, if we return to social learning theory, these socialization patterns make sense. Presumably, although not tested directly by Jennings and his colleagues, when parents do not share the same party affiliation, children were more in line with their mother's partisanship because they spent more time with their mothers than fathers. Thus, mothers should have been a source of partisan cues more often than fathers. Affinity toward parents certainly matters: Children were more likely to feel closer to mothers than fathers, contributing to the higher incidence of mother–child partisan agreement (Jennings and Langton 1969). Finally, the politicization of the parents is relevant. When parents have different party identifications, children identify more often with the party of the parent whose identification is stronger and whose level of political activity is higher.

For both measures of politicization, however, children gravitate more toward their mothers if she is the more politicized parent than toward their fathers if he is more politicized. "What seems to happen is that when [the mother's] activity and [partisan] intensity levels increase the mother becomes a much more visible and salient source of political information. She reaps corresponding benefits as her relative position improves" (Jennings and Niemi 1974, 172; see also Jennings and Langton 1969).

Gender Dynamics and Socialization in Recent Times

These past studies provide a window into family socialization patterns of the 1960s. To update this work, I examine the transmission of party identification from mothers and fathers to their children in two recent years, 1997 and 2012. My expectation is that mothers will have continued to be more influential than fathers because of the parental distribution of childcare responsibilities and societal attitudes toward gender roles.

Mothers have been more likely to work outside the home than in the 1960s. One result could be that young and adolescent children spend less time with their mothers than previous generations did. That, in fact, has not happened. Mothers' time spent on childcare did decrease slightly from 1965 through 1995, but then increased in 2000. Throughout the 2000s, mothers spent an average of 14 hours per week on childcare compared to 10 hours per week in 1965 (Bianchi 2011). As mothers have increased their hours of paid work and hours of childcare, they are spending fewer hours on routine housework (Bianchi et al. 2012; Gauthier, Smeeding, and Furstenberg 2004). This reality suggests that children are not spending less time with mom and are perhaps encountering as many opportunities to observe and take partisan cues from her as did past generations of children. Importantly, though, we need to consider overtime changes in cue-taking opportunities from both parents, specifically how much time children spend with mothers *relative to* fathers. The time that fathers devote to childcare has increased over recent decades: from 2.5 hours per week in 1965 to around seven hours in the 2000s (Bianchi 2011). Across the decades, then, it has been the case that more child-rearing is done by mothers than by fathers, although moms used to devote four times as many hours to childcare as dads, whereas now their hours only double dads' hours. Finally, not all childcare work is created equal. Parents must tend to a child's physical needs (e.g., feeding, dressing, bathing), but they also talk, play, read, and otherwise engage with their children. Such engagement might be the times when partisan cue-giving and political discussions between parents and children are most likely to occur. Overtime trends indicate that time devoted to playing and interacting with children has increased for both mothers and fathers, although the increase has been greater for fathers, resulting in a narrowing gap between parents (Sayer, Bianchi, and Robinson 2004). Among dual-working couples who were new parents in 2008 through 2010, while mothers overall devoted more hours to childcare than fathers, considering only child engagement activities, mothers' weekly hours were only slightly higher than fathers' (6.3 versus 4.5; Yavorsky, Kamp-Dush, and Schoppe-Sullivan 2015).

Taking only these family work–home dynamics into account might lead us to expect the mother–child party identification correspondence to be lessened, although perhaps only slightly. On the other hand, gender role expectations have evolved since the 1960s. The view that politics is a domain strictly for men while women's proper place is in the private domain of family and home has become less widespread (Burns et al. 2016). These broad societal changes should have implications for socialization within families. For one, parent politicization within families might have been altered such that mothers are more likely to be politically engaged than in the past. Also, as women's political activity has become more broadly acceptable, children might be even more likely to look to their mothers as sources of political orientations. Of course, even when politics was more closed to women in the 1960s, mothers were still more likely to transmit their partisanship to their children than were fathers. Liberalization of attitudes toward women's roles since then might result in an even greater correspondence between mothers and their children than occurred previously. Thus, I hypothesize that the influence of mothers will be as strong in the 1990s and 2010s as it had been in the 1960s.

Gender Dynamics and Socialization in the 1990s

For my first attempt to explore parental transmission of partisanship since the 1960s, I analyze data from the 1997 wave of Jennings and Niemi's study. In this final wave, children of the original high school students of 1965 were interviewed (Jennings and Stoker 2004). Before proceeding, it is important to note that in 1965, for approximately one-third of the high schoolers, both of their parents were interviewed, but of the publicly available data sets from the 1997 wave, direct survey measures are included from only one parent. If married, this parent was asked to report the party identification of his or her spouse.[3] Given the likelihood of misreporting another person's partisanship, this situation is not ideal. Furthermore, because only one parent was interviewed, data to replicate some of the analyses that were conducted by Jennings and his colleagues are not available, as noted below.

The other notable variation between the 1965 and 1997 waves pertains to the ages of the children. Because the original sampling unit for the 1965 wave was high school seniors, the children in this wave were 17 or 18 years old. In 1997, children of these former high school seniors were interviewed (provided they were at least 15 years old) at the time one of their parents—the high school student from the 1965 wave—was reinterviewed. Because of these sampling differences, the average age is older and the age range is greater among the 1997 compared to the 1965 children.[4] These age discrepancies are taken into account in the following analyses.

Before focusing on parent–child partisanship agreement separately for mothers versus fathers, it is worth recalling that overall the transmission of party affiliation from parents to their teenaged offspring was high in both the 1960s and 1990s, despite the substantial changes in family composition over this time. Seventy-six percent of the high school seniors with homogeneously partisan parents adopted the party identification of their parents in 1965, as did 76 percent of the 15- to 18-year olds surveyed in 1997.[5] In line with the impressionable years model, parent–child agreement among the older offspring of the 1990s dropped: 63 percent of those aged 19–26 and 64 percent of those over age 26 shared their parents' partisanship.

To explore partisan agreement between offspring and their mothers versus agreement with fathers, first I present child–mother and child–father bivariate (Pearson's r) correlation coefficients (refer to Figure 2.1).[6] Overall, the correlation between a child and his or her mother is slightly higher (.406; 697 cases) than the correlation with the father (.365; 647 cases), thus demonstrating the continued stronger influence of mothers than fathers over their children's party identification. Second, I analyzed parent–child agreement for only those children whose parents have different party affiliations. Such partisan heterogeneous parents are a small portion of the sample (only 155 total cases), but I include such results in order to replicate Jennings and Niemi's 1965 analyses. Among these families, 38.7 percent of the offspring identified with the same party as their mother, compared to 32.3 percent who shared the partisanship of their father. This gap of 6.4 percentage points is slightly higher than the five percentage points observed in 1965.

When we consider the youngest age group in 1997, the tendency for children to follow their mother's party is significantly greater. Recall that the 1965 children surveyed were all 17 or 18 years old. In 1997, for a similar age group, children of heterogeneous parents were 20 percentage points more likely to have the same party affiliation as their mother (52 percent compared to 32 percent). The number of cases for this analysis is very low (only 25), so we should be cautious in drawing conclusions. The pull of the mother's partisanship for 19- to 26-year olds (95 cases), while reduced to 7.4 percentage points, is still evident in this age group. Finally, among the oldest offspring (35 cases), agreement with fathers was actually 5.7 percentage points higher than with mothers. Perusing further down Figure 2.1, we see these age patterns mostly replicated in the correlational analyses. Across all of the families (not only those with partisan heterogeneous parents), the gap in the size of the mother–child versus father–child correlations is especially large among 15- to 18-year olds, smaller for those aged 19–26, and nonexistent for those older than 26. It is somewhat unclear what to make of the results for this oldest group, however. Because we do not have party identification data from when they were younger, we cannot be certain whether

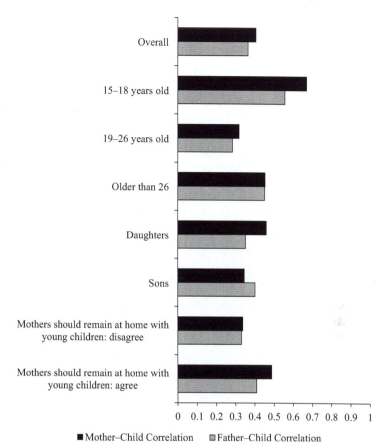

FIGURE 2.1 Mother–Child and Father–Child Correlations for Party Identification, 1997

Note: All correlations are significant at p < .001. The number of cases for the Mother–Child correlation ranges from 104 to 697; for the Father–Child correlation the range is 101 to 647.

they have always been more closely aligned with their fathers, or whether their party identification changed in the direction of their fathers sometime after their mid-twenties.

The same-sex partisan transmission patterns were the same in 1997 as they had been in 1965: Daughters are more likely to align with their mothers while sons show a tendency to agree more with their fathers. This pattern is evident in Figure 2.1. Indeed, of all the categories presented in this figure, only for sons is the father–child correlation larger than the mother–child relationship. The same pattern emerges when examining families with partisan heterogeneous parents. The 81 daughters in this analysis were 22.2 percentage points more likely to adopt mom's versus dad's partisanship whereas the 73 sons were 12.4 percentage points more likely to agree with their fathers than their mothers. Thus, as was the case in 1965, the pull of daughters toward mothers is greater than the pull of sons toward fathers.

To understand why children were more likely to share their mother's partisanship in the 1960s, Jennings and his colleagues considered the children's affinity to their parents and the relative level of politicization of the parents. Unfortunately, due to unavailable data from the 1997 wave, I am unable to examine either. The political knowledge level of the interviewed parent was assessed then, though.[7] Thus, while I cannot explore relative parental knowledge, I can consider one parent's level of knowledge for each child. Among offspring whose mother was interviewed, the mother–child partisan correlation was .447 for mothers with high levels of political knowledge compared to .304 for those with lower levels of knowledge.[8] The father–child correlation is also higher for high versus low knowledge fathers, although the discrepancy is not as large as it was for mothers: .423 versus .325.[9] The mothers' level of politicization therefore seems to affect offspring more than does the fathers', as was also the case in the 1960s.

My expectation that the differential rate of mother–child over father–child agreement would have persisted into the 1990s was based in part on the assumption that children with more progressive views toward gender roles would be more likely to adopt their mother's partisanship compared to those with more traditional views. The results do not support this prediction.[10] First, I explored views toward women's equality. Regardless of whether offspring believed that women should have an equal role as men in business and government or believed that a woman's place is in the home, mother–child was higher than father–child correspondence.[11] Second, I considered views regarding whether mothers should stay at home with young children rather than engage in paid work outside the home. Somewhat counterintuitively, offspring holding the more traditional view actually demonstrate a greater tendency of following their mothers' rather than their fathers' partisanship (see the bottom of Figure 2.1).

Finally, I take up the topic of defection from parents, asking, when a child identifies with a party other than that of a parent, is he or she more likely to defect from the mother's or the father's party? Across various analyses I conducted among children of partisan heterogeneous parents, there is evidence that children were more likely to defect away from their fathers than their mothers, a conclusion also reached in 1965. For instance, among all 141 children of partisan fathers in non-homogeneous parent families, 41 percent defected from their father's party to identify with the other party. The percentage of partisan-defecting children among the partisan mothers was lower, 33 percent (135 cases).

Gender Dynamics and Socialization in the 2010s

To explore the transmission of partisanship within families for more recent times, I turn to survey data collected by Jennifer Lawless and Richard Fox. In 2012, they conducted a study of young adult's political ambition, surveying 2,163

13- to 17-year-old high school students and 2,117 college students (aged 18–25) from across the United States.[12] Their survey contained a number of questions relevant to parent–child socialization, including asking the respondents about the party identification of their parents. As previously mentioned, children's reporting of their parents' partisanship is less reliable than are the parents' own self-reports because children might assume that their parents' attitudes are similar to theirs. On the other hand, there is no reason to suspect that children would be more likely to project their attitudes on to their mothers versus their fathers or vice-versa (Beck and Jennings 1975). In other words, the *difference* in mother–child compared to father–child correspondence is still meaningful, even though levels of correspondence are inflated for both parents.

In 2012, as had been the case in the past, when parents share partisanship, their children adopt that party affiliation. Indeed, 89.5 percent of children with partisan homogeneous parents had the same party identification as their parents. The parent–child agreement within these families was predictably higher among high school than college students (92.7 percent versus 86 percent). Here we see the first evidence of inflated parent–child agreement, likely due to the projection just mentioned. Moreover, children were asked to identify the partisanship of a parent only if they lived with or had regular contact with the parent, which was truer of mothers than fathers. Thus, there are higher rates of party identification information for mothers than fathers.[13] Excluded from the analyses are parents when children indicated they did not know a parent's party affiliation (21 percent of mothers, 18 percent of fathers). Also excluded are the 28 percent of respondents who did not consider themselves Democratic, Republican, or Independent.[14] After these exclusions, there is partisanship information for 2,420 mother–child pairs and 1,976 father–child pairs.

Replicating the 1997 analyses for 2012, I draw many similar conclusions. First, overall, children's partisanship continued to be more in line with their mothers than fathers, although the difference between parents was smaller than in the past (correlations of .777 for mothers and .751 for fathers; see Figure 2.2). In families where the parents identify with different parties, 49.3 percent of children have the same partisanship as their mothers compared to 39.2 percent who share their fathers' party affiliation, a 10 percentage point difference.[15] For both high school and college students, there was closer partisan correspondence with mom than dad, although the gap between the mother–child and father–child correlation was greater for the younger group and nearly nonexistent for the older (.857 compared to .813 for high schoolers; .700 versus .692 for college).[16] Unlike in previous years, both sons and daughters displayed higher partisan agreement with their mothers than their fathers, although when considering only the college students in 2012, we see the familiar trend of daughters aligning more with mothers and sons more with fathers.[17] Finally, focusing on children of partisan heterogeneous parents, 38.9 percent of those with partisan fathers identify with the party other than their father's compared to 30 percent who opt for the party

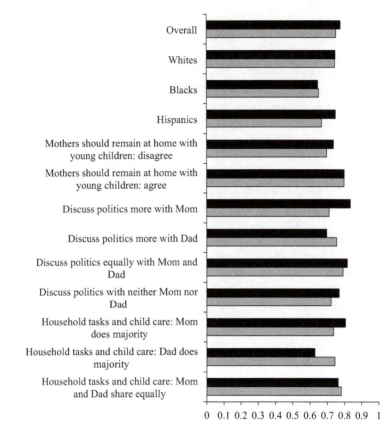

FIGURE 2.2 Mother–Child and Father–Child Correlations for Party Identification, 2012

Note: All correlations are significant at p < .001. The number of cases for the Mother–Child correlation ranges from 125 to 2,420; for the Father–Child correlation the range is 126 to 1,976.

other than their partisan mother's.[18] Thus, defections away from the father continue to be more common than away from the mother.

In addition to updating previous findings, the Lawless-Fox data permit some new analyses. The 2012 survey respondents were diverse, with sufficient numbers of Whites, Blacks, and Hispanics for reliable analysis. As demonstrated in Figure 2.2, the tendency of mothers to transmit their partisanship to their children more successfully than fathers emerges only in Hispanic families. Among Blacks, the mother–child and father–child correlations are nearly identical. The same is true for Whites. Without comparable data from earlier years, we cannot know whether such patterns are new. We can, however, conclude that the earlier stronger mother–child compared to father–child correspondence among Whites had disappeared by 2012. Also of note is that parental transmission of partisanship is highest for Hispanic mothers and White parents (of either sex). Correlations are lowest for Black parents. Probing the transmission patterns by party within Black families suggests that the strong national association of Blacks with the Democratic Party disrupts parental transmission of partisanship for Black parents who are not Democrats. Among the Black Democrats, children are extremely likely to adopt the Democratic partisanship of their parents (96 percent follow mom's party and 94 percent agree with dad). For the (admittedly relatively) few Black Republican and Independent parents, a slight majority of their offspring aligned with their parents' partisanship, with a third or more identifying as Democratic. A similar, although less pronounced, pattern exists for Hispanic fathers. In contrast, large majorities of Hispanic children adopt the partisanship of their mothers (86 percent when mom is Democratic, 80 percent when Republican).

Turning to gender role attitudes, recall that, contrary to my expectations, in 1997 offspring who believed in equal gender roles or who thought it fine for mothers to work for pay outside the home were not more likely to follow their mothers' versus their fathers' partisanship. The 2012 survey contained an item assessing whether mothers of young children should remain at home.[19] This year, the results were somewhat different than before, yet still do not provide strong support for my initial expectation. Those who disagreed with this sentiment did have slightly higher partisanship correlations with their mothers than fathers (see Figure 2.2). Agreeing was related to higher correlations for both parents (comparing to disagreeing), however, and nearly identical correlations for mothers as for fathers.

Finally, I explore political discussions within families and parental involvement in childcare. Some children are more likely to discuss politics with their mothers, of course, whereas others have more political conversations with dad. Not surprisingly, the parent with whom a child is more likely to discuss politics is the parent with whom the child is more likely to share party affiliation. What about when political discussions occur with both parents equally or do not occur with either parent? In both cases, the mother–child correlation is higher than the father–child. On the one hand, this confirms an earlier finding, that the politicization of the mother is a stronger pull for children's partisanship than is the father's politicization. On the other hand, factors other than political engagement are also clearly at play, given the results for families that do not engage in political conversations. The 2012 survey also asked respondents whether their mother or father "takes care of the majority of the household tasks and child care." Congruent with national trends, more children indicated that their mother does the majority (56 percent), although 7 percent come from families where dad does the majority of these tasks and for 37 percent the parents share this work equally. As for how this family feature maps onto parent–child partisan correlations, children whose moms do the majority of the work align with her partisanship more than dad's. Yet, dads more successfully transmit their party affiliation than moms in families when the work is shared equally and, especially, when dads do the majority of the work.

Conclusion and Future Research Directions

Several conclusions emerge from this examination of the socialization of party identification. First, family mattered in 1997 and 2012, as it had in past decades. When parents see eye-to-eye in terms of partisanship, their children are very likely to hold the same party identification as mom and dad. Second, mothers continue to transmit their partisanship to their children at a higher rate than fathers do, even if the differences in 2012 are smaller than in 1997. Furthermore, by 2012, the stronger pull of mom's versus dad's partisanship was restricted to fewer groups, notably high school-aged children, daughters, and Hispanics. As Grace Deason, Jill Greenlee, and Carrie Langner discuss in their chapter in this book, discussions of motherhood and politics often focus on the negative consequences of parenthood for women's political activity. In contrast, peering inside families highlights the important influence that mothers have in shaping the political views of their children, especially daughters. Social learning theory suggests some reasons why, although more explicit theorizing and more detailed empirical explorations of mother–daughter dynamics would help to illuminate this relationship.

   Third, the political and social times of one's adolescence and early adult years also matters, particularly changes in gender roles and norms as well as attitudes regarding gender roles. Between the 1960s and 2010s, fathers became more involved in child-rearing, there was a liberalization of attitudes toward women's roles (especially in politics), and women increased their political activity. My analyses suggest that changes in the distribution of household tasks perhaps best accounts for overtime changes in parental transmission of partisanship. This, of course, is what social learning theory would predict. As for the political activity of mothers, children are indeed more likely to share mom's than dad's partisanship when they discuss politics more with their mother than their father. Yet, this closer connection to mothers also exists for children who discuss politics equally with both parents or with neither parent, suggesting that increased political discussions with mothers cannot fully account for the aggregate patterns of parental partisanship transmission. Finally, results regarding attitudes about gender roles were inconsistent, suggesting that aggregate changes in such beliefs are not contributing to gendered socialization patterns within families.

   In both the 1960s and more recently, there is evidence of children more commonly defecting away from their fathers' party affiliation than from their mothers'. At the same time, my analyses demonstrate some closer partisan ties between fathers and children when or after the offspring are in their twenties. A complex picture thus emerges of children's relationships with their fathers.

Some children are (eventually) drawn to their father's partisanship whereas others defect from dad to identification with the opposite party. Such cross-cutting currents do not emerge when considering the partisan ties between children and their mothers. More work needs to be done to explain such divergent patterns.

There are some topics related to family socialization that neither the present nor earlier analyses fully address. The samples for the existing surveys were nearly exclusively drawn from children of heterosexual parents and primarily from White families. Whether differences in mother–child versus father–child correlations exist across same-sex parent families is thus a topic that I could not address. It seems likely, however, that the factors that are relevant for partisan socialization among children of heterosexual parents (division of childcare duties, relative politicization of parents, etc.) would be similarly relevant for children of homosexual parents. Psychological research exploring socialization of non-explicitly political behaviors, values, and motivations, for example, points to similar socialization outcomes in families with same-sex versus different-sex parents (Patterson, Farr, and Hastings 2015). I was able to explore differences across racial and ethnic communities only for 2012, finding closer mother–child compared to father–child partisanship among Hispanics but among neither Whites nor Blacks. Group differences in partisanship, notably the strong Democratic affiliation among Blacks, seem to contribute to this finding. Differences across racial and ethnic communities regarding motherhood, fatherhood, parenting styles, and contact with extended family members might also contribute to the patterns I uncovered (Smetana, Robinson, and Rote 2015). Finally, the socialization of political attitudes other than partisanship is important, yet has received much less attention, from either survey designers or socialization scholars. More comprehensive research designs, incorporating the diversity of Americans and of political issues, are clearly warranted.

With appropriate data, reciprocal communication within families could also be explored in future research. In their study of partisanship in Britain and Germany, Alan Zuckerman, Josip Dasović, and Jennifer Fitzgerald (2007) conclude that the wife/mother plays a central role in the political communication network of the family. Not only do they influence the partisanship of their husbands and children, but, in Germany, they are influenced by both their husbands and offspring. If such patterns exist in the United States, stronger mother–child compared to father–child partisan agreement might be due, in part, to the reciprocal processes of mothers bringing their partisanship in line with the children as children are aligning with their mothers.

Finally, future analyses of partisanship in the United States should account for affective polarization, or the tendency of partisans to greatly dislike members of the other party. It is even the case that parents today are much more likely than parents of the past to hope their children do not marry out-of-party (Iyengar, Sood, and Lelkes 2012). What does such polarization portend for parental transmission of partisanship? On the one hand, fewer heterogeneous partisan parents may exist in coming decades. Couple this with parents communicating more negative cues about the opposite party to their children and parent–child partisan correspondence might increase in adolescence. On the other hand, any hyper-partisanship displayed by parents could push their children to partisan independence, especially during early adulthood. Indeed, this process might be underway. Whether turned off by the partisan political environment or by partisan parents, the proportion of political independents is higher among Millennials than older generations today (Pew Research Center 2014). Future examinations of mother versus father transmission of party identification should therefore emphasize even more within-family political factors such as the relative politicization or relative strength of parental partisanship.

Notes

1. *Acknowledgments*: Earlier versions of this project were presented at the 2013 Annual Meeting of the American Political Science Association and at the College of Wooster in spring 2015. Useful feedback was provided by audience members at both presentations. Paul Allen Beck and Herbert Weisberg provided much welcomed early encouragement of this work. This research would not have been possible without the data collection efforts of two teams of scholars: Kent Jennings, Richard Niemi, and Laura Stoker and Richard Fox and Jennifer Lawless. I thank them for conducting these studies and, most especially, for making their data available for analysis.
2. For more detailed information regarding the design of this study, particularly the 1965 and 1997 waves, refer to Jennings and Niemi (1974, appendix) and Jennings, Stoker, and Bowers (2009).
3. In total, interview data exists for 769 parent–child pairs from the 1997 wave. Of these, party identification data exists for 613 father–mother–child triads.
4. The mean age for the 1997 children was 23 years old, with a range of 15 to 38 years old. Only 4 percent of these respondents were older than 30.
5. To determine whether parents were homogeneous or heterogeneous, I followed the approach of Jennings and colleagues (see Jennings and Langton 1969, 334; Jennings and Niemi 1974, 53). First, I collapsed the seven-point party identification scale into three points, including the partisan leaners in with the partisans. Second, homogeneous parents are those where both are Democratic, both are Independent, or both are Republican. Similarly, parents–child agreement exists if all are Democratic, all are Independent, or all are Republican (using the collapsed party identification scale).
6. Because of the nature of the data collection (parents were asked the partisanship of spouses), only parents who were married at the time of the survey are included in the analyses.
7. The respondents' "general level of information about politics and public affairs" was supplied by the interviewer. High knowledge parents were those whose level was rated as "very high" or "fairly high." I classified "average," "fairly low," and "very low" respondents as possessing low knowledge.
8. Both correlations are significant at $p < .001$; numbers of cases are, respectively, 150 and 242.
9. Both correlations are significant at $p < .001$; numbers of cases are, respectively, 182 and 150.

10. To assess support for women's equality, a seven-point scale was used. Respondents were grouped into those selecting a point on the "Equal role for women and men" side of the scale versus those on the "Women's place is in the home" side. Those choosing the scale midpoint were not included in the analysis. Similarly, those selecting "Neither agree nor disagree" when asked whether they agreed that mothers with young children should stay at home were not included in the analysis for that item.

11. Among supporters of equal gender roles, the mother–child and father–child correlations are, respectively, .338 (N = 452) and .290 (N = 416). Correlations for those believing women's proper place is in the home are .448 for mothers (N = 202) and .429 for fathers (N = 191). All correlations are significant at $p < .001$.

12. For more details about their study, see Lawless and Fox (2015, chap. 1).

13. Party identification data is missing for 396 mothers versus 1,070 fathers.

14. Not surprisingly, about two-thirds of children who do not know the party affiliation of one or both parents think of themselves as not partisan.

15. These results are for the 306 children who reported partisanship data for both parents and whose parents do not share the same partisanship. When adding the cases for those children who reported partisanship for only one parent, the pull of mom's partisanship is even stronger: 71.9 percent of children had the same partisanship of their mothers versus 51.2 percent of their fathers. However, many of these added cases are from children of single mothers, so the children are not receiving any partisan cues from their fathers.

16. All four correlations are significant at $p < .001$; numbers of cases are, respectively, 1,150, 953, 1,270, and 1,023.

17. Among the college students, the mother–daughter correlation was .698 (N = 658) compared to .662 for fathers and daughters (N = 522). For college-aged sons, the correlation with the mothers was .703 (N = 612) versus .728 for fathers (N = 501). All correlations are significant at $p < .001$.

18. Again, these results are restricted to the 306 non-homogeneous partisan parent families where children reported partisanship data for both parents. Of these, 234 have partisan fathers whereas 231 have partisan mothers.

19. Unlike in 1997, however, the 2012 respondents were not provided a "neither agree nor disagree" option.

References

ABC. 2015. "Elephant in the Room." *black-ish*, Season 1, Episode 23. Accessed January 17, 2016. http://abc.go.com/shows/blackish/episode-guide/season-01/123-elephant-in-the-room#recap.

Bandura, Albert. 1969. "Social-Learning Theory of Identificatory Processes." In *Handbook of Socialization Theory and Research*, edited by David A. Goslin, 213–262. Chicago: Rand McNally and Company.

Bandura, Albert. 1986. *Social Foundations of Thought and Action: A Social Cognitive Theory*. Englewood Cliffs, NJ: Prentice-Hall.

Beck, Paul Allen. 1977. "The Role of Agents in Political Socialization." In *Handbook of Political Socialization: Theory and Research*, edited by Stanley Allen Renshon, 115–141. New York: The Free Press.

Beck, Paul Allen, and M. Kent Jennings. 1975. "Parents as 'Middlepersons' in Political Socialization." *Journal of Politics* 37: 83–107.

Beck, Paul Allen, and M. Kent Jennings. 1991. "Family Traditions, Political Periods, and the Development of Partisan Orientations." *Journal of Politics* 53: 742–763.

Bianchi, Suzanne M. 2011. "Family Change and Time Allocation in American Families." *Annals of the American Academy of Political and Social Science* 638: 21–44.

Bianchi, Suzanne M., Liana C. Sayer, Melissa A. Milkie, and John P. Robinson. 2012. "Housework: Who Did, Does or Will Do It, and How Much Does It Matter?" *Social Forces* 91: 55–63.

Burns, Nancy, Ashley E. Jardina, Donald Kinder, and Molly E. Reynolds. 2016. "The Politics of Gender." In *New Directions in Public Opinion* (2nd ed.), edited by Adam J. Berinsky, 124–145. New York: Routledge.

Campbell, Angus, Philip E. Converse, Warren E. Miller, and Donald E. Stokes. 1960. *The American Voter*. New York: John Wiley.

Campbell, Ernest Q. 1969. "Adolescent Socialization." In *Handbook of Socialization Theory and Research*, edited by David A. Goslin, 821–859. Chicago: Rand McNally and Company.

Dinas, Elias. 2013. "Why Does the Apple Fall Far from the Tree? How Early Political Socialization Prompts Parent-Child Dissimilarity." *British Journal of Political Science* 44: 827–852.

Gauthier, Anne, Timothy M. Smeeding, and Frank F. Furstenberg, Jr. 2004. "Are Parents Investing Less Time in Children? Trends in Selected Industrialized Countries." *Population and Development Review* 30: 647–671.

Greenstein, Fred I. 1961. "Sex-Related Differences in Childhood." *Journal of Politics* 23: 353–371.

Iyengar, Shanto G., Guarav Sood, and Yphtach Lelkes. 2012. "Affect, Not Ideology: A Social Identity Perspective on Polarization." *Public Opinion Quarterly* 76: 405–431.

Jennings, M. Kent, and Kenneth P. Langton. 1969. "Mothers versus Fathers: The Formation of Political Orientations among Young Americans." *Journal of Politics* 31: 329–358.

Jennings, M. Kent, and Gregory B. Markus. 1984. "Partisan Orientations over the Long Haul: Results from the Three-Wave Political Socialization Panel Study." *American Political Science Review* 78: 1000–1018.

Jennings, M. Kent, and Richard G. Niemi. 1968. "The Transmission of Political Values from Parent to Child." *American Political Science Review* 62: 169–184.

Jennings, M. Kent, and Richard G. Niemi. 1974. *The Political Character of Adolescence: The Influence of Families and Schools*. Princeton: Princeton University Press.

Jennings, M. Kent, and Richard G. Niemi. 1981. *Generations and Politics: A Panel Study of Young Adults and Their Parents*. Princeton, NJ: Princeton University Press.

Jennings, M. Kent, and Laura Stoker. 2004. *Study of Political Socialization: Parent-Child Pairs Based on Survey of Youth Panel and Their Offspring, 1997*. Ann Arbor, MI: University of Michigan, Center for Political Studies/Survey Research Center [producer]. Ann Arbor, MI: Inter-university Consortium for Political and Social Research [distributor].

Jennings, M. Kent, Laura Stoker, and Jake Bowers. 2009. "Politics across Generations: Family Transmission Reexamined." *Journal of Politics* 71: 782–799.

Kinder, Donald R. 2006. "Politics and the Life Cycle." *Science* 312: 1905–1908.

Lawless, Jennifer L., and Richard L. Fox. 2015. *Running from Office: Why Young Americans Are Turned off to Politics*. Oxford: Oxford University Press.

Leeper, Thomas J., and Rune Slothuus. 2014. "Political Parties, Motivated Reasoning, and Public Opinion Formation." *Advances in Political Psychology* 35 (Supplement 1): 129–156.

Levendusky, Matthew. 2009. *The Partisan Sort: How Liberals Became Democrats and Conservatives Became Republicans.* Chicago: University of Chicago Press.

Maccoby, Eleanor E., Richard E. Matthews, and Anton S. Morton. 1954. "Youth and Political Change." *Public Opinion Quarterly* 18: 23–39.

Nogee, Philip, and Murray B. Levin. 1958. "Some Determinants of Political Attitudes among College Voters." *Public Opinion Quarterly* 22: 449–463.

Patterson, Charlotte J., Rachel H. Farr, and Paul D. Hastings. 2015. "Socialization in the Context of Family Diversity." In *Handbook of Socialization: Theory and Research* (2nd ed.), edited by Joan E. Grusec and Paul D. Hastings, 202–227. New York: Guilford Press.

Pew Research Center. 2014. "Millennials in Adulthood: Detached from Institutions, Networked with Friends." Accessed January 18, 2016. http://www.pewsocialtrends. org/2014/03/07/millennials-in-adulthood/#fnref-18663-1.

Saenz, Michael. 2016. "Family Ties." Encyclopedia of Television. *Museum of Broadcast Communications.* Accessed January 17, 2016. http://www.museum.tv/eotv/familyties. htm.

Sayer, Liana C., Suzanne M. Bianchi, and John P. Robinson. 2004. "Are Parents Investing Less in Children? Trends in Mothers' and Fathers' Time with Children." *American Journal of Sociology* 110: 1–43.

Smetana, Judith G., Jessica Robinson, and Wendy M. Rote. 2015. "Socialization in Adolescence." In *Handbook of Socialization: Theory and Research* (2nd ed.), edited by Joan E. Grusec and Paul D. Hastings, 60–84. New York: Guilford Press.

Stewart, Susan. 2007. "The Parents Ate Sprouts: The Kids Stole the Show." *New York Times,* February 25. Accessed January 17, 2016. http://www.nytimes.com/2007/02/25/ arts/television/25stew.html.

Stoker, Laura, and Jackie Bass. 2011. "Political Socialization: Ongoing Questions and New Directions." In *The Oxford Handbook of American Public Opinion and the Media,* edited by Robert Y. Shapiro and Lawrence R. Jacobs, 453–470. Oxford: Oxford University Press.

Stoker, Laura, and M. Kent Jennings. 2008. "Of Time and the Development of Partisan Polarization." *American Journal of Political Science* 52: 619–635.

Yavorsky, Jill E., Claire M. Kamp-Dush, and Sarah J. Schoppe-Sullivan. 2015. "The Production of Inequality: The Gender Division of Labor across the Transition to Parenthood." *Journal of Marriage and Family* 77: 662–679.

Zuckerman, Alan S., Josip Dasović, and Jennifer Fitzgerald. 2007. *Partisan Families: The Social Logic of Bounded Partisanship in Germany and Britain.* Cambridge: Cambridge University Press.

3

PROMOTING ADOLESCENT GIRLS' CIVIC ENGAGEMENT AND ACTIVISM[1]

Britney G Brinkman

Sara Pesi is a senior at a small liberal arts college in Pittsburgh, Pennsylvania, majoring in Public Policy. When Sara was an adolescent, she was stalked and harassed by an adult she worked with and she was unable to get a restraining order under the Pennsylvania state law. Despite filing a complaint, Sara was told that her relationship to the perpetrator did not fit the law's specifications. At the age of 14, Sara turned her personal experiences into a campaign to change the state law, ensuring that minors would have complete access to protective orders (Andren 2012). As a college student, Sara continued to advocate for the bill, which finally passed.

Sara's story is a testament to the active engagement of girls and young women in the political sphere. However, Sara is likely not the image that comes to mind when most people think of a political activist. Citizen activists within the United States tend to be from advantaged groups, particularly White, middle to upper class, and male (Verba, Schlozman, and Brady 1995). In particular, men engage in more formal political activities than do women (Burns, Schlozman, and Verba 2001). One of the key reasons for this gender difference involves the fact that women are less likely to be politically oriented than men, resulting from differences in political socialization of boys and girls—a process explored throughout this volume.

Despite assertions that girls are less interested in political activities than boys, girls have long been engaged in activism, although their efforts have traditionally been either ignored or tokenized by researchers and adult activists (Taft 2010). Although traditional political participation (like voting) among young adults is on the decline, activism related to social issues and causes that youth care about is increasing (Soler-i-Marti 2015). Girls' activism includes activities that are usually considered nonpolitical, but as evidenced by Sara's story, this activism may in fact be directly connected to more traditional political spheres. Further, there has been a recent surge of interest in "girl power"—and along with that, explorations of girls' civic engagement.

In this chapter, I scrutinize girls' civic engagement within the United States by addressing how different definitions of civic engagement, political participation, and activism may impact our conclusions. I am particularly interested in examining girls' activism—defined as the ways in which they work to promote social or political change. I draw upon Verba, Schlozman, and Brady's (1995) Civic Volunteerism Model, which posits that three main types of factors influence civic participation: resources, recruitment, and psychological orientation. In particular, I ask: Do girls have an orientation to civic engagement? Do they have resources available to them to facilitate their participation in civic activities and activism? And can a program designed to promote activism among girls increase their orientation to or engagement in activism? I provide data from a study to further explore the influence of motivation, knowledge, and self-efficacy on girls' activism.

Defining "Girl"

In order to understand the engagement of girls it is essential to explore the way in which girls' gendered identities influence their experiences. Understanding the girl as activist means understanding girlhood—a dynamic and diverse phenomenon itself. One aspect to understanding the political and activist lives of girls requires exploring research on gender differences in political engagement. However, this exploration is not done to dichotomize or essentialize gender or gendered experiences. I utilize the term "girl" itself from an intersectional approach—emphasizing that individuals who identity as girls differ considerably in their internal lives and external experiences based on their race/ethnicity, nationality, social class, sexuality, and gender identity. I understand femininity and "girlness" itself to exist on a continuum—girls are not all the same and are not opposite of boys. However, girls may share similar experiences in terms of gendered socialization and oppression that influence the ways in which they conceptualize political life and how they choose to engage as citizens and/or activists.

Differentiating Civic Engagement, Political Participation, and Activism

Civic engagement, political participation, and activism are related, yet distinct, constructs; defining them is necessary to conducting any research on girls' civic engagement. Michael Delli Carpini (2000) describes civic engagement as actions that address issues of public concern. A key element to developing civic engagement involves having a civic identity (Colby and Damon 1992; Hatcher

2011)—meaning seeing oneself as being an active participant in society com-
mitted to making social changes (Colby and Sullivan 2009). Definitions of civic
engagement often link individual activities to citizenship and its accompanying
rights and responsibilities. As a result, many think of civic engagement as being
innately political, though as Putnam (2000) argues, civic engagement involves a
range of nonpolitical activities in which people connect to their communities.
Civic engagement can include actions that both seek to support current structures
(e.g., volunteering in a soup kitchen) and those that promote change (e.g., writing a letter to a politician asking them to change laws impacting homeless youth).
Civic engagement can include voluntary activities not explicitly connected to
governmental agencies or bodies. In contrast, Verba, Schozman, and Brady (1995)
define political participation as including "activity that is intended to or has the
consequence of affecting, either directly or indirectly, government action" (9). I
focus on the factors influencing girls' and young women's activism—actions
intended to promote social change, which may or may not be political.

While clarifying these constructs can be helpful in distinguishing among types
of participation, they often overlap in ways that may complicate our ability to
study civic engagement amongst girls. Girls may be more likely to participate
in some forms of civic engagement than others. The operationalization of these
constructs varies across studies, making it difficult to draw conclusions. Later, I
explore the ways these definitions may impact girls' motivation for these
activities.

Orientation to Civic Engagement and Activism

Developing an orientation to activism increases the likelihood that girls will
become engaged citizens and participate in activities such as voting and community organizing. Such an orientation can include having an interest in particular
issues, being motivated to engage in activism, and having a feeling of self-efficacy
regarding one's ability to engage in activism. Some research on political engagement among youth has suggested that girls view politics as being a masculine
endeavor and therefore are less likely to develop an orientation toward political
participation (Burns, Scholzman, and Verba 2001). Additionally, adult women
are more likely to engage in informal, rather than formal, political actions
(Cicognani et al. 2011), and studies have shown small, but meaningful differences
in the political engagement of men and women (Verba, Schlozman, and Brady
1995). To the extent that gender differences exist, they have often been attributed
to gender role socialization in childhood (Owen and Dennis 1988).

When one considers the definitions of civic engagement and activism as
including both political and nonpolitical forms of participation, the question
of gender differences in engagement becomes more complicated. Research
assessing such differences has been mixed, and the findings vary considerably
based on what and how questions are asked. For example, in their comprehensive

study of school children, Alozie, Simon, and Merrill (2003) found that girls surpassed boys in their political interest and activity. In particular, girls were significantly more likely than boys to see voting as important, to express interest in political activity at school or at home, and to engage in media to follow election campaigns.

Unfortunately, assumptions that girls are not interested in politics have often lead researchers to exclude girls from research on citizenship and political engagement (Taft 2014) or to frame studies using definitions of political involvement based on the types of activities in which men are more likely to participate (Alozie, Simon, and Merrill 2003). As a result, scholarship about girls' activism and civic engagement is limited. Taft (2014) asserted that understanding girls' civic engagement may require first redefining and conceptualizing what is meant by politics and political engagement. In fact, some qualitative research with girls/young women has suggested that while they may endorse a disinterest in "politics," many express an interest in and engagement in social movements, social issues, and social change. Briggs (2008) found that young women who were disinterested in party politics expressed deep interest in political issues, such as reproductive rights, wars, and policy decisions. In fact, "even girls with critical perspectives on many deeply political issues may state that they are 'not political'" (Taft 2014, 263).

Clarifying the differences between civic engagement, activism, and political participation highlights the nuance surrounding findings indicating that girls are less politically engaged than boys. Understanding girls' involvement in activism that may not be "political" contributes to a complete picture of the civic engagement of young women. These activities in and of themselves provide value to the community and offer girls opportunities to develop personal attributes. Girls' social and civic participation also increases the likelihood of them participating in political endeavors and increases political interest (Cicognani et al. 2012). These types of activities can also influence engagement in more directly political acts in adulthood (Youniss and Yates 1999). Thus, understanding girls' orientation toward activism, be it political or not, is important. It contributes to the landscape of girls' civic engagement as well as increasing our understanding of youth (and later adult) political engagement.

Numerous studies have shown that parental influence can be an important factor in the development of girls' orientation to civic engagement and activism (e.g., Burns, Scholzman, and Verba 2001; Gniewosz, Noack, and Buhl 2009) as well as party identification (see Oxley in this volume). Adolescents' whose parents are interested in politics are more likely to be interested as well (Schulz et al. 2010). Parents' perceived involvement in social, civic, and political activities impacts their children's involvement such that children were more likely to engage in the activities their parents engaged in (Cicognani et al. 2012). In one study of youth activists in Canada, the majority of the activists had family members who were engaged in activism as well (Jennings 2002).

The development of girls' civic identity, orientation to activism, and political orientation is also impacted by girls' experiences and identities related to social class and ethnicity. This is particularly true for minority youth who may experience disenfranchisement and discrimination. One study found that White children showed a higher orientation to politics than Black, Asian, Hispanic, or Native American children (Alozie, Simon, and Merrill 2003). This finding is congruent with research with adults demonstrating that Whites are more likely to engage in political or civic behavior than African Americans or Latinos (Verba, Schlozman, and Brady 1995).

It may be that White children have a greater sense of trust in political systems because of their own experiences (either positive experiences or a lack of negative experiences) with social systems and adults in authority. Rubin (2007) argues that civic identity of youth is constructed and is impacted by their racial and economic backgrounds, as well as their experiences inside and outside of school, and their interpretations of these experiences. She found that students' perceptions of either congruence (where they felt that the cultural ideals of America and realities of citizenship matched up) or disjuncture (where they experience a gap between ideal and actual experiences) influenced the way they discussed their intentions towards civic participation. White students and immigrant students were more likely than students of color to experience congruence. White students often argued that their own experiences of personal safety and prosperity were "proof" of such congruence, while immigrant students frequently compared the United States to other nations, describing how citizens in the U.S. have more freedoms. Students of color and students from low-income communities reported more experiences of disjuncture, sharing stories of their experiences of discrimination as evidence that the civic ideals they learn about in class are in conflict with people's lived experiences of injustice.

Thus, girls' orientation toward civic engagement and activism will be shaped not only by their experiences within civic organizations but also by the way they interpret these events and how they conceptualize their own role within society. Girls from all ethnic groups may decide not to engage in political processes or activism, but their reasons for the disengagement might vary depending upon their ethnic identity and experiences. Rubin (2007) found students from privileged backgrounds often indicated that they did not need to participate in civic life because they should just be grateful for what they had. In contrast, youth who experienced disjuncture often reported a hopelessness regarding civic participation, indicating that there was no point to trying to change the system (Rubin 2007). In fact, many African American and Asian American youth report that politics is a way for those already in power to maintain that power (Marcelo, Lopez, and Kirby 2007).

However, there are girls who decide that they should play a role in changing how their society functions. Although these girls likely face barriers to civic engagement, one should not assume that they, like ethnic minority youth, are not engaged in politics or activism. Youth of color engage in a variety of civic activities, including volunteering for nonpolitical groups, being involved in community problem-solving and participating in charity events (Marcelo, Lopez, and Kirby 2007).

Resources for Civic Engagement

Having a civic identity may lead one to developing a plan for civic engagement, but is not sufficient to lead to action, which requires resources, including social capital and civic skills. Disparities in political participation among different groups are not merely a result of lack of motivation but also reflect unequal access to these resources (Verba, Schlozman, and Brady 1995).

Numerous political scientists have noted the importance of social capital, the "connections among individuals—social networks and the norms of reciprocity and trustworthiness that arise from them" (Putnam 2000, 19). Many adolescents believe that they can make a difference in their community (Marcelo, Lopez, and Kirby 2007) but may feel uncertain about how to do so. Girls' involvement in formal and informal community groups can impact their civic engagement (Albanesi, Cicognani, and Zani 2007) and later engagement in political action (Cicognani et al. 2012). Relationships with other activists and the structures that support them are crucial (Kennelly 2009). Belonging to a like-minded group can provide the relationships that youth need in order to dig deeper and take risks. Activism groups provide opportunities for girls to learn from each other and share ideas. Networks of recruitment increase the likelihood that an individual will engage in political activity because they provide opportunities for individuals to be asked to be involved (Verba, Schlozman, and Brady 1995). Groups can also provide existing networks to allow activism to happen—especially when one wants to take quick action on an urgent matter ("Kennelly" 2009).

In addition to acquiring social capital, girls will be more likely to engage in activism if they learn civic skills (Brady, Verba, and Schlozman 1995). Schools in particular can teach civic skills through involvement in clubs and activities (Burns, Scholzman, and Verba 2001) and through social studies courses (Hahn 2001). For example, involvement in Gay-Straight Alliances (GSAs) can lead to individual and collective empowerment and help these adolescents become agents for change (Russell et al. 2009). Girls may also gain civic skills by participating in programs offered outside of schools that teach adolescent girls about social issues, some of which directly encourage participation in social activism. For example, girls within the organization SPARK (Sexualization Protest: Action, Resistance, Knowledge) participate in online forums, blogs, and marches addressing concerns related to the sexualization of young women (Edell, Brown, and Tolman 2013). Youth who participate in either school-based or community-based programs are more likely to stay politically engaged as adults, and many go through a developmental process in which they transition from being a program participant to an engaged citizen (Borden and Serido 2009). I explore whether a program designed to teach activism skills can increase orientation to and participation in activism.

Girls, Activism, and Social Change Community-Based Research Program

The Girls, Activism and Social Change (GASC) Program was developed to examine young women's perceptions about activism and to design and evaluate a program to promote activism. As the lead investigator, I was invited to develop the program by the principal of the upper school of an all-girl's school in a large city in the Mid-Atlantic region of the United States. In line with Participatory Action Research (Brinkman 2012; Kidd and Kral 2005), in which scholars and community members work together to develop research projects that meet the needs of a community, the lead investigator and principal met to discuss the goals and outcome of the program and research study.

Workshops

There were four main goals of the GASC Program, including that the students would 1) learn about girls/women who have engaged in activism to promote social change; 2) learn about current social issues and how they impact girls' lives; 3) generate skills to participate in activism for social change; and 4) develop a social change proposal plan.

The program consisted of seven, 2.5 hour workshops spread throughout the academic year. The workshops were designed and implemented by the program team consisting of the lead investigator, two advanced graduate students in Counseling Psychology, and five undergraduate Women's Studies interns. The workshops focused on awareness building, skills training, and/or community engagement. Students were provided training in the following activism-related skills: using technology and social media, conducting a needs assessment, exploring and capitalizing on individual strengths, establishing allies, and creating an action plan. Four of the workshops took place at the girls' school. Three workshops consisted of field trips that provided opportunities for conversations about community engagement, including a visit to the university where the lead investigator works, a visit to the local city building with a talk by a female councilwoman, and a visit to a natural history museum exhibit about empowering women around the globe. In the initial session, the students were asked to develop a list of the most important social issues facing girls today and then voted on the top three, which were sexism, lack of opportunities, and freedom of speech. These three topics were then woven into the program and used to develop examples in the skill building activities.

The program was offered as part of the school's Community Connections curriculum. All freshman, sophomores, and juniors were required to participate in one year-long community engagement project within the school curriculum. Students in the school learned about the possible projects during an assembly in which the Community Connections Coordinator gave an overview of the projects. The lead investigator was present at the assembly and described the GASC Program. Students were informed that they would be asked to participate in a research project if they were placed in this program but would be allowed to participate even if they did not elect to be in the research component. All 12 students assigned to the GASC Program provided parental consent and their own assent and became participants in the study.

Participants

The participants for this study included 12 girls ranged in age from 14 to 16 years ($M = 14.83$, $SD = .835$) in grade Freshman (50 percent), Sophomore (17 percent), or Junior (33 percent). The students self-identified their ethnicity as White non-Hispanic (75 percent), African American/Black (8 percent), Multi-racial (7 percent), or undisclosed (8 percent). All participants reported their parents received at least some post-secondary education.

Research Study Procedures and Measures

A mixed methods approach was used to capitalize on the strengths of both quantitative and qualitative methodologies. By utilizing open-ended questions in addition to quantitative measures, the perspectives of the young women are portrayed in their own words. In addition to pre- and post-test questionnaires, the girls participated in in-depth interviews at the end of the program. In this chapter, I report only on the survey findings.

The students completed questionnaires on the first and last day of the program (taking approximately 20 minutes to complete). The questionnaires consisted of the following measures: a demographic questionnaire, the Engagement in Activism Scale (EAS), the Activism Orientation Scale (Corning and Myers 2002), and open-ended questions about the girls' perceptions of activism. The orientation to activism scale measured the extent to which the girls self-reported the likelihood they would engage in 35 different activism behaviors. Higher scores on the AOS indicated greater likelihood that the participant would engage in activism behaviors. The Engagement in Activism Scale was developed by the research team to assess how frequently girls engage in political, social, financial, and personal behaviors related to activism.

Results

Repeated measures ANOVA was utilized to examine whether the participants changed in their orientation to activism or engagement in activism behaviors from the beginning to the end of the year. The results revealed significant changes from pre-test to post-test (F (2, 12) = 7.37, p < .05, partial η^2 = .69). Follow-up analyses revealed an increase in orientation to activism (pre-test M = 62.11; post-test M = 69.22, $F(1, 12)$ = 4.88, p = .058, partial η^2 = .38) and an increased engagement in activism behaviors (pre-test M = 2.23; post-test M = 2.60, $F(1, 12)$ = 14.70, p < .01, partial η^2 = .65).

Before the program, the items on the Activism Orientation Scale with the highest means included: encourage a friend to join a political organization, try to change a friend's mind about a social or political issue, and invite a friend to attend a meeting of a political organization. After the program, the highest means were for items: likely to wear a t-shirt or button with a political message, purchase an item with a political message, and display a poster or bumper sticker with a political message. Before the program, the girls reported the behaviors they had most often engaged in, including: voting in an election (including school elections), making a donation (including material donations like clothes or books) to a campaign or non-profit organization, and assisting with a group engaged in community problem-solving. The girls reported the least participation in a protest or boycott. After the program, frequencies for all of the activist behaviors increased, with voting in an election, making a donation, and volunteering for a non-profit organization having the highest item means. Participating in a protest or boycott remained the lowest.

In addition to measuring girls' intentions to engage and actual engagement in various activist behaviors, we were interested in knowing more about what girls thought about the role they play in social change as well as their levels of confidence in their ability to engage in activism. The students were asked to indicate the extent to which they agreed with three statements about activism on a four-point likert scale with 1 being *strongly disagree* and 4 being *strongly agree*. On average, students indicated agreement with all three statements about activism (see Table 3.1), with higher scores of agreement on statements one

TABLE 3.1 Extent of Agreement with Statements about Activism

Statement	Pre-Test			Post-Test		
	M	*SD*	*Range*	*M*	*SD*	*Range*
It is important for young women to engage in activism to promote social change	3.82	.15	3.44–4.00	3.50	.18	3.15–3.96
It is important for me personally to engage in activism to promote social change	3.55	.17	3.15–3.96	3.5	.17	3.15–3.96
I feel confident in my ability to engage in activism to promote social change	3.00	.11	2.63–3.15	2.90	.24	2.46–3.54

Note: Higher scores indicate greater level of agreement with statement; scale range from 1–4, Strongly Disagree to Strongly Agree

("It is important for young women to engage in activism to promote social change") and two ("It is important for me personally to engage in activism to promote social change") compared to statement three ("I feel confident in my ability to engage in activism to promote social change"). Repeated measures MANOVA found no significant change over time on participants' extent of agreement with statements about activism (F (3, 9) = .50, p = .69), although with a small sample size the lack of a significant difference should be interpreted with caution.

The girls were asked to explain their level of agreement with each activism statement in an open-ended format. Students' open-ended responses were analyzed by a team of researchers using qualitative content analysis informed by grounded theory (Charmaz 2006, 2014). Four categories of codes emerged from the data (see Table 3.2): motivation for activism, activism to challenge cultural limitations, personal engagement in activism, and confidence to engage in activism. McNemar's chi-square was used to assess whether there were differences in codes in the

TABLE 3.2 Themes from Responses to Activism Statements

Theme	Category	Pre-test frequency	Post-test frequency	McNemar's chi-square p value
Motivation				.38
	Activism ability	3	4	
	Activism obligation	6	4	
	Personal benefits	2	2	
	N/A	1	2	
Challenge cultural limitations				.07
	Yes	8	2	
	No	4	10	
Personal engagement				.06
	Desire/need for change	8	2	
	Responsibility	1	7	
	Importance of youth perspective	2	1	
	No answer	1	2	
Confidence				*Unable to calculate; cell sizes too small*
	Confident	7	4	
	Not confident	1	4	
	Inexperienced	2	2	
	Needs resources	1	0	
	No answer	1	2	

pre- and post-test responses. No significant differences were found for any of the themes; however, again we must consider the small sample size.

Examinations of the qualitative data suggest that there were slight shifts in the way the girls explained their reasons for their level of agreement with the statements about activism. Eight students on the pre-test questionnaires wrote about the desire to change cultural limitations as a motivation for activism, while that theme was present for only two of the students at post-test. Before the program began, eight of the students wrote that their desire/need for social change would be the reason they would personally become involved in activism, as evidenced in one girl's response, "It is important to me to promote social change because to see the change, you have to believe in the change." However, at the end of the program, only two students had this theme, while seven of the students indicated that they had a responsibility to personally be involved in activism. As one girl wrote, "I believe that it is all of our responsibility to better the condition of our fellow humans."

Discussion and Implications of the Program

The findings from our study support the emerging body of research suggesting that adolescent girls are invested in activism and civic engagement, despite some research to the contrary. Our data indicate that girls do see themselves as having a role to play in social change, they possess an orientation toward activism and they engage in a variety of activist behaviors. The GASC Program was designed to provide girls with tools to do this work, and our preliminary results suggest that it was effective in doing so. The girls increased in their orientation to activism and engagement in activism behaviors from the beginning to the end of the program. Our study also supported the importance of social capital and the development of civic skills as necessary resources. Additional research using a larger sample size and a control group could provide further evidence of the impact of programs designed to promote activism skills among girls.

Our findings indicate that the girls at the start of our study already possessed some amount of orientation toward activism, which increased by the end of the program. In addition to girls reporting that they would be more likely overall to engage in activism, the types of behaviors they were most likely to do changed. At pre-test the highest scores on the AOS were for items related to interpersonal conversations about social issues while at post-test their highest scores were for items that indicated public displays of opinions. It is possible that programs like ours encourage girls to shift from more private to more public forms of civic engagement.

The girls in our study articulated a belief that young women should be involved in activism for social change, and that they have a special contribution to make. As one of our participants wrote, "Young women have just as much to say about activism as anyone else, they also look at things in different ways."

At the end of the program, the girls indicated more themes related to their own individual responsibility to engage in activism, not just the belief that young women should be involved, writing statements like, "I want to be able to say, 'I helped make this happen' or, 'I was the one who solved this.'"

Our study also supported research indicating that social capital and the acquisition of civic skills are important in understanding girls' engagement in activism behaviors by turning one's motivations regarding civic life into actions (Putnam 2000). Girls may not always have access to social capital or may struggle to find adult allies and role models to support them in being activist. As one our participants noted in her pre-test questionnaire, "Yes, I do believe I can [engage in activism], however the right support and team work from others in my community can prove to be difficult or just having more women role models to show how it is done." Programs designed to teach girls activism skills, especially ones that challenge ideas that youth activism occurs in isolation, can be impactful in providing girls the support they need to transform an interest into action.

The program's goal was to help girls develop specific skills to increase their ability to engage in activism. While we did see an increase in activist behaviors, we were surprised to find that the girls' endorsement of their confidence decreased slightly (although not statistically significantly so). In their written responses regarding their assessment of their confidence, on the pre-test measure many girls directly endorsed feeling confident to engage in activism, even if they admitted that they had not actually done so. One girl wrote, "If I took the time to engage in activism I feel I could use my abilities to help in the cause." In contrast, the responses at post-test were less likely to include a statement directly citing confidence, but indicated they now had tools and knowledge that would help them act on their motivations to make social change. Such statements included: "I know more on how I can be engaged and what can be most effective" and "I feel equipped now that I know what to do with my ideas." It may be that girls' overt statements of confidence before the program reflected a lack of understanding of what is actually needed in order to engage in activism. The program's emphasis on skill building appeared to be successful in offering the girls tools they need to participate in activist behaviors.

The Future of Girls' Civic Engagement and Activism

In this chapter, I investigated girls' civic engagement within the United States, examining activism in particular. Overall, I argue that many girls are in fact interested in and engaged in activism behaviors, and that programs to promote such behaviors can be valuable. One reason for the need for the current research is the body of literature suggesting that girls are more likely to participate in nonpolitical rather than political forms of civic engagement. In some ways, girls' engagement in activism and civic activities that are outside the scope of "traditional" methods may itself constitute a form of activism. Girls and young women are finding ways to resist being defined by those in power and are seeking their own ways to promote social change. However, it is important to not dismiss the likelihood that girls' engagement in underground or informal political acts is also a result of being excluded (or expecting to be excluded) from more traditional forms of engagement. While we can (and should) celebrate the strength and resiliency that girls show by engaging in activism and informal civic actions, we should not do so in place of tackling very real barriers limiting girls and women. Gender differences in political engagement do matter as those who are inactive risk having their interests and preferences ignored by policymakers (Burns, Scholzman, and Verba 2001). Although girls may vary in their type and quantity of participation in political endeavors, it is important to continue to seek to understand why and how.

Redefining "Citizenship" and "Activism"

Understanding girls' civic engagement and activism within the United States today and in the future requires an exploration of shifting definitions. Anita Harris (2004) argued that the merging of neoliberal values and feminist inclinations at the beginning of the 21st century has resulted in a new conceptualization of the "ideal" girl-citizen—one she refers to as the "can-do girl." This ideal expects girls to be consumer citizens, independent, and responsible. The redefining of citizenship into consumerism means that citizen status is gained not by reaching a particular age or participating in political processes, but by achieving financial independence from one's family and the government (Harris 2004). Civic engagement and/or activism itself is portrayed to be linked to the power to spend money. Harris proposed that these ideals are conveyed to girls in messages by governmental institutions concerned with economic uncertainly and motivated to discourage young women from becoming reliant on government forms of social support. Marketers have also capitalized on this movement toward valuing the "consumer citizen" with attempts to package female empowerment as a product to be purchased and conveying shopping as a form of activism (Gill 2012; Lamb and Brown 2006). In this way, girls are given the message that consumerism can (and should) replace other forms of civic engagement.

The "can-do girl" is a vision of girlhood that is inaccessible to girls with limited financial resources and girls who value community over independence. Not only is the emphasis on consumer power limiting, the focus on individualism as the number one value is likely unappealing to girls whose cultural values emphasize family and community. Such discourses that offer a narrow view of political engagement limit the possibilities for empowerment of a diverse range of girls (Taft 2014). This conceptualization of the shopper as citizen/activist has been critiqued by young women who question its validity and applications. In a study of college women's reflections on media representations of empowerment, 50 percent of the participants indicated that media messages encourage consumerism among girls and young women—that they are given the message that having power comes from being perfect, and being perfect comes from using the "right" products. (Brinkman et al. 2015). In exploring girls' civic engagement, it is important to be aware of the pressures that girls experience to adopt the consumer-citizen model and examine the ways in which girls may resist or accept this model.

The future of girls' activism is likely also greatly influenced by technology. Quaye (2004) argues that youth activism of the 21st century looks qualitatively different than activism that has come before it, often targeting smaller changes and emphasizing coalition-building. Technology has broadened the scope of activism, with greater access for production and consumption of information (Kahn and Kellner 2004). Girls are able to utilize social media as a free and accessible source for engagement (Hirzalla and van Zoonen 2010). Activism taking place online is often scrutinized by scholars and adult activists who prefer more "traditional" forms of action. Some refer to these forms of activism as "slacktivism"—a word used to describe activities (many of them online) that ask minimal effort of individuals such as liking a Facebook post, sharing a blog, retweeting a tweet, or posting a photo of themselves wearing a particular color. The term is used derisively to indicate that the person engaging in the action is a "slacker" or too lazy to do more "meaningful" activism. While this term may be applied to individuals of any age who engage in activism via social media, the proportions of young adults utilizing social media sites suggests that girls will more commonly be targeted with this criticism than adult activists.

Although girls may be accused of being "slacktivist" while engaging in activism through social media, many youth are combining modes of activism through online and offline activities (Hirzalla and van Zoonen 2010). Online activism can have direct impacts on social issues. For example, Vie (2014) examined the use of the Human Rights Campaign (HRC) logo on Facebook as an example of social media activism. An HRC movement in March 2013 encouraged Facebook users to change their profile photo to a red logo designed to represent marriage equality. The image was shared by over 78,000 users within the first 24 hours, garnered media attention, and was adapted and adopted in numerous ways. Vie (2014) argues that this quickly spreading meme had real power as an action within the gay rights movement itself. The widespread use of the image temporarily changed the culture of Facebook. In contrast to the more common microaggressions that LGBT individuals face within social media this meme provided a tangible sign of support for a marginalized community.

Expressing one's opinions on social media and engaging in online activism can facilitate participation in offline political action (Valenzuela 2013). Seeking news information through social media sites has been shown to positively predict political participation (de Zuniga, Jung, and Valenzuela 2012). Understanding girls' civic engagement and activism will require continued research on the ways social media impact activism.

Conclusions

Despite American myths about rugged individuals creating social change on their own (e.g., Rosa Parks), the reality is that most change movements occur and are successful when people tap into social capital. Unfortunately, girls may acquire the perception that activism is often done in solitude based on the way media portray youth activists—focusing on one individual and ignoring the contexts (and other people) that surrounded that individual. In her book, *Rebel Girls* (2010), Jessica Taft explored the theme of exceptionalism—the idea that only exceptional and unique individuals are able to make real change—often highlighted in the media. Although initially it may seem complimentary to refer to a girl activist as "exceptional," this narrative can become problematic when it is the prevailing one. It sends the message that not all young adults are, can be, (or want to be) activists, and that youth activism occurs in isolation. The message that activists "do it alone" may create a barrier for a girl who is considering engaging in activism, but fears that she will lack support (Taft 2010). Adults can work as allies for girl activists, challenging the myth of exceptionalism and providing scaffolding for girls to work toward their own social change goals.

Sara is not the only girl who will face discrimination and legal barriers, nor is she the only one who will decide she wants to contribute to making social and political changes. As scholars we can continue to better understand girls' engagement in activism, including barriers that may keep them from developing an orientation toward political life or prevent them from acting on their hopes for social change. Girls and young women have enormous potential to make important contributions to civic life. One young woman fighting for change is a human interest story. Girls working together for social change create a movement.

Note

1. The research project would not have been possible without the efforts of Allison Jedinak and Aliya Kahn, who I thank tremendously for their efforts. Thanks also to Alexis DeRiggi for her editorial assistance on the manuscript.

References

Albanesi, Cinzia, Elvira Cicognani, and Bruna Zani. 2007. "Sense of Community, Civic Engagement, and Social Well-Being in Italian Adolescents." *Journal of Community and Applied Social Psychology* 17: 387–406.

Alozie, Nicholas O., James Simon, and Bruce D. Merrill. 2003. "Gender and Political Orientation in Childhood." *The Social Science Journal* 40: 1–18.

Andren, Kari. 2012. "Rostraver Teenager Pushes Legislation to Boost Protection against Stalking, Harassment." *TribLive.* Accessed March 15, 2016. http://triblive.com/home/2467228-74/pesi-victims-protection-harassment-legislation-order-stalking-area-belle-dated#axzz3u34lho7g.

Borden, Lynne, and Joyce Serido. 2009. "From Program Participant to Engaged Citizen: A Developmental Journey." *Journal of Communication Psychology* 37: 423–438.

Brady, Henry E., Sidney Verba, and Kay Lehman Schlozman. 1995. "Beyond SES: A Resource Model of Political Participation." *American Political Science Review* 89: 271–294.

Briggs, Jacqueline Ellen. 2008. "Young Women and Politics: An Oxymoron?" *Journal of Youth Studies* 11: 579–592.

Brinkman, Britney G. 2012. "More PAR Please! Why Schools and Universities Should Be Doing More Programming to Reduce Prejudice." In *The Psychology of Prejudice: Interdisciplinary Perspectives on Contemporary Issues*, edited by Dale W. Russell and Cristel Antonia Russell, 203–218. New York: Nova Publishers.

Brinkman, Britney G., Aliya Khan, Allison Jedinak, and Laura Vetere. 2015. "College Women's Reflections on Media Representations of Empowerment." *Psychology of Popular Media Culture* 1: 2–17. Accessed March 15, 2016. http://dx.doi.org/10.1037/ppm0000043.

Burns, Nancy, Kay Lehman Scholzman, and Sydney Verba. 2001. *The Private Roots of Public Action.* Cambridge: Harvard University Press.

Charmaz, Kathy. 2006. *Constructing Grounded Theory: A Practical Guide through Qualitative Research.* London: Sage Publications Ltd.

Charmaz, Kathy. 2014. *Constructing Grounded Theory.* Los Angeles, CA: Sage.

Cicognani, Elvira, Bruna Zavi, Bernard Fournier, Claire Gavray, and Michael Born. 2012. "Gender Differences in Youth's Political Engagement and Participation: The Role of Parents and Adolescents' Social and Civic Participation." *Journal of Adolescence* 3: 561–576.

Colby, Anne, and William Damon. 1992. *Some Do Care: Contemporary Lives of Moral Commitment.* New York: Free Press.

Colby, Anne, and William Sullivan. 2009. "Strengthening the Foundations of Student's Excellence, Integrity, and Social Contribution." *Liberal Education* 1: 22–29.

Corning, Alexandra, and Daniel J. Myers. 2002. "Individual Orientation toward Engagement in Social Action." *Political Psychology* 4: 703–729.

Delli Carpini, Michael X. 2000. "Gen.com: Youth, Civic Engagement, and the New Information Environment." *Political Communication* 4: 341–349.

de Zuniga, Homero Gil, Nakwon Jung, and Sebastian Valenzuela. 2012. "Social Media Use for News and Individuals' Social Capital, Civic Engagement and Political Participation." *Journal of Computer-Mediated Communication* 3: 319–336.

Edell, Dana, Lyn Miken Brown, and Deborah Tolman. 2013. "Embodying Sexualization: When Theory Meets Practice in Intergenerational Feminist Activism." *Feminist Theory* 3: 275–284.

Gill, Rosalind. 2012. "Media, Empowerment and the 'Sexualization of Culture' Debates." *Sex Roles* 11–12: 736–745.

Gniewosz, Burkhard, Peter Noack, and Monika Buhl. 2009. "Political Alienation and Adolescence: Associations with Parental Role Models, Parenting Styles, and Classroom Climate." *International Journal of Behavioral Development* 4: 337–346.

Hahn, Carole L. 2001. "Student Views of Democracy: The Good and Bad News." *Social Education* 7: 456–460.

Harris, Anita. 2004. *Future Girl: Young Women in the Twenty-First Century.* New York: Routledge.

Hatcher, Julie A. 2011. "Assessing Civic Knowledge and Engagement." *New Directions for Institutional Research* 149: 81–92.

Hirzalla, Fadi, and Liesbet van Zoonen. 2010. "Beyond the Online/Offline Divide: How Youth's Online and Offline Civic Activities Converge." *Social Science Computer Review* 4: 481–498.

Jennings, Kent M. 2002. "Generation Units and the Student Protest Movement in the United States: An Intra- and Intergenerational Analysis." *Political Psychology* 2: 303–324.

Kahn, Richard, and Douglas Kellner. 2004. "New Media and Internet Activism: From the 'Battle of Seattle' to Blogging." *New Media and Society* 1: 87–95.

Kennelly, Jacqueline Joan. 2009. "Youth Cultures, Activism, and Agency: Revisiting Feminist Debates." *Gender and Education* 3: 259–272.

Kidd, Sean A., and Michael J. Kral. 2005. "Practicing Participatory Action Research." *Journal of Counseling Psychology* 3: 367–379.

Lamb, Sharon, and Lyn Mikel Brown. 2006. *Packaging Girlhood: Rescuing Our Daughters from Marketers' Schemes.* New York: St. Martin's Griffin.

Marcelo, Karlo Barrios, Mark Hugo Lopez, and Emily Hoban Kirby. 2007. "Civic Engagement among Minority Youth." *Center for Information and Research on Civic Learning and Engagement.* Accessed March 15, 2016. http://www.civicyouth.org/PopUps/FactSheets/FS_Civic_Eng_Minority Youth.

Owen, Diana, and Jack Dennis. 1988. "Gender Differences in the Politicization of American Children." *Women and Politics* 2: 23–41.

Putnam, Robert D. 2000. *Bowling Alone: The Collapse and Revival of American Community.* New York: Simon and Schuster.

Quaye, Stephen John. 2004. "Hope and Learning: The Outcomes of Contemporary Student Activism." *About Campus* 2: 2–9.

Rubin, Beth. 2007. "'There's Still Not Justice': Youth Civic Identity Development amid Distinct School and Community Contexts." *The Teachers College Record* 2: 449–481.

Russell, Stephen T., Anna Muraco, Aarti Subramaniam, and Carolyn Laub. 2009. "Youth Empowerment and High School Gay-Straight Alliances." *Journal of Youth and Adolescence* 7: 891–903.

Schulz, Wolfram, John Ainley, Julian Fraillon, David Kerr, and Bruno Losito. 2010. *Initial Findings from the IEA International Civic and Citizenship Education Study.* Amsterdam: IEA.

Soler-i-Marti, Roger. 2015. "Youth Political Involvement Update: Measuring the Role of Cause-Oriented Political Interest in Young People's Activism." *Journal of Youth Studies* 3: 396–416.

Taft, Jessica K. 2010. *Rebel Girls: Youth Activism and Social Change across the Americas.* New York: New York University Press.

Taft, Jessica K. 2014. "The Political Lives of Girls." *Sociology Compass* 3: 259–267.

Valenzuela, Sebastian. 2013. "Unpacking the Use of Social Media for Protest Behavior: The Role of Information, Opinion Expression, and Activism." *American Behavioral Scientist* 7: 920–942.

Verba, Sidney, Kay Lehman Scholzman, and Henry E. Brady. 1995. *Voice and Equality: Civic Volunteerism in American Politics.* Cambridge, MA: Harvard University Press.

Vie, Stephanie. 2014. "In Defense of 'Slacktivism': The Human Rights Campaign Facebook Logo as Digital Activism." *First Monday* 19.

Youniss, James, and Miranda Yates. 1999. "Youth Service and Moral-Civic Identity: A Care for Everyday Morality." *Educational Psychology Review* 11 (4): 361–376.

4

THE GENDER GAP IN PUBLIC OPINION

Exploring Social Role Theory as an Explanation

Mary-Kate Lizotte

In President Obama's 2015 State of the Union Address, he proposed a childcare tax cut: "my plan will make quality childcare more available and more affordable for every middle-class and low-income family with young children in America" (State of the Union 2015). Feminist women lauded the remarks while many right-wing women pointed out that the plan would not apply to stay-at-home moms (Friedman 2015; Miller 2015). Ultimately, women from both the left and the right wanted the government to do more and spend more; in particular, these views seemed to come from women with children. But, do the opinions of these women differ from the opinions of men and fathers? Are all parents equally supportive of childcare spending or are there gender differences whereby men with children are not as supportive as women with children? This pattern need not be unique to spending on childcare, but could apply to other policy areas; indeed, we might expect that mothers' preferences would differ from other subsets of the population on public school spending and the provision of government services.

The gender gap in public opinion is of considerable interest. Gender gaps on policy issues likely contribute to gender differences in partisanship and voting, which are of interest because women are more likely to turn out to vote than men (CAWP 2015). This chapter begins with an overview of gender differences on political issues—that, generally, women are more likely than men to hold liberal positions on a variety of issues. The focus of the chapter is explaining these differences using Social Role Theory, which purports that men and women inhabit different social roles (for example, women as caregivers, men as bread-winners) that then leads to opinion differences, because individuals are socialized to adopt the traits necessary for these roles (Diekman and Schneider 2010). Such traits include anti-conflict and compassionate for women compared to assertive and tough for men. These social roles can be both diffuse (e.g., a woman; a man) and specific (e.g., a mother, a nurse, or a schoolteacher; a father, a soldier, or a police officer).

Gender differences in issue positions have notable political consequences rendering them worthy of investigation. Policymakers heed public opinion; changes in public opinion influence policymakers' decisions (Page and Shapiro 1983; Zaller 1992). Gender differences consistently appear for several policy areas. Specifically, women are less likely to support the use of force and are more likely to support increasing government spending for various social programs (Carroll 2006a; CAWP 2012; Norrander 2008; Sapiro 2002). Lastly, gender differences in issue positions contribute to the gender gap in voting (Chaney, Alvarez, and Nagler 1998; Clark and Clark 2008).

Certain issue gaps may be the result of the political effects of roles, in particular the intersection of gender and parenthood. These social roles are likely not independent but rather intersect in ways that produce meaningful and varied political perspectives. Analyzing the 1980–2012 cumulative American National Election Study (ANES) data, this chapter tests the supposition that gender differences in public opinion are largest when diffuse roles (i.e., being a woman) and specific roles (i.e., being a parent) intersect. For example, support should be highest among mothers for maternity leave. The specific role of mother would lead to support because of self-interest; the diffuse role of woman should lead to the adoption of particular personality traits, such as compassionate, empathetic, and helpful, that in turn leads to support for maternity leave. The intersection of both of these roles should produce the highest level of support compared to fathers and childless men and women.

The key finding from my analysis is that mothers significantly differ from fathers on a number of policy questions related to children and families. Specifically, mothers are more likely than fathers to support increased childcare spending, to support increased spending on public schools, and express a desire for more government services. Moreover, motherhood partially explains the origins of the gender gaps on these policies. The chapter concludes with implications of the results for the study of the gender gap as well as for applications in American political elections.

Gender Differences in Issue Positions

Differences in policy preferences exist between men and women on many policy areas. Prior research documents gender differences in attitudes toward force, compassion, and traditionalism (Shapiro and Mahajan 1986), and gender gaps are often robust to the inclusion of party identification (Kaufmann and Petrocik 1999). A consistently significant and sizeable—8–12 percentage points on average—gender gap has been documented for force issues with women less supportive of military interventions (Huddy, Cassese, and Lizotte 2008b; Norrander 2008). Evidence of gender differences in support for intervention existed for all the major wars since World War II (Conover and Sapiro 1993; Huddy et al. 2005;

Shapiro and Mahajan 1986). The force gap also extended to domestic force issues with women more likely to support gun control (Howell and Day 2000).

Women have been consistently more supportive of the government helping the less fortunate and providing for the general welfare (Howell and Day 2000; Huddy, Cassese, and Lizotte 2008b; Norrander 2008). In recent years, this gap has also hovered around 10 percentage points (Norrander 2008). Scales of social welfare attitudes, including questions on government guaranteed jobs, government provision of services, and government spending on food stamps, social security, the homeless, public schools, childcare, and the poor produced sizeable gender gaps (Howell and Day 2000). Analysis of individual items revealed gaps on welfare, foreign aid, spending on AIDS research, spending on the poor, spending on social security, spending on public schools, and spending on childcare (Sapiro 2002). Women were also more likely to support increased government involvement in providing and/or regulating health care and health insurance including higher levels of favorability toward the Affordable Care Act (Howell and Day 2000; Lizotte in press/2015).

Finally, gaps on moral issues, environmental issues, and women's issues such as abortion and equal rights have been less consistent and smaller in size (Huddy, Cassese, and Lizotte 2008b; Norrander 2008). Though women have been more supportive of gay rights (CAWP 2012), they were less supportive of the legalization of marijuana and of extramarital affairs (Eagly et al. 2004). Modest and, at times, significant gender differences in environmental attitudes have been found with women tending to report greater environmental concern (Norrander 2008). With respect to equal rights and abortion attitudes, gender differences have been very small or nonexistent (Chaney, Alvarez, and Nagler 1998; Huddy, Cassese, and Lizotte 2008b; Lizotte 2015; Mansbridge 1985; Shapiro and Mahajan 1986).

Gender differences in issue positions are dynamic and contribute to the gender gap in voting. Research has shown that the gender gap in policy preferences fluctuates in size (Kellstedt, Peterson, and Ramirez 2010). Issue gaps influence vote choice; the gender gap in vote choice substantially decreased in a statistical simulation for more than one election where men's issue preferences were given to women (Chaney, Alvarez, and Nagler 1998). Although most research focuses on women as the cause of the gender gap in party identification and vote choice, there is evidence that men's movement caused the gender gap in voting to emerge (Kaufmann and Petrocik 1999). Men, particularly White men, realigned to the Republican Party (Kaufmann, Petrocik, and Shaw 2008). Race, racial attitudes, regional identity, and differences in social welfare attitudes all appear to contribute to this variability (Ondercin 2013).

Origins of Gender Differences

There are several theories for why gender differences exist. Gender differences in personality traits, with women more altruistic and less assertive/dominant than men (Costa, Terracciano, and McCrae 2001), may explain some of the observed gender gaps on compassion and force issues. Differences in the endorsement of core values such as women's greater endorsement of egalitarianism (Howell and Day 2000) may lead women to differ from men on various social welfare and equal treatment policies. Research on these two explanations has been limited; the other theories discussed in detail below have received greater attention and investigation (for more see Huddy, Cassese, and Lizotte 2008a).

There is some evidence that feminist identity contributed to various gender gaps including military interventions, defense spending, and spending on social security, food stamps, and childcare (Conover 1988; see Mansbridge 1985 for divergent findings). Feminist consciousness may not directly explain political differences between men and women, but it might work via resultant differences in political outlook. Feminist identity correlated with a greater endorsement of egalitarianism as well as lower endorsements of traditionalism and symbolic racism, which may explain why feminists were less supportive of military interventions and more supportive of social welfare spending compared to men and non-feminist women (Conover 1988).

Relatedly, it may be that professional, economically independent women and/ or psychologically independent women are causing some of these gaps. This theory originated with the emergence of the voting gap in 1980 coinciding with higher divorce rates and increasing proportions of women working outside the home. Autonomous women, whether divorced, single, widowed, or married but working outside the home, are not economically dependent on or psychologically interdependent with men leading them to have opinions or to vote based on their own material interests. Women have been more likely to work in the public sector including in public schools and as health providers, and therefore, may support Democrats and funding policies that would benefit that sector (Carroll 1988; Huddy, Cassese, and Lizotte 2008b). Evidence has been mixed for this with respect to the gender gap in voting; some research found support (Carroll 1988; Manza and Brooks 1998) and others have not (Huddy, Cassese, and Lizotte 2008b).

Differences in the average economic circumstances of women compared to men offers another explanation. Women have made up a larger proportion of the economically disadvantaged than men (Kimenyi and Mbaku 1995; Pressman 1988). Therefore, gender differences may exist because certain policies have differential impacts on men and women; for example, cutting social services has a disproportionate effect on women, because more women receive such services (Sapiro 2002). In this volume, Bullock and Reppond review the evidence that self-interest explains gender differences in support for redistributive policies. Times-series analysis revealed a relationship between the percentage of economically vulnerable women and the size of the gender gap in party identification (Box-Steffensmeier, De Boef, and Lin 2004). There is limited evidence for this explanation with respect to gender differences in voting, as income did not consistently mediate the gender gap (Carroll 1988; Huddy, Cassese, and Lizotte 2008b).

In sum, issue gaps exist on a number of policy positions, and gender differences in issue positions are meaningfully tied to the gender gap in voting. Past research has investigated a number of possible explanations for these gender differences, though limited support for each of these explanations suggests that different explanations contribute to different issue gaps and multiple explanations simultaneously contribute to individual gaps. Encouragingly, Social Role Theory hypothesizes quite specific expectations for why certain issues are likely to have a significant gender gap.

Social Role Theory

Social Role Theory, a biosocial approach to gender differences, takes into account evolved characteristics, socialization, and societal division of labor to posit that gender differences in political attitudes emerge as the result of gender role socialization (Diekman and Schneider 2010; Eagly et al. 2004). In this approach, sex differences are caused by distal factors including physical characteristics, such as men's strength and women's reproductive responsibilities and the features of the local environment, in particular the reliance on foraging versus hunting (Eagly and Koenig 2006). SRT argues that an interaction between physical characteristics and the features of the local environment produce a male–female division of labor (Eagly and Koenig 2006). For example, men would hunt because of their strength while women would care for children because of their capacity for pregnancy and lactation.

The division of labor leads to gender roles, including socialization of gender expectations, which are a proximal, or an immediate, cause of sex differences (Eagly and Koenig 2006). Research on gender stereotypes has indicated different societal expectations of men and women in terms of agentic versus communal traits (Eagly and Wood 2012; Wood and Eagly 2012). Agentic traits include being assertive and aggressive while communal traits include being compassionate and nurturing. To return to the example of a hunting reliant society, gender role socialization would lead to expectations of men being aggressive and women being nurturing, because these traits are seen as necessary for the particular roles of hunting and child-rearing.

Gender roles are diffuse in that women are virtually always expected to embody communal traits and men are supposed to demonstrate agentic traits. Indeed, SRT is primarily an explanation for gender stereotypes, or the belief that men and women will tend to possess certain characteristics. Parents socialize their children to adhere to gender roles; differences in adherence to gender roles could be the result of discrepancies in socialization (i.e., gender-neutral socialization) or differences in internalization of such expectations (Eagly and Koenig 2006). Social Role Theory purports that socialization into gender roles leads men and women to display on average different behaviors and attitudes (Wood and Eagly 2002).

There is a great deal of empirical and cross-cultural support for SRT (e.g., Eagly and Koenig 2006; Wood and Eagly 2002). Observed sex differences in attitudes on social and political issues support the expectations of SRT. Prior research found that women are more likely than men to express a more liberal perspective on compassion issues and hold traditional positions on moral issues, which supported SRT's expectations for women to have been socialized to be compassionate and moral to fill the roles of mother and caretaker (Eagly et al. 2004). According to a 1996 ANES analysis, women with children were significantly more liberal than men with children on a scale of social welfare questions including several items among which were public school and childcare spending; the gender gap was not significant among those without children (Howell and Day 2000).

Soccer Moms, Security Moms, and Parenthood

During recent presidential elections, the news media has focused on the political leanings of certain subgroups of women such as 'soccer moms' and 'security moms.' This is not an entirely new phenomenon; political parties, activists, campaigns, and candidates have used targeted appeals to mothers for a long time (Deason, Greenlee, and Langner 2015; Greenlee 2014). Since the 1980s, political parties and the media coverage of elections have made increasing reference to the family (Elder and Greene 2012). Deason, Greenlee, and Langner (2015), mainly focusing on the implications for female political candidates, put forward the notion of Politicized Motherhood referring to the current emphasis on and salience of motherhood both culturally and politically (also see their chapter in this volume).

Carroll (2006b) argued how campaign and media focus on soccer moms in the 1996 and 2000 presidential elections as well as security moms in 2004 diverted attention away from the issues of importance to women and away from other subgroups of women. The soccer mom media frame during the 1996 Presidential Election focused on White, middle-class, suburban mothers (Carroll 1999). Therefore, the campaigns failed to focus on certain issues of importance to various subgroups of women like health care, employment, and childcare instead emphasizing school uniforms (Carroll 1999).

Limited evidence exists supporting that these particular subgroups of women, in particular security moms, are politically consequential. First with regard to defining security moms, the news usually described security moms as White, middle-class, formerly soccer moms, and most concerned with the future possibility of terrorism (Carroll 2008). Turning to the evidence, women with children at home, compared to women without children at home, were more likely to vote for Bush in 2000 but not in 2004 (Kaufmann, Petrocik, and Shaw 2008). White, married mothers were less likely than White, married fathers to pick terrorism as the most important issue affecting their presidential choice in 2004 exit poll data (Carroll 2008). Moreover, all women feared a future terrorist attack with unmarried mothers the most worried, and women worried about a future terror attack were actually more likely to vote for Kerry (Carroll 2008). Similarly, analysis of the 2004 ANES did not provide support for the media categories of security moms with no mother gap on security issues (Elder and Greene 2007).

Although soccer moms and security moms did not appear to be politically meaningful, there is evidence that motherhood has had important effects on political attitudes. Motherhood appears to have a liberalizing effect on women's attitudes toward compassion issues and on women's presidential vote choice. In particular, mothers differed from fathers on social welfare attitudes. Motherhood predicted more liberal positions on social welfare attitudes including aid to the poor, health care, and the provision of government services (Elder and Greene 2006, 2007, 2012). Results have not been entirely consistent, but have been suggestive, that mothers were, at times, more liberal on childcare spending, school spending, and food stamps spending (Greenlee 2014). Fatherhood did not appear to have a significant effect on social welfare attitudes (Elder and Greene 2006). In some election years, mothers compared to fathers were significantly more likely to vote for the Democratic Presidential Candidate and to identify as a Democrat (Huddy, Cassese, and Lizotte 2008a).

SRT predicts that women will be more compassionate on certain issues and more traditional on others. Because society expects women to be more morally virtuous and mothers to instill morality in their children, SRT predicts women will be more likely than men to hold traditional views for certain issue areas (Eagly et al. 2004). Women and mothers were more traditional than men on a variety of issues including legalization of marijuana, extramarital affairs, divorce, school prayer, and endorsement of traditional values (Eagly et al. 2004; Greenlee 2010, 2014). A higher percentage of Tea Party and Republican women identifiers compared to women nationally hold traditional views on marriage equality, gay rights, government assistance to the poor, and the death penalty; but, these women were less conservative than their male counterparts on these issues and motherhood was not explored as part of the explanation for their conservative views (Deckman 2012).

To summarize, notable differences between women with children and women without children exist (Elder and Greene 2007, 2012; Howell and Day 2000), and this extant literature points to SRT as a possible explanation. The evidence does not support the idea of soccer moms and security moms, but becoming a parent appears to have more of an effect on the political attitudes of women than men and that effect is for the most part a liberalizing one (Elder and Greene 2006, 2007). Research to date, however, has not investigated whether diffuse and specific gender roles intersect to produce particular gender gaps (Diekman and Schneider 2010). For example, women with children may express greater support for childcare subsidization policies compared to women without children.

The analysis in this chapter makes two important contributions to the existing literature. First, the analysis offers a test of the intersectional hypothesis of diffuse and specific social roles. Prior tests of SRT or the effects of motherhood on political attitudes have largely looked at social welfare or compassion attitudes more generally. This chapter isolates and investigates policies where the intersection of the diffuse role of woman and the specific role of mother should produce gaps: public school spending, childcare spending, and government services. Likewise, Bejarano's chapter in this volume also investigates the importance of intersectional research with a discussion of the need to include race/ethnicity in the study of gender differences in political behavior. Second, this analysis extends earlier findings in that it includes data for a longer and/or updated time period.

Hypotheses

My analysis focuses on the intersection of diffuse and specific gender roles, comparing women with children to other groups on political issues that should be of particular importance to women with children: government spending on childcare and public schools as well as general government provisions of services. *Hypothesis 1* posits that women with children will prefer increased spending and more government services compared to men with children and women without children. Mothers should be most supportive because of the intersection of the diffuse role of woman that has led to the adoption of traits such as compassion, which then leads to support for government programs to help people, with the specific role of parent, which would lead to support for these particular government programs out of self-interest. Unfortunately, the data does not allow for analysis that would distinguish this from a purely self-interest explanation. *Hypothesis 2* proposes that men with children will not as substantially differ on these issues from men without children. Finally, *Hypothesis 3* posits that the inclusion of motherhood will fully or partially mediate the gender gaps on these three issues. This third hypothesis tests to what extent SRT, specifically the intersection of woman and parent, accounts for the gender differences on these issues. In other words, what looks like a gender gap is actually caused by a subset of women, mothers.

Data, Measures, and Analysis Plan

Sample

I use the American National Election Study (ANES) cumulative data 1980–2012. The ANES is an established data set with a nationally representative sample that has been widely used in previous studies of the gender gap in issue preferences, party identification, and voting.

Measures

Dependent Variables

The spending questions ask respondents if spending should be decreased (1), kept the same (2), or increased (3). These questions ask respondents about their attitudes toward government spending for various programs including childcare and public schools. Both spending questions use the following question stem: "If you had a say in making up the federal budget this year, for which programs would you like to see spending increased and for which would you like to see spending decreased."[1] The third dependent variable is a question that asks respondents to place themselves on a continuum concerning the provision of government services. The question wording is as follows: "Some people think the government should provide fewer services, even in areas such as health and education, in order to reduce spending. Other people feel that it is important for the government to provide many more services even if it means an increase in spending. Where would you place yourself on this scale, or haven't you thought much about this?"[2] The coding is 1 for the belief that government services should be greatly reduced and 7 for the belief that the government should provide more services.

Key Independent Variables

Female equals 1 and male is coded as 0. The measure of having children is unfortunately imperfect and was not asked of all respondents in all years. This question asks respondents how many children under the age of 18 are either in their family or living in their household. In 1980, the survey simply asked the respondent how many children s/he has. Data are not available for 1994 or 2000 and for only a small subset of the 2002 data. This variable has been coded as dichotomous so that 1 equals having children and 0 equals not having children.[3] The mother variable is an interaction between the female and the children variables.

Control Variables

I include a number of demographic controls including race, income, education, region, age, and marital status. These are dummy variables: Race is 1 for White or 0 for all other races; income is 1 for below the 33rd percentile; education is 1 for bachelor's degree or more; region is 1 for South; and marital status is 1 for married. I include a dummy variable for Protestant and another for Catholic, and control for church attendance. I include a dummy variable for Republican presidential administration, 1 for the Reagan and both Bush administrations and 0 for Clinton and Obama. Finally, I control for party identification. I use the standard 7-point measure (1 = strong Republican, 2 = Republican, 3 = Independent that leans Republican, 4 = Independent, 5 = Independent that leans Democrat, 6 = Democrat, 7 = strong Democrat) with higher values indicating Democratic identification.

Analysis Plan

I perform multivariate analyses including the control variables. For the spending questions, I use ordered logistic regression because these items are ordered but not continuous: 1 for decrease spending, 2 for stay the same, and 3 for increase spending. Finally, for the government services question, I use ordinary least squares

(OLS) regression with higher values indicating greater support for the government providing more services. For simplicity of understanding the motherhood interaction variable, I also report the marginal effects, i.e., predicted probabilities, which provides the probability of support for increased spending or more government services for mothers, fathers, childless women, and childless men.

My analysis investigates whether having children mediates the gender gap. I run the analyses for each dependent variable including all respondents with and without the measures of children and mother to see if the inclusion of these variables has an effect on the gender gap. For mediation to exist the effect of the independent variable, gender, on the dependent variable should reduce with the inclusion of the meditational variable (Baron and Kenny 1986). I report the results of the Sobel–Goodman mediation test in STATA 11 SE 64-bit, which provides an overall percent mediation.

My analysis also investigates whether motherhood moderates attitudes. I run the analyses separately for women and men to investigate differences in how having children influences these policy positions. Thus, the analysis is an example of moderated mediation (Preacher, Rucker, and Hayes 2007). In this analysis, the effect of the mediator, having children, on the dependent variable (i.e., public school spending, childcare spending, and government services) is moderated by the independent variable, gender. Therefore, the conditional indirect effect of having children on support for increased spending or more services is reliant on the value of the gender variable. Again, I hypothesize that for men having children does not affect these policy positions but for women having children leads to more support for increased spending and services.

Results

I find support for *Hypothesis 1* that the intersection of the diffuse role of woman and specific role of mother leads to greater support for increased government spending on public schools, for increased government spending on childcare, and for more government services. In support of *Hypothesis 2*, having children is a strong predictor for these positions only among women. For men, having children does not significantly predict their positions on these issues. Supporting *Hypothesis 3*, the inclusion of the mother variable partially mediates the effect of gender.

Public Schools

As shown in Model 1 of Table 4.1, gender is significant, with women more likely than men to support increased government spending on public schools. In Model 2, the gender gap remains significant with the inclusion of the children and mother variables, neither of which are significant. Comparing the men only and women only models, for women, having children is associated with being more likely to support increased government spending on public schools, while

TABLE 4.1 Support for Increased Public School Spending, Childcare Spending, and Government Services

	Public Schools				Childcare				Government Services			
	Model 1	Model 2	Men Only	Women Only	Model 3	Model 4	Men Only	Women Only	Model 5	Model 6	Men Only	Women Only
Female	0.27** (0.04)	0.25** (0.05)			0.26** (0.05)	0.18** (0.06)			0.29** (0.03)	0.22** (0.04)		
Children		0.11 (0.07)	0.10 (0.08)	0.19** (0.07)		0.07 (0.07)	0.07 (0.08)	0.24** (0.07)		-0.05 (0.04)	-0.03 (0.05)	0.13** (0.04)
Mother		0.03 (0.09)				0.19* (0.10)				0.18** (0.06)		
Race 1 = White	-0.69** (0.06)	-0.68** (0.06)	-0.84** (0.08)	-0.56** (0.08)	-0.72** (0.06)	-0.70** (0.06)	-0.77** (0.08)	-0.63** (0.07)	-0.50** (0.03)	-0.49** (0.03)	-0.60** (0.05)	-0.41** (0.05)
Married	-0.05 (0.05)	-0.09+ (0.05)	-0.07 (0.08)	-0.09 (0.07)	-0.07 (0.05)	-0.10* (0.05)	-0.04 (0.08)	-0.19** (0.07)	-0.15** (0.03)	-0.16** (0.03)	-0.17** (0.05)	-0.17** (0.04)
Edu 1 = BA	0.09+ (0.05)	0.10+ (0.05)	0.01 (0.07)	0.24** (0.08)	0.02 (0.06)	0.03 (0.06)	-0.03 (0.08)	0.12 (0.08)	-0.19** (0.03)	-0.19** (0.03)	-0.27** (0.05)	-0.08+ (0.05)
Region 1 = South	0.08+ (0.05)	0.08+ (0.05)	0.14* (0.07)	0.02 (0.07)	-0.09+ (0.05)	-0.09+ (0.05)	-0.05 (0.07)	-0.12+ (0.07)	-0.11** (0.03)	-0.11** (0.03)	-0.11* (0.04)	-0.10* (0.04)
Income 1 = Low	0.19** (0.06)	0.19** (0.06)	0.32** (0.09)	0.11 (0.07)	0.35** (0.06)	0.35** (0.06)	0.50** (0.08)	0.25** (0.08)	0.27** (0.03)	0.27** (0.03)	0.22** (0.05)	0.32** (0.05)
Age	-0.02** (0.00)	-0.02** (0.00)	-0.02** (0.00)	-0.02** (0.00)	-0.01** (0.00)	-0.01** (0.00)	-0.01** (0.00)	-0.01** (0.00)	-0.01** (0.00)	-0.01** (0.00)	-0.01** (0.00)	-0.01** (0.00)
Protestant	-0.17* (0.07)	-0.17* (0.07)	-0.08 (0.10)	-0.29** (0.11)	-0.09 (0.07)	-0.09 (0.07)	-0.06 (0.10)	0.11 (0.11)	-0.11** (0.05)	-0.11* (0.05)	-0.02 (0.06)	-0.22** (0.07)

(Continued)

TABLE 4.1 (Continued)

	Public Schools				Childcare				Government Services			
	Model 1	Model 2	Men Only	Women Only	Model 3	Model 4	Men Only	Women Only	Model 5	Model 6	Men Only	Women Only
Catholic	-0.17* (0.08)	-0.17* (0.08)	0.00 (0.10)	-0.35** (0.11)	-0.02 (0.08)	-0.02 (0.08)	0.04 (0.11)	-0.06 (0.12)	0.01 (0.05)	0.01 (0.05)	0.08 (0.07)	-0.08 (0.07)
Church Attendance	-0.02 (0.02)	-0.02 (0.02)	-0.04+ (0.02)	0.01 (0.02)	-0.05** (0.02)	-0.05** (0.02)	-0.07** (0.02)	-0.04+ (0.02)	-0.03** (0.01)	-0.03** (0.01)	-0.04** (0.01)	-0.02+ (0.01)
Party Identification	1.06** (0.07)	1.06** (0.07)	1.17** (0.10)	0.96* (0.09)	1.14** (0.07)	1.14** (0.07)	1.34** (0.10)	0.99** (0.09)	1.22** (0.04)	1.22** (0.04)	1.47** (0.06)	1.00** (0.06)
Republican Presidency	-0.16 (0.12)	-0.17 (0.12)	-0.01 (0.18)	-0.32+ (0.17)	0.04 (0.11)	0.03 (0.11)	-0.06 (0.17)	0.08 (0.14)	0.08+ (0.04)	0.08+ (0.04)	0.08 (0.06)	0.07 (0.06)
N	10408	10408	4639	5769	8477	8477	3775	4702	12216	12216	5597	6619
Pseudo/Adj. R^2	0.06	0.06	0.07	0.06	0.07	0.07	0.07	0.06	0.15	0.15	0.17	0.12

Note: ANES data 1980–2012. Public schools and childcare spending are 1 = decrease spending, 2 = maintain spending, and 3 = increase spending; I use ordered logistic regression. Government services is a 7-point scale with higher values indicating support for more services. I use OLS regression. $+ p < 0.10$, $* p < 0.05$, and $** p < 0.01$. To retain respondents, the analysis includes a missing income variable (not shown).

it is not a significant predictor of men's attitudes. According to the Sobel–Goodman test, including the mother variable mediates 34 percent of the effect of gender.[4]

I also calculated the predicted probabilities for men without children, fathers, women without children, and mothers. These predicted probabilities are calculated as marginal effects, also known as partial effects, and hold all other variables at their means (Brambor, Clark, and Golder 2006). In this analysis, the marginal effect gives the probability that each subgroup will support increasing public school spending while controlling for the effect of all of the other variables in the model. In other words, this information tells us how likely members of each subgroup are to support increasing public school spending. Men without children have the lowest predicted probability of 0.65 for choosing the increase spending option. Fathers have the second lowest with a probability of 0.68. Women without children have a probability of 0.71 and mothers have a probability of 0.74. Even holding all other variables at their means, mothers are the most likely to endorse increased spending on public schools.

Childcare

As shown in Model 3, the fifth column of Table 4.1, women are significantly more likely than men to support increased government spending on childcare. In Model 4, the gender gap remains significant with the inclusion of the children and mother variables. The mother variable is also significant; women with children are more likely to support increased government spending on childcare. Comparing the men only and women only models, for women, having children is associated with being more likely to support increased government spending on childcare while it is not a significant predictor of men's attitudes. The Sobel–Goodman test reports a percent mediated of 38 percent.

The predicted probabilities for the increase spending option are displayed in Figure 4.1. As shown in Figure 4.1, men without children have the lowest predicted probability of 0.55. Men with children have the second lowest with a probability of 0.57. Having children does not have a significant influence on men's attitudes toward childcare spending. Women without children have a probability of 0.59 and women with children have a probability of 0.65. Women without children are more likely than men to support increased spending on childcare, and having children leads to even greater support.

Government Services

As shown in Model 5, in the ninth column of Table 4.1, the gender gap is significant with women more likely than men to support more government services. In Model 6, the gender gap remains significant with the inclusion of the children and mother variables; the mother variable is significant and is

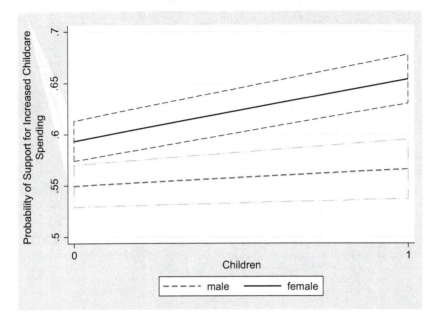

FIGURE 4.1 Probability of Support for Increased Childcare Spending

Note: Marginal effects calculated from Model 4 in Table 4.1 with variables held at their means with 95 percent confidence intervals.

associated with wanting more services. Comparing the men only and women only models, for women, having children leads to wanting more services while it is not a significant predictor of men's attitudes. The Sobel–Goodman test reports that including the motherhood variable mediates 21 percent of the effect of gender.

I also calculated the predicted values on the scale from 1 to 7 with higher values indicating support for more government services. Similar to the findings for the other two dependent variables, men with children have the lowest predicted value of 4.06. Men without children have the second lowest predicted value of 4.11. Women without children have a predicted value of 4.33 and women with children have a predicted value of 4.46.

As predicted, women with children do not significantly differ from men or women without children on other issues for which there is a gender gap (analysis not shown). This is the case for environmental regulation, social security spending, economic retrospections, economic prospections, defense spending, the use of force, foreign aid, and spending to help the homeless. SRT would not predict that the intersection of the diffuse role of woman and specific role of mother would contribute to the gender gap on these issues.

To summarize, the analyses show that the intersection of diffuse and specific roles produces notable differences in policy positions. Specifically, women with children have very different attitudes than men with children on these particular issues. Supporting *Hypothesis 1*, compared to women without children, mothers are more likely to support increased spending on public schools and childcare as well as report a preference for more government services. In support of *Hypothesis 2*, parenthood does not have the same influence on men's attitudes. Finally, motherhood partially mediates the gender gaps on these issues, which provides support for *Hypothesis 3*.

Discussion and Conclusions

The gender gap in issue positions is of importance to public opinion researchers and political campaign strategists, alike. This chapter demonstrates the explanatory power of Social Role Theory to answer key questions related to the gender gap: If we should expect women to differ from men, parents to differ from non-parents, and mothers to differ from fathers, childless women, and childless men on their preferences for public school spending, childcare spending, and general orientation toward the provision of government services. The analysis indicates that there are differences in political attitudes between women with children and women without children, and the effects of parenthood on political attitudes are not the same for women and men. Women with children are more likely than women without children, men with children, and men without children to support increased government spending on childcare and public schools and to express a desire for increased government services. Controlling for motherhood partially mediates the gender gaps on these issues adding to our understanding of what causes these gender differences.

Future work should investigate other intersections of diffuse and specific roles as well as how the intersection of diffuse and specific roles account for gender differences in issue salience. Another interesting way to test how the intersection of diffuse and specific roles influences political attitudes would be an investigation of women in communal, nurturing occupations such as elementary school teachers (Diekman and Schneider 2010). Women are more likely to work in jobs close to government and are more likely to vote Democrat (Andersen 1999). Therefore, women in these types of professions could be causing some of the issue gaps.

Researchers should also investigate how parental involvement moderates these effects. Among mothers but not fathers, higher levels of parental involvement predict liberal positions on childcare and health care (Elder and Greene 2008). It will be interesting to see if these gender differences decrease as gender roles change. With fathers becoming more engaged in the rearing of children over time, men with children may become more similar to women with children on certain issues. SRT acknowledges that gender roles are not rigid over time; modern times have led to a decrease in the gendered division of labor (Eagly and Koenig 2006). Therefore, SRT would likely predict a closing of these gender gaps as fathers become more involved in child-rearing.

Issue salience may also serve as another important component of understanding how social roles influence political attitudes (Diekman and Schneider 2010). Men are more conservative in their social welfare attitudes and these attitudes matter more for men than for women with respect to voting (Kaufmann, Petrocik, and Shaw 2008). In 2004, attitudes toward government spending for the poor had more influence on women's vote (Clark and Clark 2008). It might be the case that mothers prioritize and rely more on attitudes toward government spending on childcare, public schools, and the provision of government services when voting. This and other examples of the intersection of diffuse and specific roles deserve further attention in terms of issue salience and issue prioritization.

Policymakers, political parties, and political candidates should continue to heed that gender matters when it comes to vote choice, party identification, and issue positions. Presidential candidates and the political parties are aware of gender differences and make appeals to women voters (Carroll 2006a). Political parties and candidates can influence the size of the gender gap by appealing to female voters using targeted advertisements (Holman, Schneider, and Pondel 2015). Candidates should consider campaign advertisements that emphasize female-congenial policy positions. Gender differences in voting could be the result of partisan and candidate differences in female-congenial issue positions, such as government subsidization of childcare (Eagly et al. 2003). Yet, it is important that candidates, campaigns, activists, and political parties appeal to and address the issues of significance to different subgroups of women including single mothers, women of color, and low-income women rather than focusing on White, married, and middle-class mothers (Carroll 2006b).

In sum, there is evidence that mothers differ from other subgroups on political issues of particular impact on their lives. This provides support for Social Role Theory, generally, and for the need to explore how diffuse and specific roles intersect to bring about variations in political attitudes and in the size of the gender gap.

Notes

1. The public schools variable began being measured in 1984 and is included in all years except 1998. The childcare variable in the cumulative ANES began being measured in 1988 and is included for all years after except 1998.
2. The government services variable began being asked in 1982 and is included for all years.
3. For cumulative data analysis, the Ns may seem small. The overlap of data for each dependent variable and the having children variable is as follows: For public schools, the N is 10,918; for childcare, the N is 9,051; and for government services, the N is 12,606.
4. The Sobel–Goodman test in STATA is intended for use with OLS regression.

References

American National Election Studies (www.electionstudies.org) Time Series Cumulative Data File 1948–2012. 2015. Stanford University and the University of Michigan.

Andersen, Kristi. 1999. "The Gender Gap and Experiences with the Welfare State." *PS: Political Science and Politics* 32: 17–19.

Baron, Reuben M., and David A. Kenny. 1986. "The Moderator–Mediator Variable Distinction in Social Psychological Research: Conceptual, Strategic, and Statistical Considerations." *Journal of Personality and Social Psychology* 51: 1173–1182.

Box-Steffensmeier, Janet M., Suzanna De Boef, and Tse-Min Lin. 2004. "The Dynamics of the Partisan Gender Gap." *American Political Science Review* 98: 515–528.

Brambor, Thomas, William Roberts Clark, and Matt Golder. 2006. "Understanding Interaction Models: Improving Empirical Analyses." *Political Analysis* 14: 63–82.

Carroll, Susan J. 1988. "Women's Autonomy and the Gender Gap: 1980 and 1982." In *The Politics of the Gender Gap: The Social Construction of Political Influence*, edited by Carol M. Mueller, 236–257, Newbury Park, CA: Sage.

Carroll, Susan J. 1999. "The Disempowerment of the Gender Gap: Soccer Moms and the 1996 Elections." *PS: Political Science & Politics* 32: 7–12.

Carroll, Susan J. 2006a. "Voting Choices: Meet You at the Gender Gap." In *Gender and Elections: Shaping the Future of American Politics*, edited by Susan J. Carroll and Richard L. Fox, 74–96. Cambridge: Cambridge University Press.

Carroll, Susan J. 2006b. "Moms Who Swing, or Why the Promise of the Gender Gap Remains Unfulfilled." *Politics & Gender* 2: 362–374.

Carroll, Susan J. 2008. "Security Moms and Presidential Politics: Women Voters in the 2004 Election." In *Voting the Gender Gap*, edited by Lois Duke Whitaker, 75–90. Champaign, IL: University of Illinois Press.

Center for American Women and Politics. 2012. "The Gender Gap: Attitudes on Public Policy Issues." Accessed August 10, 2015. http://www.cawp.rutgers.edu/sites/default/files/resources/gg_issuesattitudes-2012.pdf.

Center for American Women and Politics. 2015. "Gender Differences in Voter Turnout." Accessed February 3, 2016. http://www.cawp.rutgers.edu/sites/default/files/resources/genderdiff.pdf.

Chaney, Carole Kennedy, R. Michael Alvarez, and Jonathan Nagler. 1998. "Explaining the Gender Gap in US Presidential Elections, 1980–1992." *Political Research Quarterly* 51: 311–339.

Clark, Cal, and Janet M. Clark. 2008. "The Reemergence of the Gender Gap in 2004." In *Voting the Gender Gap*, edited by Lois Duke Whitaker, 50–74. Champaign, IL: University of Illinois Press.

Conover, Pamela J. 1988. "Feminists and the Gender Gap." *The Journal of Politics* 50: 985–1010.

Conover, Pamela J., and Virginia Sapiro. 1993. "Gender, Feminist Consciousness, and War." *American Journal of Political Science* 37: 1079–1099.

Costa, Paul, Jr., Antonio Terracciano, and Robert R. McCrae. 2001. "Gender Differences in Personality Traits across Cultures: Robust and Surprising Findings." *Journal of Personality and Social Psychology* 81: 322–331.

Deason, Grace, Jill S. Greenlee, and Carrie A. Langner. 2015. "Mothers on the Campaign Trail: Implications of Politicized Motherhood for Women in Politics." *Politics, Groups, and Identities* 3: 133–148.

Deckman, Melissa. 2012. "Mama Grizzlies and the Tea Party." In *Steep: The Vertiginous Rise of the Tea Party*, edited by Christine Trout and Larry Rosenthal, 171–191. Berkeley: University of California Press.

Diekman, Amanda B., and Monica C. Schneider. 2010. "A Social Role Theory Perspective on Gender Gaps in Political Attitudes." *Psychology of Women Quarterly* 34: 486–497.

Eagly, Alice H., Amanda B. Diekman, Mary C. Johannesen-Schmidt, and Anne M. Koenig. 2004. "Gender Gaps in Sociopolitical Attitudes: A Social Psychological Analysis." *Journal of Personality and Social Psychology* 87: 796–816.

Eagly, Alice H., Amanda B. Diekman, Monica C. Schneider, and Patrick Kulesa. 2003. "Experimental Tests of an Attitudinal Theory of the Gender Gap in Voting." *Personality and Social Psychology Bulletin* 29: 1245–1258.

Eagly, Alice H., and Anne M. Koenig. 2006. "Social Role Theory of Sex Differences and Similarities: Implication for Prosocial Behavior." In *Sex Differences and Similarities in Communication*, edited by Daniel J. Canary and Kathryn Dindia, 161–178. Mahwah, NJ: Lawrence Erlbaum.

Eagly, Alice H., and Wendy Wood. 2012. "Social Role Theory." In *Handbook of Theories of Social Psychology*, edited by Arie W. Kruglanski, Paul A. M. Van Lange, and Tory Higgins, 458–476. Thousand Oaks, GA: Sage.

Elder, Laurel, and Steven Greene. 2006. "The Children Gap on Social Welfare and the Politicization of American Parents, 1984–2000." *Politics & Gender* 2: 451–472.

Elder, Laurel, and Steven Greene. 2007. "The Myth of 'Security Moms' and 'Nascar Dads': Parenthood, Political Stereotypes, and the 2004 Election." *Social Science Quarterly* 88: 1–19.

Elder, Laurel, and Steven Greene. 2008. "Parenthood and the Gender Gap." In *Voting the Gender Gap*, edited by Lois Duke Whitaker, 119–140. Champaign, IL: University of Illinois Press.

Elder, Laurel, and Steven Greene. 2012. "The Politics of Parenthood: Parenthood Effects on Issue Attitudes and Candidate Evaluations in 2008." *American Politics Research* 40: 419–449.

Friedman, Ann. 2015. "Can We Solve Our Child-Care Problem?" *NYmag.com*. Accessed February 3, 2016. http://nymag.com/thecut/2015/01/can-we-solve-our-child-care-problem.html.

Greenlee, Jill S. 2010. "Soccer Moms, Hockey Moms and the Question of 'Transformative' Motherhood." *Politics & Gender* 6: 405–431.

Greenlee, Jill S. 2014. *The Political Consequences of Motherhood*. Ann Arbor: University of Michigan Press.

Holman, Mirya R., Monica C. Schneider, and Kristin Pondel. 2015. "Gender Targeting in Political Advertisements." *Political Research Quarterly* 68: 816–829.

Howell, Susan E., and Christine L. Day. 2000. "Complexities of the Gender Gap." *Journal of Politics* 62: 858–874.

Huddy, Leonie, Erin Cassese, and Mary-Kate Lizotte. 2008a. "Gender, Public Opinion, and Political Reasoning." In *Political Women and American Democracy: Critical Perspective on Women and Politics Research*, edited by Christina Wolbrecht, Karen Beckwith, and Lisa Baldez, 31–49. New York, NY: Cambridge University Press.

Huddy, Leonie, Erin Cassese, and Mary-Kate Lizotte. 2008b. "Sources of Political Unity and Disunity among Women: Placing the Gender Gap in Perspective." In *Voting the Gender Gap*, edited by Lois Duke Whitaker, 141–169. Champaign, IL: University of Illinois Press.

Huddy, Leonie, Stanley Feldman, Charles Taber, and Gallya Lahav. 2005. "Threat, Anxiety, and Support of Antiterrorism Policies." *American Journal of Political Science* 49: 593–608.

Kaufmann, Karen M., and John R. Petrocik. 1999. "The Changing Politics of American Men: Understanding the Sources of the Gender Gap." *American Journal of Political Science* 43: 864–887.

Kaufmann, Karen M., John R. Petrocik, and Daron R. Shaw. 2008. *Unconventional Wisdom: Facts and Myths about American Voters*. New York, NY: Oxford University Press.

Kellstedt, Paul M., David A. M. Peterson, and Mark D. Ramirez. 2010. "The Macro Politics of a Gender Gap." *Public Opinion Quarterly* 74: 477–498.

Kimenyi, Mwangi S., and John Mukum Mbaku. 1995. "Female Headship, Feminization of Poverty and Welfare." *Southern Economic Journal* 62: 44–52.

Lizotte, Mary-Kate. 2015. "The Abortion Attitudes Paradox: Model Specification and Gender Differences." *Journal of Women, Politics & Policy* 36 (1): 22–42.

Lizotte, Mary-Kate. In press. "Investigating Women's Greater Support of the Affordable Care Act." *The Social Science Journal*. Accessed August 10, 2015. http://dx.doi.org/10.1016/j.soscij.2014.12.003.

Mansbridge, Jane J. 1985. "Myth and Reality: The ERA and the Gender Gap in the 1980 Election." *Public Opinion Quarterly* 49: 164–178.

Manza, Jeff, and Clem Brooks. 1998. "The Gender Gap in US Presidential Elections: When? Why? Implications?" *American Journal of Sociology* 103: 1235–1266.

Miller, Lisa. 2015. "Obama's Right-Wing Feminist Critics." *NYmag.com*. Accessed February 3, 2016. http://nymag.com/daily/intelligencer/2015/01/obamas-right-wing-feminist-critics.html.

Norrander, Barbara. 2008. "The History of the Gender Gaps." In *Voting the Gender Gap*, edited by Lois Duke Whitaker, 9–32. Champaign, IL: University of Illinois Press.

Ondercin, Heather. 2013. "What Scarlett O'Hara Thinks: Political Attitudes of Southern Women." *Political Science Quarterly* 128: 233–259.

Page, Benjamin I., and Robert Y. Shapiro. 1983. "Effects of Public Opinion on Policy." *American Political Science Review* 77: 175–190.

Preacher, Kristopher J., Derek D. Rucker, and Andrew F. Hayes. 2007. "Addressing Moderated Mediation Hypotheses: Theory, Methods, and Prescriptions." *Multivariate Behavioral Research* 42: 185–227.

Pressman, Steven. 1988. "At Home: The Feminization of Poverty: Causes and Remedies." *Challenge* 31: 57–61.

Sapiro, Virginia. 2002. "It's the Context, Situation, and Question, Stupid: The Gender Basis of Public Opinion." In *Understanding Public Opinion* (2nd ed.), edited by Barbara Norrander and Clyde Wilcox, 21–41. Washington, DC: CQ Press.

Shapiro, Robert Y., and Harpreet Mahajan. 1986. "Gender Differences in Policy Preferences: A Summary of Trends from the 1960s to the 1980s." *Public Opinion Quarterly* 50: 42–61.

State of the Union Address. 2015. "Remarks by the President in State of the Union Address." Accessed February 3, 2016. https://www.whitehouse.gov/the-press-office/2015/01/20/remarks-president-state-union-address-january-20-2015.

Wood, Wendy, and Alice H. Eagly. 2002. "A Cross-Cultural Analysis of the Behavior of Women and Men: Implications for the Origins of Sex Differences." *Psychological Bulletin* 128: 699–727.

Wood, Wendy, and Alice H. Eagly. 2012. "Biosocial Construction of Sex Differences and Similarities in Behavior." In *Advances in Experimental Social Psychology*, edited by James M. Olson and Mark P. Zanna, 55–123. Burlington: Academic Press.

Zaller, John. 1992. *The Nature and Origins of Mass Opinion*. New York, NY: Cambridge University Press.

Gender Gaps in Public Opinion, Public Policy, and Political Action

5

ECONOMIC INEQUALITY AND THE GENDERED POLITICS OF REDISTRIBUTION

Heather E. Bullock and Harmony A. Reppond

Quite frankly, of all the wealthy nations, we have the lowest safety net and the highest poverty, because we're not willing to accept the fact that sometimes an American needs help.

U.S. Representative Sheila Jackson Lee, D-Texas (2014, H23-H24)

But we don't want to turn the safety net into a hammock that lulls able-bodied people to lives of dependency and complacency, that drains them of their will and their incentive to make the most of their lives.

Speaker of the U.S. House of Representatives Paul Ryan, R-Wisconsin (quoted in Delaney and McAuliff 2012, para 6)

The first quote by U.S. Representative Sheila Jackson Lee, an African American woman and Democrat, and the second by Speaker of the U.S. House of Representatives Paul Ryan, a European American man and Republican, underscores deep ideological divides found across gender, racial and ethnic groups, and political parties. Yet, redistributive attitudes are complex, intersecting across identities and interacting with other beliefs. For example, the Democratic contenders for the 2016 presidential nomination defied traditional gendered trends of greater female support for redistribution with Bernie Sanders possessing a stronger record on these issues than front-runner Hillary Clinton.

The relationship of demographic characteristics to poverty and economic vulnerability is more straightforward. Women bear the brunt of economic inequality, remaining overrepresented among the world's poor and underrepresented among high earners. Women's status in the U.S., the richest nation in the world, starkly illustrates the depth and pervasiveness of gendered economic disparities. Although women now comprise over half of U.S. college graduates and nearly half of the workforce, women continue to have lower annual earnings than men, disproportionately work in low-wage jobs, and live in poverty. Women of color are particularly hard hit: For every dollar earned by White men in 2013, White women earned 77 cents, Black women 64 cents, and Latinas only 56 cents (National Women's Law Center 2015). Wealth (assets minus debt) is even more concentrated, with U.S. women holding 36 cents for every dollar of wealth owned by men (Chang 2010).

Redistributive programs and policies that shift resources to low-income groups, such as social welfare programs (e.g., Temporary Assistance to Needy Family, TANF) and progressive taxation (e.g., Earned Income Tax Credit, EITC), can help reduce gender inequities. Yet, redistributive policies are highly contested with fractures in support occurring across political, economic, racial, ethnic, and gender lines. Greater support for redistributive policies has been found among lower status (e.g., women, low-income groups, people of color) than higher status groups (e.g., men, higher income groups, European Americans) (Hunt and Bullock 2016). These differences have important implications for social policy and continued economic inequality.

This chapter examines attitudes toward redistributive policies, particularly those that can directly benefit women and their families, with the dual goals of illuminating patterns of support across diverse groups and understanding the social psychological and political underpinnings of both policy support and opposition. We address three broad questions: 1) How is gender related to economic vulnerability and redistributive programs?; 2) Which demographic groups tend to support redistributive programs and which groups tend to oppose redistribution?; and 3) Which attitudes and beliefs are related to support for redistribution? Special attention is given to understanding gender differences in policy attitudes and theories that seek to explain differential support (e.g., self-interest). Emphasis is also placed on understanding how stereotypes and legitimizing beliefs (e.g., individualism, meritocracy) influence policy attitudes. We also consider the role and potential of female policymakers in supporting and advancing redistributive policies. We conclude with strategies for increasing support for redistributive policies and policies that enhance women's economic advancement. We begin with a brief overview of U.S. redistributive policies.

Redistributive Policies and Their Impact on Poverty and Economic Inequality

The Basics of Redistribution

Redistributive policies transfer resources, typically income from taxes, from one group to another group (Sefton 2006). Progressive taxation, which taxes high-income earners at a higher percentage than low-income earners, is a central facet of redistribution. The U.S. employs a progressive taxation system; however, it is less progressive than is typically assumed. Although it is widely believed that the richest Americans pay a disproportionately high share of taxes, each income group actually pays an amount that is similar to their total share of the nation's income (Citizens for Tax Justice 2015). In a progressive tax system, millionaires would not be taxed at roughly equivalent rates as families earning $100,000 annually (Citizens for Tax Justice 2015). The Earned Income Tax Credit (EITC), which reduces the taxes paid by low and moderate income taxpayers based on their income and family size, is the most progressive aspect of the U.S. tax policy program.

By distributing resources to less well-off groups, redistributive policies are an important strategy for promoting equality. Redistribution is often perceived solely in terms of direct, immediate benefits, particularly the transfer of income from economically secure groups to poor groups (Denhardt, Denhardt, and Blanc 2014). However, redistributive policies also contribute to greater long-term equality via better education, enhanced job prospects, and improved health. Major redistributive initiatives can be categorized into the following groups: 1) income stabilization programs such as Social Security and unemployment benefits; 2) social welfare programs such as Temporary Assistance to Needy Families (TANF) and the Supplemental Nutrition Assistance Program (SNAP); and 3) health care programs such as Medicaid and Medicare (Denhardt, Denhardt, and Blanc 2014).

Some redistributive programs, such as Social Security, are referred to as universal because they aim to include nearly everyone, whereas others (e.g., TANF) are considered targeted because they only reach low-income individuals and families who meet means-tested criteria (i.e., have incomes that fall below designated thresholds). Targeted programs tend have less broad-based, public support than universal programs, in part because they serve a specific segment of the population and other interest groups perceive themselves as competing for these limited resources (Skocpol 1991).

Poverty, Redistribution, and Women

Redistributive programs are crucial to poverty alleviation, particularly for women. Single-female headed households comprise the majority of TANF caseloads, with women constituting approximately 85 percent of adult recipients (Falk 2014). In 2014, the EITC lifted the incomes of more than 5.6 million people above the poverty line, including 2.5 million adults of whom almost 1.6 million were women. Of the 2 million people lifted above the poverty line by housing subsidies, almost 1.4 million were women (Bell, Robbins, and Vogtman 2015). Women also benefit from SNAP, with women making up approximately 1.1 million of the 1.7 adults whose poverty was reduced by the program. Many more women and their families could be helped if greater investments were made in these programs.

Cross-country comparisons consistently show a strong relationship between increased welfare expenditures and poverty reduction. In Kenworthy's (1999) analysis of 15 wealthy countries between 1960–1991, social welfare policies helped reduce poverty, however, the effects were smaller in the U.S. than in countries with more generous benefits. Similarly, a study of European Union countries and countries that are members of the Organisation for Economic Co-operation and Development (OECD) found that redistributive programs had the smallest effects on poverty in Korea and the United States (Caminada and Goudswaard 2010). Relative to other industrialized nations, U.S. income tax and cash benefits also do less to decrease income inequality (Organisation for Economic Co-operation and Development 2015).

The TANF program powerfully illustrates the limited reach and low benefits of U.S. redistributive programs targeting low-income groups. In 2014, only 23 of every 100 eligible low-income families received TANF benefits, down from 68 families of every 100 in 1996 (Floyd and Schott 2015). Shorter time limits than required by law, strict work requirements, and stringent application processes all contribute to the program's declining reach since its inception in 1996. Failing to keep pace with the cost of living, TANF benefits in 2015 were so low that benefits for a family of three were below 50 percent of the poverty guidelines (Floyd and Schott 2015). SNAP benefits are also minimal, averaging just $1.40 per person per meal (Keith-Jennings 2015). Adults' higher hospital admission rates for low-blood sugar at the month's end when food is low, and children's higher test scores and lower number of disciplinary infractions at school earlier in the monthly benefit cycle, are but two illustrations of the human cost (Keith-Jennings 2015).

Redistributive policies are considered "gender-blind" yet as the World Health Organization (2010) observed, "Gender-blind policies, though they may appear to be unbiased, are often, in fact, based on information derived from men's activities and/or the assumption that all persons affected by the policies have the same needs and interests as males" (194). For example, Social Security benefits are paid to senior citizens based on the 35 years in which they earned the most money, but this approach fails to take into account gender differences in workforce trajectories. Women tend to earn lower wages, work part-time rather than full-time, and leave the paid labor market for extended periods of time to attend to caregiving responsibilities. The financial impact of these diverse pathways is reflected in the lower Social Security benefits typically paid to women 65 years of age and older ($13,500) versus men ($17,600) (Entmacher and Robbins 2015). Moreover, women rely on Social Security more than men, both because they tend to live longer and because they have fewer other sources of income to draw on in old age. Social Security is pivotal to poverty reduction, however, its impact would be enhanced if other forms of labor such as unpaid caregiving were considered.

Unemployment insurance (UI) is plagued by similar gendered "blind spots." It is estimated that women are 10 percent less likely than men to receive unemployment benefits due to eligibility rules that disproportionately disqualify female workers (e.g., earnings criteria, limitations on part-time workers, narrow allowable reasons for unemployment; Mitchell 2010). In recent years, legislative initiatives have broadened the reasons that are accepted as "good cause" for leaving a job, such as family violence (Institute for Women's Policy Research 2015). Nevertheless, most states require documentation that violence has occurred for an individual to be eligible for unemployment benefits, and this can be difficult to obtain. Similarly, even in caregiving-friendly states, women must document their reasons for leaving a job and show that the employer offered no alternatives to resigning (Ben-Ishai, McHugh, and Ujvari 2015). Stronger unemployment protection is important for all women but particularly those who experience high rates of joblessness—women of color, single mothers, and women with disabilities.

In sum, lower earnings, higher rates of poverty, caregiving responsibilities, and longer life expectancy make strong redistributive programs crucial to women's well-being across the lifespan. Examining attitudes toward redistribution and economic inequality can help us understand why this is the case.

Support for Redistributive Programs: Convergence, Fractures, and Fault Lines

Attitudes toward Redistribution

Public opinion polls over the past 30 years consistently find that approximately 6 in 10 Americans perceive the distribution of income and wealth in the U.S. as unfair (Newport 2015). Support is also evident in attitudes toward taxing the rich, albeit not as strongly. In 2015, a high of 52 percent of Gallup respondents supported redistributing wealth via heavy taxes on the rich, while 45 percent of respondents opposed doing so (Newport, 2015). And while support for a government safety net slipped from 63 percent in 2009 to 59 percent in 2012, it remains the case that a majority of Americans believe that it is the government's responsibility to help take care of people who cannot take care of themselves (Pew Research Center 2012).

Overall support for redistribution, however, does not necessarily translate into positive attitudes toward specific programs. Public attitudes vary across redistributive initiatives, with universal programs like Social Security receiving stronger support than targeted ones, particularly those that serve the poor (Brady and Bostic 2015). In Quadagno and Pederson's (2012) analysis of polling data from 2000 and 2010, four-fifths of respondents regarded spending on Social Security as either too low or about right. And, despite discussion of cutting Social Security, support for the program remains solid. More than half (53 percent) of respondents in one poll favored raising Social Security taxes so that the benefits can be kept the same for everyone, and in another poll the majority of respondents disapproved of raising the retirement age for Medicare and Social Security (56 percent each) (Stokes 2013).

Attitudes toward targeted programs, especially those that assist low-income groups, are less positive. The former Aid to Families with Dependent Children (AFDC), now Temporary Assistance to Needy Families (TANF), is among the most unpopular. Although the Personal Responsibility and Work Opportunity Reconciliation Act of 1996 (PRWORA) ushered in TANF's more restrictive welfare reform policies (e.g., a 60-month lifetime limit on receipt of benefits, requirements that recipients work outside the home, establishment of paternity), opposition to "welfare" persists. A 2014 survey found that nearly half of respondents (49 percent) believed that anti-poverty programs increase poverty, and a plurality (44 percent) believed that the government spends too much on poverty programs (Rasmussen Reports 2014).

Welfare, more than other forms of assistance, is viewed as fostering long-term dependency on the state that is at times characterized as "pathological." This dislike can appear paradoxical—while many Americans believe that the current distribution of wealth is unfair, express support for redistributive initiatives, and generously donate billions of dollars to charity, "welfare" and program recipients have long been the focus of intense scrutiny (Gilens 1999). Indeed, a large body of research documents more negative reactions to "welfare" than "the poor," finding that the source of this attitudinal divide lies in racist, sexist, and classist stereotypes about the weak work ethic and sexual promiscuity of low-income women, especially women of color, fears about the erosion of the nuclear family and the prevalence of single motherhood, and beliefs about the immorality of poor people (Bullock 2013; Gilens 1999; Henry, Renya, and Weiner 2004; Smith 1987).

Gender and Other Intergroup Differences in Support for Redistribution

While important, levels of overall support conceal meaningful intergroup differences and political fractures in support for redistribution. Groups differ considerably not only in relation to lived experience and socioeconomic status but also in terms of the power they hold to effect change. Analysis of beliefs across diverse groups provides insight into how redistributive attitudes correlate with social and material position, and reveals potential political coalitions that could be formed based on shared beliefs and needs.

Political affiliation is strongly correlated with attitudes toward redistributive programs. Every U.S. president from Theodore Roosevelt through Jimmy Carter (1901–1981) has supported some form of redistributive policy, but this changed with President Reagan and subsequent presidents through George W. Bush, all of whom pursued initiatives to limit and/or reduce redistributive programs (Denhardt, Denhardt, and Blanc 2014, 58). President Obama's health care plan and increased taxes on the wealthy reversed this trend. Among the general public, attitudes toward redistribution (along with other issues) have grown more polarized, with Democrats voicing greater support than Republicans for redistributive programs for the poor. A Pew Research Center (2015a) poll found that only about one-third of Republicans perceived the government as having a major role in helping people move out of poverty (36 percent) and ensuring access to health care (34 percent), whereas approximately three-quarters of Democrats supported government involvement in these areas. A smaller but still sizeable 21-point gap divides Democrats' (80 percent) and Republicans' (59 percent) endorsement of government responsibility for providing basic income to people over 65 years of age (Pew Research Center 2015a). Gender is important here as well. Women are more likely to identify as Democrats, whereas men are more evenly divided between the two major U.S. parties (Pew Research Center 2015b). This holds true across educational level (Pew Research Center 2015b).

Just as gender affects economic status and experiences with redistributive programs, gender informs redistributive attitudes. Overall, women hold more favorable attitudes toward a broad range of redistributive programs than men. In this volume, Lizotte's analysis of American National Election Study (ANES) data between 1980–2012 shows that mothers were more likely than fathers to support increased government spending on childcare, public schools, and other services. Women are also bigger supporters of a strong safety net for the poor, with a 2012 poll finding that 64 percent of female versus 54 percent of male respondents believed that the government should guarantee food and shelter for all citizens (Stokes 2013). Compared to men, women also express greater support for maintaining Social Security and opposition to privatization (Barrett and Barrett 2006).

Higher levels of support for redistribution are also documented among poor people and people of color, groups that along with women tend to be more economically vulnerable and hold less institutional power (Alesina and Ferrara 2005). People of color, the poor, and senior citizens express greater support for maintaining Social Security than European Americans, those with higher incomes, and younger age groups (Alesina and Ferrara 2005). Similar findings emerge for welfare programs, with women, people of color, and low-income groups supporting more progressive initiatives and increased funding. Race, socioeconomic status, and other key identities operate independently of and intersect with gender. Bejarano's chapter in this volume speaks to the importance of moving beyond one-dimensional analyses of whether "race trumps gender," "gender trumps race," or "class trumps them both" to fully examine overlapping identities. This approach is embodied in Keely and Tan's (2008) study of redistributive support. They found significant variation in redistributive preferences, with people of color and young, European Americans with low maternal education expressing strong support for redistribution, while other European American men and older White women who were not from low socioeconomic backgrounds opposing redistribution.

Collectively, these findings tell us much about the "who" but little about the "why" of redistributive support. We now turn our attention to explanations for gender and other intergroup differences in redistributive attitudes.

Understanding Attitudes toward Redistribution

Social scientists from a broad range of fields including psychology, political science, and sociology have sought to explain intergroup differences in support for redistribution. We review major explanations, both those focused on self-interest and those emphasizing belief systems. No single theory can fully explain gendered support for redistributive programs, rather different explanations complement each other, and some are more effective than others.

Is Support for Redistribution Simply a Matter of Self-Interest?

Self-interest theory—that program beneficiaries and those at greatest risk of needing support are more likely to endorse supportive programs—is frequently invoked to explain why women and other economically and socially disadvantaged groups hold more favorable attitudes toward redistribution. However, it is far from the only influence on attitudes. For example, in a five-country study, Breznau (2010) found that egalitarian economic beliefs (e.g., belief that the gap between the rich and the poor is too large) were more predictive of support for welfare policies than characteristics associated with self-interest (i.e., income, education, gender, age). Other research finds that women endorse egalitarian beliefs more strongly than men (Blekesaune and Quadagno 2003), suggesting that what appears to be simple self-interest may instead reflect ideological differences, or be the result of complex interactions among these and other contextual and experiential factors.

Garcia et al.'s (2005) study of support for redistributive workplace policies illustrates these complexities. Gender differences were found, but only among participants who knew that their organizations had adopted comparable worth and affirmative action policies benefitting women. These respondents expressed policy attitudes that aligned with their gender group's interests, while those without this workplace experience did not. Men with conscious experience of these policies expressed more opposition to them, as well as greater sexist and meritocratic beliefs compared to men without this policy experience (Garcia et al. 2005). The reverse pattern was found for women, with those with conscious experience of these redistributive policies expressing greater support for them than their counterparts without these experiences. These findings underscore the shortcomings of fully attributing attitudinal differences to self-interest and the need to consider multiple influences, particularly beliefs, context, and personal experience, on attitudes toward redistribution.

The Impact of Beliefs about Meritocracy and Individualism on Redistribution

A vast network of attitudes and beliefs is related to support for redistributive policies. Opposition to redistributive programs is associated with a belief in a just world (i.e., that people experience the outcomes that they deserve), social dominance orientation (i.e., support for hierarchy and belief in the superiority of some groups over others), authoritarianism, and belief in the Protestant work ethic. These beliefs are considered hierarchy-enhancing because of their role in justifying current economic and social arrangements (Jost and Hunyady 2005). We focus here on two of the most powerful and fundamental legitimizing beliefs in U.S. popular and political culture—meritocracy and individualism.

Meritocratic beliefs emphasize that anyone, regardless of their family of origin or other characteristics, can advance through hard work and perseverance. Not surprisingly, belief in meritocracy is correlated positively with opposition to redistributive programs, while perceiving mobility as blocked is associated with support for redistributive programs, likely because these initiatives are viewed as correcting structural obstacles (Alesina and La Ferrara 2005). In Luo's (1998) analysis of attitudes toward unemployment in Great Britain and the U.S., respondents who believed that opportunities for intergenerational mobility are limited were also more likely to believe that the government is responsible for reducing income inequality. Despite limited prospects for mobility and rising income inequality, Americans continue to overestimate prospects for class mobility (Kraus and Tan 2015).

Individualism focuses on independence and personal responsibility for achievement whereas collectivism prioritizes interdependence and group welfare (Bullock 2008). In this vein, individualism is about being your own "support" system and "pulling yourself up by your bootstraps" rather than turning to the government for assistance. The cultural dominance of individualism in the U.S. is documented by national and cross-cultural analyses. Public opinion polls find that in the U.S. greater value is placed on freely pursuing life goals without state interference than on having the government ensure that nobody is in need (Stokes 2013). Conversely, citizens of Great Britain, Spain, Germany, and France prioritize government guarantee of freedom from want over individual freedom (Stokes 2013). Individualism directly informs redistributive support via beliefs about the limited scope and responsibility of government, as well as through other beliefs. In cultures that are characterized by low institutional collectivism such as the U.S., individuals tend to perceive themselves as being different from others around them. Similar findings have been documented for gender, with men tending to see themselves as less similar to others than women do (Ott-Holland et al. 2014). These perceived distinctions contribute to distancing from perceived outgroups (e.g., the poor) and may be a source of gender differences in redistributive attitudes.

Individualism and meritocratic beliefs are integral to perceiving social class as an earned or deserved status rather than an ascribed position. As a consequence, in the U.S. social class is widely viewed as resulting from personal effort, with both poverty and wealth predominantly attributed to individualistic over structural causes (Bullock 2013). With respect to wealth, individualistic attributions are positive, focusing on highly valued characteristics—perseverance, good business sense, and hard work—but this is not the case for poverty. Instead, individualistic explanations for poverty focus on negative characteristics and the role of the individual in creating her or his own poverty (e.g., lack of motivation, lack of thrift, "loose" morals) (Bullock 2008). In both instances, individualistic explanations are grounded in classist stereotypes that legitimize socioeconomic disparities and reinforce the status quo. In contrast, structural attributions focus on societal and institutional factors. Low wages, discrimination, and underfunded schools are common structural explanations for poverty, while preferential tax policies and attending elite schools are structural attributions for wealth (Bullock, 2008). As hierarchy-enhancing beliefs, individualistic attributions focus on individual rather than institutional change, whereas structural attributions are hierarchy-attenuating beliefs due to their promotion of group-based equality and structural reform (Hunt and Bullock 2016).

When asked to rate different potential causes of poverty, Feagin (1975) found that Americans endorsed individualistic explanations more strongly than structural attributions. Subsequent research has replicated this tendency (Hunt and Bullock 2016; Kluegel and Smith 1986). Yet, paralleling attitudes toward redistribution, lower status groups (e.g., women, African Americans, low-income groups) tend to favor structural over individualistic causes, whereas more powerful groups (e.g., men, European Americans, and higher income groups) endorse individualistic over structural explanations (Bullock 2013; Kluegel and Smith 1986). Greater likelihood of experiencing discrimination (e.g., sexism, racism) and economic hardship may contribute to women's heightened acknowledgement of structural barriers to financial security. Political divides persist as well, with conservatives endorsing individualistic attributions and progressives preferring structural explanations.

These groups vary considerably in their power and control of resources, and these attributional differences have meaningful implications for support for redistributive programs, particularly those that target the poor. Individualistic explanations for poverty are positively correlated with reduced support for welfare spending and restrictive welfare policies; the reverse is true of structural attributions (Hunt and Bullock 2016; Kluegel and Smith 1986). As such, attributions for poverty have important consequences not only for the level of income inequality an individual perceives as just or unjust, but also whether government intervention is viewed as warranted (Schneider and Castillo 2015). Collectively, these patterns demonstrate that groups with greater political power tend to hold beliefs that are associated with reduced support for government redistribution.

While it is relatively obvious why groups with greater distance from economic hardship may support individualistic attributions and more restrictive welfare policies (e.g., less personal experience with poverty, self-interest), support among less powerful groups can be more challenging to understand.

Gender, Marginalization, and System Justification

Shared structural beliefs and support for redistribution among women and other marginalized groups could spur coalition-building and fuel demand for institutional change, but individuals who are disadvantaged by economic and political systems often uphold these structures by distancing themselves from others who share these experiences or by endorsing system-justifying beliefs. While class-based stigma and negative stereotypes associated with poverty and welfare receipt may fuel conscious distancing from others receiving assistance (e.g., denying receiving aid, scapegoating), unconscious cognitive biases may minimize recognition of structural sources of inequality (Seccombe 2011). One common cognitive bias is the actor–observer effect, the tendency of individuals to attribute their own (negative) outcomes to situational factors but the (negative) outcomes of others to personal causes (Jones and Nisbett 1972). For example, Seccombe (2011) found that welfare recipients explained their own economic hardship in structural terms (e.g., discrimination, low wages) but attributed others' poverty to individualistic causes (e.g., laziness). Such beliefs may fuel scapegoating and stereotyping within and across groups. Moreover, it is not uncommon for marginalized groups, particularly people of color and low-income groups, to endorse both structural and individualistic attributions for poverty. This "dual consciousness" reflects the complexities of exposure to U.S. individualism and experiences of sexism, racism, classism, and other structural inequities (Hunt and Bullock 2016). Despite stronger endorsement of structural attributions, relatively high support for individualistic attributions may temper the more systemic critique associated with structural explanations for inequality.

When advantaged groups support system-justifying beliefs, it generates little surprise because these beliefs typically align with maintaining one's own privilege. This is not the case for marginalized groups. System justification theory (SJT)—that "people are motivated to justify and rationalize the way things are, so that existing social, economic, and political arrangements tend to be perceived as fair and legitimate"—offers insight into why disadvantaged groups endorse beliefs and policies that work against their material self-interest (Jost and Hunyady 2005, 260). A study of high school students vividly illustrates this phenomenon. While girls and low SES students rationalized school success and failures through the belief that people get what they deserve, this connection was weaker for boys and high SES students (Wiederkehr et al. 2015). The researchers posit that low-status students are more motivated than their higher status peers to legitimize the current system because for them, having a diploma is crucial to climbing the socioeconomic ladder. And, for low-status students, but not their higher status peers, they found that being reminded of the highly competitive university selection process paradoxically led to even greater endorsement of school meritocracy (Wiederkehr et al. 2015).

Although such findings may seem counterintuitive and self-defeating, system-justifying beliefs serve important psychologically protective functions among marginalized groups. McCoy et al. (2013) found that among low SES women and women of color, belief in meritocracy was positively correlated with well-being, with perceived control mediating this relationship. As such, system-justifying beliefs may be "beneficial" to the extent that they foster perceived control over future outcomes and belief in the possibility of upward mobility. Yet, these same beliefs may limit blunt structural critique of inequality and support for redistribution.

Racist, Sexist, and Classist Stereotypes

The impact of beliefs on support for redistribution, particularly cash aid (e.g., AFDC, TANF), comes into sharper focus when considering intersections of racist, classist, and sexist stereotypes. Portrayals of welfare recipients as negligent single mothers who devalue education, marriage, work, and mainstream values tap into long-standing stereotypes that associate people of color with laziness and criminality, poor women with promiscuity, and poverty with immorality (Bullock 2013). As Henry, Renya, and Weiner (2004, 52–53) explain:

> Stereotypes of those on welfare portray them as lazy people who are capable of working, but instead choose to engage in morally questionable strategies in order to increase their monthly welfare checks. This stereotype stands in opposition to American values that those who work hard should get the rewards that society has to offer, and those who do not work hard do not deserve such rewards.

Derogatory labels such as "welfare queen," popularized by President Reagan in the 1970s, draw their power from these beliefs.

Extensive research documents the negative impact of racist, sexist, and classist stereotypes on support for welfare programs. Opposition to gender and ethnic discrimination is associated with support for the welfare state, whereas gender traditionalism and racist beliefs depress this support (Calzada et al. 2014). From a gender "traditionalist" vantage point, the state supplants the role of fathers by providing financial support and in doing so encourages single motherhood, particularly among women of color. Racist stereotypes emphasize the role of welfare in fostering laziness and encouraging dependency on the state. Gilens (1999) found that perceiving welfare recipients as "undeserving" and African Americans as lazy were the strongest predictors of anti-welfare attitudes among European Americans. The overestimation of poverty rates among ethnic minorities, particularly African Americans, intensifies anti-welfare attitudes; the media reinforces this bias (Gilens 1999; Kelly 2010; van Doorn 2015). In portrayals of welfare mothers in television news coverage between 1992–1997, 58 percent of the public assistance recipients profiled were African American (Kelly 2010). This was an overrepresentation of the actual percentage of African American AFDC/TANF recipients (39 percent) during this timeframe (Kelly 2010). Further evidence of the overrepresentation of African Americans in news stories about poverty and welfare comes from van Doorn's analysis of photos published alongside articles published between 1992–2010. Interestingly, however, Hispanics were underrepresented. These over- and underrepresentations, respectively, reinforce stereotypes of African Americans as lacking a strong work ethic and Latino/as as hardworking.

Experimental research documents the negative consequences of media priming of racist stereotypes. In a first study, Johnson and his colleagues (2009) primed racist stereotypes of "criminality" by showing White participants photographs of "looting" after Hurricane Katrina. Respondents exposed to the prime were less supportive of policies to assist Black evacuees-in-need but the prime did not affect support for needy White evacuees. In a second experiment, stereotypes about "Black female promiscuity" were primed via exposure to sexualized rap music (Johnson et al. 2009). White respondents who were exposed to the prime were less supportive of policies to assist a hypothetical Black pregnant woman-in-need but once again the prime had no impact on judgments of a similar White target. Perhaps even more troubling is the finding that European Americans who follow politics closely tend to rely more heavily on racial stereotypes in forming their opinions of welfare and food stamp policies (Goren 2003).

Although welfare has received more attention than other redistributive programs, "welfare racism" extends beyond anti-Black attitudes and cash aid. Soroka, Harell, and Iyengar (2013) found that Whites in the United States, United Kingdom, and Canada were less generous toward poor people of color, regardless of their ethnic and racial background, or whether assistance was means-tested or contribution-based (e.g., unemployment benefits). Collectively, these findings underscore the importance of examining intersections of racism, sexism, and classism across the full range of redistributive programs (see also Bejarano 2016).

Beliefs in Context: Does Rising Inequality Influence Redistributive Support?

Attitudes and beliefs do not exist in a vacuum, making it crucial to also consider the influence of broader social and economic context on redistributive support. Common sense suggests that rising inequality drives increased public support for redistribution, but recent evidence is mixed. Counterintuitively, studies by Kelly and Enns (2010) and Luttig (2013) found that rising U.S. income inequality promotes conservatism rather than liberalism among both high- and low-income

Americans, and is not associated with greater support for redistribution. Johnston and Newman (2016) challenge these conclusions, with their analysis yielding a weak positive relationship between inequality and policy liberalism. Other more focused analyses report stronger effects. In Bleksaune and Quadagno's (2003) multi-nation study, high unemployment rates were associated with greater public support for welfare policies, particularly programs targeting the unemployed. These effects were stronger at the national than individual level (e.g., being unemployed oneself), suggesting that when unemployment is more widespread, it is more likely to be perceived as a shared public problem. Micro-level analyses illustrate that even neighborhood context can influence support: Residents of Chicago neighborhoods with a higher African American population were more likely than their counterparts in neighborhoods with a low Black population to support welfare programs (Abner 2011).

Women as Policymakers and Support for Redistributive Policies

A sizeable body of research indicates that women at all levels of U.S. government are more likely than their male counterparts to support and promote so-called "women's issues," including abortion, education, social services, and family and children's issues as well as redistributive programs related to health care and welfare (Jeydel and Taylor 2003; Little, Dunn, and Deen 2001). Even after controlling for party, ideology, and measures of constituency concerns, Poggione (2004) found that female state legislators were more supportive of liberal welfare policies than their male counterparts. Similarly, Little, Dunn, and Deen (2001) found that the percentage of women-friendly issues prioritized by women state legislators was more than 25 percent higher than that of their male counterparts. Women's legislative representation, in particular, appears to be more closely associated with women-friendly policy than women's executive representation (Caiazza 2004).

Men continue to dominate governing bodies and a wide range of factors outside of women's control—the institutional resources available to women, gender role attitudes, and party strength—influence the types of policies that are considered and whether women legislators' initiatives are adopted (Caiazza 2004). Although some redistributive issues, such as poverty, are stereotyped as being "women's issues," women legislators are not deferred to in these areas. Gender bias limits women's impact as legislators and tempers their potential to advance redistributive initiatives. Securing desired committee assignments influences legislators' ability to "pursue their multiple goals of achieving reelection, making good public policy, and wielding influence" (Frisch and Kelly 2003, 2). These assignments are gendered and tied to other power dynamics. Both Democratic and Republican women in the U.S. House of Representatives have been found to be disadvantaged in their first-term committee assignments (Frisch and Kelly 2003). After the first term, Democratic women tended to obtain their preferred assignments, but this was not the case for Republican women. The researchers attribute the continued "shut-out" of Republican women to their distance from the party median and their greater liberalism relative to their male colleagues (Frisch and Kelly 2003). Caucuses, organizations within the legislature that unite subgroups of legislators, often from both parties, are one avenue for women legislators to join together around shared priorities.

Ultimately, power is crucial to women's ability to advance redistributive initiatives. Smith's (2014) city-level analysis documents this point. She found that when women held key positions in city governments, especially mayoral and council seats, and when the offices they held had greater power relative to other municipal positions, cities were more likely to endorse expenditures related to childcare, youth, abused and battered spouses, and abused and neglected children (Smith 2014). Such findings speak to the importance of synergy across levels of government, offering insight into both possibilities and challenges for women legislators. Male legislators, particularly Democrats, may be powerful allies in advancing redistributive initiatives. As U.S. politics grows increasingly polarized, strong bridges across gender, party, and other markers of difference will become even more pivotal to legislative effectiveness.

Toward Greater Economic Inequality: Obstacles and Opportunities

Redistributive programs play a crucial role in advancing economic security, particularly among women, but the "gender neutral" approach taken in the U.S. shortchanges women by overlooking women's work and caregiving trajectories. Social Security, welfare (e.g., TANF), and unemployment benefits provide much-needed assistance but adopting gender-targeted rather than gender-neutral redistributive approaches to these programs would boost both reach and impact. Recognizing that political and economic inequities disadvantage women, gender-redistributive policies seek to rebalance power structures to foster more equitable relationships between women and men (World Health Organization 2010, 195). In concrete terms, this would require recognizing caregiving labor in the calculation of Social Security and other benefits, strengthening unemployment benefits for part-time workers, and expanding welfare benefits. It would also require embracing the belief that women and other marginalized groups have the potential to build on supportive conditions to empower themselves (World Health Organization 2010). Deeply embedded sexism, racism, and classism in welfare policies offers just one illustration of the challenges to greater equality and the need for comprehensive feminist reform (Bullock 2013).

Current record-setting rates of income and wealth inequality could create an opportune social and economic climate for stronger redistributive support and policy change. Public opinion polls indicate that a majority of Americans perceive the distribution of resources as unfair (Newport 2015). The Occupy movement of the late 2000s is another indication of growing unrest with the concentration of wealth, as is the surge in support for Senator Bernie Sanders, a 2016 Democratic presidential candidate, whose platform was based on taking on "Wall Street" and reducing economic inequality. Women's increasing involvement in legislative and other government positions is also promising.

Yet, significant obstacles remain. Individualism, meritocracy, and other legitimizing beliefs dominate public attitudes and political discourse. Even in the wake of the Great Recession, Americans gravitate toward individualistic explanations for socioeconomic status. In a multi-nation public opinion poll, 73 percent of American respondents rated hard work as very important to getting ahead and 57 percent disagreed with the statement "Success in life is pretty much determined by forces outside our control" (Pew Research Center 2014). These percentages are higher than in the other industrialized countries polled, and far above the global medians of 50 and 38 percent, respectively. In this same poll, only one-quarter of U.S. respondents perceived government economic policies as responsible for inequality. Building broad-based political momentum for redistributive programs is contingent on challenging these beliefs.

Gender is a central facet of redistributive politics, both in terms of beneficiaries of and support for redistributive programs. System justification research makes clear that even those who are disadvantaged by current economic arrangements—women, people of color, and low-income groups—may support them. Nevertheless, low-status groups are more likely than high-status groups to recognize discrepancies between system goals and system outcomes, express dissatisfaction with the U.S. system, and prefer policies that would attenuate hierarchies (Zimmerman and Reyna 2013). The full participation of women and other marginalized groups in the political process is essential to challenging racist, classist, and sexist stereotypes that undermine support for redistribution, and to bringing diverse economic experiences to the forefront of political consciousness. Only then can we genuinely take on the challenge Associate Supreme Court Justice Louis Brandeis identified decades ago, "We must make our choice. We may have democracy, or we may have wealth concentrated in the hands of a few, but we can't have both" (cited in Lonergan 1941, 42).

References

Abner, Kristin S. 2011. "Determinants of Welfare Policy Attitudes: A Contextual Level Analysis." *Sociological Spectrum* 31 (4): 466–497.

Alesina, Alberto, and Eliana La Ferrara. 2005. "Preferences for Redistribution in the Land of Opportunities." *Journal of Public Economics* 89 (5): 897–931.

Bell, Amelia, Katherine Gallagher Robbins, and Julie Vogtman. 2015. *Public Programs Lift Millions of Women and Children Out of Poverty.* National Women's Law Center. Accessed March 15, 2016. http://nwlc.org/resources/public-programs-lift-millions-women-and-children-out-poverty/.

Ben-Ishai, Liz, Rick McHugh, and Kathleen Ujvari. 2015. *Access to Unemployment Insurance Benefits for Family Caregivers: An Analysis of State Rules and Practices.* Washington, DC: Association for Retired Persons Public Policy Institute.

Blekesuane, Morten, and Jill Quadagno. 2003. "Public Attitudes toward Welfare State Policies: A Comparative Analysis of 24 Nations." *European Sociological Review* 19 (5): 415–427.

Brady, David, and Amy Bostic. 2015. "Paradoxes of Social Policy: Welfare Transfers, Relative Poverty, and Redistribution Preferences." *American Sociological Review* 80 (2): 268–298.

Breznau, Nate. 2010. "Economic Equality and Social Welfare: Policy Preferences in Five Nations." *International Journal of Public Opinion Research* 22 (4): 458–484.

Bullock, Heather E. 2008. "Justifying Inequality: A Social Psychological Analysis of Beliefs about Poverty and the Poor." In *The Colors of Poverty: Why Racial and Ethnic Disparities Persist,* edited by Ann Chih Lin and David R. Harris, 52–75. New York: Russell Sage.

Bullock, Heather E. 2013. *Women and Poverty: Psychology, Public Policy, and Social Justice.* Chichester, UK: Wiley-Blackwell.

Caiazza, Amy. 2004. "Does Women's Representation in Elected Office Lead to Women-Friendly Policy? Analysis of State-Level Data." *Women & Politics* 26 (1): 35–70.

Calzada, Ines, Maria Gomez-Garrido, Luis Moreno, and Francisco Javier Moreno-Fuentes. 2014. "It Is Not Only about Equality: A Study on the (Other) Values That Ground Attitudes to the Welfare State." *International Journal of Public Opinion Research* 26 (2): 178–201.

Caminada, Koen, and Kees Goudswaard. 2010. "How Well Is Social Expenditure Targeted to the Poor?" In *Social Security, Poverty and Social Exclusion in Rich and Poorer Countries, International Studies on Social Security,* Vol. 16, edited by Peter Saunders and Roy Sainsbury, 97–112. Belgium: Intersentia.

Chang, Mariko Lin. 2010. *Shortchanged: Why Women Have Less Wealth and What Can Be Done about It.* New York, NY: Oxford University Press.

Citizens for Tax Justice (CTJ). 2015. *Who Pays Taxes in America in 2015.* Accessed March 15, 2016. http://ctj.org/ctjreports/2015/04/who_pays_taxes_in_america_in_2015.php.

Delaney, Arthur, and Michael McAuliff. March 20, 2012. "Paul Ryan Wants 'Welfare Reform Round 2'." *Huffington Post.* Accessed March 15, 2016. http://www.huffington post.com/2012/03/20/paul-ryan-welfare-reform_n_1368277.html.

Denhardt, Robert B., Janet V. Denhardt, and Tara A. Blanc. 2014. *Public Administration: An Action Orientation* (7th ed.). Boston, MA: Wadsworth.

Entmacher, Joan, and Katherine Gallagher Robbins. 2015. *Women and Social Security.* National Women's Law Center. Accessed March 15, 2016. http://nwlc.org/resources/women-and-social-security/.

Falk, Gene. 2014. "Temporary Assistance for Needy Families (TANF): Size and Characteristics of the Cash Assistance Caseload." *Green Book.* Congressional Research Service. Accessed March 15, 2016. http://greenbook.waysandmeans.house.gov/2014-green-book/chapter-7-temporary-assistance-for-needy-families/temporary-assistance-for-needy-1.

Feagin, Joe R. 1975. *Subordinating the Poor.* Englewood Cliffs, NJ: Prentice Hall.

Floyd, Ife, and Liz Schott. 2015. *TANF Cash Benefits Have Fallen by More Than 20 Percent in Most States and Continue to Erode.* Center on Budget and Policy Priorities. Accessed March 15, 2016. http://www.cbpp.org/research/family-income-support/tanf-cash-benefits-have-fallen-by-more-than-20-percent-in-most-states.

Frisch, Scott A., and Sean Q. Kelly. 2003. "A Place at the Table: Women's Committee Requests and Women's Committee Assignments in the U.S. House." *Women & Politics* 25 (3): 1–26.

Garcia, Donna M., Serge Desmarais, Nyla R. Branscombe, and Stephen S. Gee. 2005. "Opposition to Redistributive Policies for Women: The Role of Policy Experience and Group Interest." *British Journal of Social Psychology* 44 (4): 583–602.

Gilens, Martin. 1999. *Why Americans Hate Welfare: Race, Media, and the Politics of Antipoverty Policy*. Chicago, IL: University of Chicago Press.

Goren, Paul. 2003. "Race, Sophistication, and White Opinion on Government Spending." *Political Behavior* 25 (3): 201–220.

Henry, P. J., Christine Renya, and Bernard Weiner. 2004. "Hate Welfare but Help the Poor: How the Attributional Content of Stereotypes Explains the Paradox of Reactions to Destitute in America." *Journal of Applied Social Psychology* 34 (1): 34–58.

Hunt, Matthew O., and Heather E. Bullock. 2016. "Ideologies and Beliefs about Poverty." In *The Oxford Handbook of the Social Science of Poverty*, edited by David Brady and Linda Burton, 93–116. New York, NY: Oxford University Press.

Institute for Women's Policy Research. 2015. *The Status of Women in the States, 2015*. Institute for Women's Policy Research. www.iwpr.org/publications/pubs/the-status-of-women-in-the-states-2015-full-report.

Jeydel, Alana, and Andrew J. Taylor. 2003. "Are Women Legislators Less Effective? Evidence from the U.S. House in the 103rd-105th Congress." *Political Research Quarterly* 56 (1): 19–27.

Johnson, James D., Nelgy Olivo, Nathan Gibson, William Reed, and Leslie Ashburn-Nardo. 2009. "Priming Media Stereotypes Reduces Support for Social Welfare Policies: The Mediating Role of Empathy." *Personality and Social Psychology Bulletin* 35 (4): 463–476.

Johnston, Christopher D., and Benjamin J. Newman. 2016. "Economic Inequality and U.S. Public Policy Mood across Space and Time." *American Politics Research* 44 (1): 164–191.

Jones, Edward E., and Richard E. Nisbett. 1972. "The Actor and the Observer: Divergent Perceptions of the Causes of Behavior." In *Attribution: Perceiving the Causes of Behavior*, edited by Edward E. Jones, David E. Kanouse, Harold H. Kelley, Richard E. Nisbett, Stuart Valins, and Bernard Weiner, 79–94. Morristown, NJ: General Learning Press.

Jost, John T., and Orsolya Hunyady. 2005. "Antecedents and Consequences of System-Justifying Ideologies." *Current Directions in Psychological Science* 14 (5): 260–265.

Keely, Louise C., and Chih Ming Tan. 2008. "Understanding Preferences for Income Redistribution." *Journal of Public Economics* 92 (5–6): 944–961.

Keith-Jennings, Byrnne. 2015. *SNAP Benefits Do Much But Are Often Too Small*. Center on Budget and Policy Priorities. Accessed March 15, 2016. http://www.cbpp.org/blog/snap-benefits-do-much-but-are-often-too-small.

Kelly, Maura. 2010. "Regulating the Reproduction and Mothering of Poor Women: The Controlling Image of the Welfare Mother in Television News Coverage of Welfare Reform." *Journal of Poverty* 14 (1): 76–96.

Kelly, Nathan J., and Peter K. Enns. 2010. "Inequality and the Dynamics of Public Opinion: The Self-Reinforcing Link Between Economic Inequality and Mass Preferences." *American Journal of Political Science* 54 (4): 855–870.

Kenworthy, Lane. 1999. "Do Social-Welfare Policies Reduce Poverty? A Cross-National Assessment." *Social Forces* 77 (3): 1119–1139.

Kluegel, James R., and Eliot R. Smith. 1986. *Beliefs about Inequality: Americans' Views of What Is and What Ought to Be*. New York, NY: Aldine De Gruyter.

Kraus, Michael, and Jacinth J. X. Tan. 2015. "Americans Overestimate Social Class Mobility." *Journal of Experimental Social Psychology* 58: 101–111.

Lee, Sheila Jackson. January 8, 2014. "The War on Poverty." *The Congressional Record* 160 (4): H23–H24.

Little, Thomas H., Dana Dunn, and Rebecca E. Deen. 2001. "A View from the Top: Gender Differences in Legislative Priorities among State Legislative Leaders." *Women & Politics* 22 (4): 29–50.

Lonergan, Raymond. 1941. "A Steadfast Friend of Labor." In *Mr. Justice Brandeis, Great American*, edited by Irving Dilliard, 42–45. St Louis, MO: Modern View Press.

Luo, Xiaowei. 1998. "What Affects Attitudes towards Government's Role in Solving Unemployment? A Comparative Study of Great Britain and the United States." *International Journal of Public Opinion Research* 10 (2): 121–144.

Luttig, Matthew. 2013. "The Structure of Inequality and Americans' Attitudes toward Redistribution." *Public Opinion Quarterly* 77 (3): 811–821.

McCoy, Shannon K., Joseph D. Wellman, Brandon Cosley, Laura Saslow, and Elissa Epel. 2013. "Is the Belief in Meritocracy Palliative for Members of Low Status Groups? Evidence for a Benefit for Self-Esteem and Physical Health via Perceived Control." *European Journal of Social Psychology* 43 (4): 307–318.

Mitchell, Michelle. 2010. "Gender and Unemployment Insurance: Why Women Receive Unemployment Benefit at Lower Rates than Men and Will Unemployment Insurance Reform Close the Gender Gap." *Texas Journal of Women and the Law* 20 (1): 55–74.

National Women's Law Center. 2015. *Closing the Wage Gap is Crucial for Women of Color and Their Families*. National Women's Law Center. https://nwlc.org/wp-content/uploads/2015/08/closing_the_wage_gap_is_crucial_for_woc_and_their_families_2015.pdf.

Newport, Frank. 2015. *Americans Continue to Say U.S. Wealth Distribution is Unfair*. Gallup Poll. Accessed March 15, 2016. http://www.gallup.com/poll/182987/americans-continue-say-wealth-distribution-unfair.aspx?g_source=income%20inequality&g_medium=search&g_campaign=tiles.

Organisation for Economic Co-operation and Development (OECD). 2015. *In It Together, Why Less Inequality Benefits All*. Accessed March 15, 2016. http://www.oecd.org/social/in-it-together-why-less-inequality-benefits-all-9789264235120-en.htm.

Ott-Holland, Catherine J., Jason L. Huang, Ann Marie Ryan, Fabian Elizondo, and Patrick L. Wadlington. 2014. "The Effects of Culture and Gender on Perceived Self-Other Similarity in Personality." *Journal of Research in Personality* 53: 13–21.

Pew Research Center. 2012. *Partisan Polarization Surges in Bush, Obama Years. Trends in American Values: 1987–2012*. Accessed August 15, 2016. http://www.people-press.org/2012/06/04/partisan-polarization-surges-in-bush-obama-years/

Pew Research Center. 2014. *Emerging and Developing Economies Much More Optimistic Than Rich Countries about the Future*. Accessed March 15, 2016. http://www.pewglobal.org/2014/10/09/emerging-and-developing-economies-much-more-optimistic-than-rich-countries-about-the-future/.

Pew Research Center. 2015a. *Beyond Distrust: How Americans View Their Government*. Accessed March 15, 2016. http://www.people-press.org/2015/11/23/beyond-distrust-how-americans-view-their-government/.

Pew Research Center. 2015b. *A Deep Dive into Party Affiliation: Sharp Differences by Race, Gender, Generation, Education*. Accessed March 15, 2016. http://www.people-press.org/2015/04/07/a-deep-dive-into-party-affiliation/.

Poggione, Sarah. 2004. "Exploring Gender Differences in State Legislators' Policy Preferences." *Political Research Quarterly* 57 (2): 305–314.

Quadagno, Jill, and JoEllen Pederson. 2012. "Has Support for Social Security Declined? Attitudes toward the Public Pension Scheme in the USA, 2000 and 2010." *International Journal of Social Welfare* 21 (s1): S88–S100.

Rasmussen Reports. 2014. *49% Believe Government Programs Increase Poverty in America.* Accessed March 15, 2016. www.rasmussenreports.com/public_content/lifestyle/general_lifestyle/july_2014/49_believe_government_programs_increase_poverty_in_america.

Schneider, Simone M., and Juan C. Castillo. 2015. Poverty Attributions and the Perceived Justice of Income Inequality: A Comparison of East and West Germany." *Social Psychology Quarterly* 78 (3): 263–282.

Seccombe, Karen. 2011. *So You Think I Drive a Cadillac? Welfare Recipients' Perspectives on the System and Its Reform* (3th ed.). Boston, MA: Allyn & Bacon.

Sefton, Tom. 2006. "Distributive and Redistributive Policy." In *The Oxford Handbook of Public Policy*, edited by Michael Moran, Martin Rein, and Robert E. Goodin, 607–623. New York, NY: Oxford University Press.

Skocpol, Theda. 1991. "Targeting within Universalism: Politically Viable Policies to Combat Poverty in the United States." In *The Urban Underclass*, edited by Christopher Jencks and Paul E. Peterson, 411–436. Washington, DC: The Brookings Institution.

Smith, Adrienne R. 2014. "Cities Where Women Rule: Female Political Incorporation and the Allocation of Community Development Block Grant Funding." *Politics & Gender* 10 (3): 313–340.

Smith, Tom W. 1987. "That Which We Call Welfare by Any Other Name Would Smell Sweeter: An Analysis of the Impact of Question Wording on Pattern Response." *Public Opinion Quarterly* 51 (1): 75–83.

Soroka, Stuart, Allison Harell, and Shanto Iyengar. 2013. *Racial Cues and Attitudes toward Redistribution: A Comparative Experimental Approach* (RSCAS 2013/59). Accessed March 15, 2016. http://cadmus.eui.eu//handle/1814/27700.

Stokes, Bruce. 2013. *Public Attitudes toward the Next Social Contract.* Pew Research Center. Accessed March 15, 2016. http://www.pewglobal.org/2013/01/15/public-attitudes-toward-the-next-social-contract/.

van Doorn, Bas W. 2015. "Pre- and Post-Welfare Reform Media Portrayals of Poverty in the United States: The Continuing Importance of Race and Ethnicity." *Politics & Policy* 43 (1): 142–160.

World Health Organization. 2010. *Gender, Women, and the Tobacco Epidemic.* Manila, Philippines: WHO.

Yang, Philip, and Nadine Barrett. 2006. "Understanding Public Attitudes towards Social Security." *International Journal of Social Welfare* 15 (2): 95–109.

Zimmerman, Jennifer L., and Christine Reyna. 2013. "The Meaning and Role of Ideology in System Justification and Resistance for High- and Low-Status People." *Journal of Personality and Social Psychology* 105 (1): 1–23.

6

POLITICAL CONSCIOUSNESS AND GENDER COLLECTIVE ACTION

A Case and Place for Self-Objectification

Rachel Calogero

The beauty practices that women engage in, and which men find so exciting, are those of political subordinates. . . . The fact that some women say that they take pleasure in the practices is not inconsistent with their role in the subordination of women.

(*Jeffreys 2005*)

Published in 1792, Mary Wollstonecraft's *A Vindication of the Rights of Woman: With Strictures on Political and Moral Subjects* served as a treatise on overcoming the oppression of women in British society and elsewhere. Here she set out her observations on the socialization of women during this era. In her view, adult women were treated as subordinate and dependent creatures, taught to regard their looks with the utmost importance, and to view appearance management as natural. For Wollstonecraft, these cultural beliefs and practices were oppressive to women. The kicker, though, was women had bought into them so deeply that they had become active participants in their own oppression—instead of rejecting these beliefs and practices.

The cultural message persists that a woman's value is based on how her body and appearance are evaluated by others. In 1920 women in the United States won the right to vote *and* in the same year the Miss America beauty pageant was established, referred to initially as the "Fall Frolic." Coincidence? Susan Faludi (1991) and other feminist scholars have said no. Coincidence or not, as women were gaining status in society, they were met with a stark reminder of their status and function as decorative sex objects. Cultural reminders of the value placed on women's appearance (such as beauty pageants) imply that women's greatest calling is to be the pretty girl, regardless of their capabilities. Recognizing this possibility,

Naomi Wolf (1991) warned that "dieting is the most potent political sedative in women's history; a quietly mad population is a tractable one. . . . It is those traits [passivity, anxiety, and emotionality], and not thinness for its own sake, that the dominant culture wants to create in the private sense of self of recently liberated women in order to cancel out the dangers of their liberation" (p. 187–88).

And still today, in the United States, girls and women learn to value and manage their youthful appearance, beauty, and sexual appeal above all else. Beauty socialization is a particular form of gender socialization, and an especially effective form occurs through the sexual objectification of women in mainstream media and culture. *Miss Representation*, a documentary released in 2011 by Jennifer Siebel Newsom, showcases the depth and scope of the harm done to girls and women by representing and viewing them in hypersexualized and demeaning ways. This film renders visible how regular encounters with sexual objectification operate as lessons for girls and women on "a woman's place" in society—and it's not in the oval office or as political leaders.

Over time and across cultures, women have been valued more for how they look than what they can do—a value system that gets internalized and impacts everyday life. Over the last decade, studies driven by campaigns aimed at reducing negative body image among girls and women report staggering statistics on the impact of appearance pressures in their lives. Of thousands of girls and women surveyed across countries and cultural contexts, over half of them report avoiding an activity (or activities) because they felt bad or were self-conscious about how they looked (Etcoff et al. 2006). Girls and women avoided giving an opinion, going on a job interview, going to the doctor, going to work, going to school, going to the beach (or pool, sauna, spa), going to social events or parties, dating, and exercising. These patterns of withdrawal from everyday life reflect a narrowing of presence—women end up taking less physical, mental, and social space in their immediate surroundings, and the world at large, because they anticipate and fear the repercussions of their appearance.

Given these historical and cultural observations on the impact of beauty socialization across so many critical life domains, this chapter focuses our attention more squarely on the potential impact this socialization process has on women's political consciousness and social activism. Drawing largely from social psychological theories and perspectives, this chapter is guided by several key questions: Were Mary Wollstonecraft's observations about women over three hundred years ago correct—does appearance consciousness interfere with their political consciousness? In particular, does the socialization of women into sexual objects contribute to a dulled political consciousness and social activism on their own behalf? If so, how does this happen and what is the short-term and long-term impact on women? Notably, this volume includes several chapters that complement this perspective in their consideration of other sociocultural factors that shape all aspects of women's socio-political life (see Oxley—Chapter 2, Brinkman—Chapter 3, Lizotte—Chapter 4).

In contemporary societies around the world, girls and women routinely encounter sexual objectification in their day-to-day lives. One consequence of living in this cultural climate is *self-objectification*—or internalized objectification—which occurs when a woman views herself through this same sexually objectified lens. This chapter begins with literature that supports a case for the role of self-objectification in women's political consciousness and activism. This analysis is followed by a summary of the research on the link between self-objectification and women's political consciousness and activism. One clear pattern to emerge is women are less willing to stand up for themselves and each other to make society function more fairly when they are thinking about and managing how they look. This research illuminates how this self-perspective ultimately limits the full potential of girls and women. To wrap up the chapter, several new directions for scientific inquiry are described.

Objecthood and the Cultural Climate of Sexual Objectification

The basis for the idea that self-objectification obstructs women's political consciousness and activism rests on an understanding of what it means to become an object. Objectification is the process by which a person is made into a thing or object (Dworkin 1997). This process is assumed to occur when a person is divested of their personhood and regarded as a means to an end (Haslam 2006; MacKinnon 1989). Philosophical insights on the objectification of others have identified 10 ways a person can be objectified: 1) when treated as a tool for their own purposes; 2) when treated as lacking self-determination and autonomy; 3) when treated as lacking agency; 4) when treated as interchangeable with others; 5) when treated as violable; 6) when treated as something to be owned; and 7) when treated as lacking subjectivity and personal experience (Nussbaum 1995). Three features were appended later to this list: 8) when reduced to a body or body parts; 9) when reduced to one's appearance; and 10) when silenced (Langton 2009). This collection of qualities and conditions that define objecthood underpin a foundational feminist framework on the objectification of girls and women—objectification theory.

Objectification theory (Fredrickson and Roberts 1997) starts from the well-established premise that cultural practices of objectifying women are pervasive in westernized societies (Calogero, Tantleff-Dunn, and Thompson 2011; Loughnan et al. 2015) and create multiple opportunities for public attention to be fixated on the female body. Sexual objectification—the process of making a woman into a sexual object—is the particular focus of this theory. We witness instances of objectifying experiences for women on a regular basis, typically within interpersonal encounters, such as being gazed at from the neck down, catcalls, appearance commentary, unsolicited touching (Gardner 1980; Macmillan, Nierobisz, and Welsh 2000; Swim et al. 2001), and visual presentations of women in media, such as magazine images, product adverts, TV programs, films, music lyrics and videos, and Internet and social networking sites (Aubrey and Frisby 2011; Reichert and Carpenter 2004). In these sexually objectifying encounters, women are treated more like bodies than full-fledged human beings, their bodies are viewed as sufficient to represent them, and their bodies are valued for the sexual purpose or function they satisfy for the perceiver (Bartky 1990; LeMoncheck 1985).

Experimental studies by social psychologists show that sexualized portrayals of women (compared to non-sexualized portrayals of women or portrayals of men) trigger perceptions of them as objects. Specifically, sexualized women are associated with less mental capability, moral status, and humanness (Heflick and Goldenberg 2009; Heflick et al. 2011; Loughnan et al. 2010; Vaes, Paladino, and Puvia 2011), viewed interchangeably with other women (Gervais, Vescio, and Allen 2012) and with objects (Bernard et al. 2012), and targeted for more violent and aggressive treatment (Aubrey, Hopper, and Mbure 2011; Rudman and Mescher 2012). Psychologists have observed this pattern even at the level of neural responses, demonstrating less activity in brain regions associated with mental state attribution when viewing sexualized women, compared to non-sexualized women and men (Cikara, Eberhardt, and Fiske 2011).

Self-Objectification: Concept and Consequences

In the objectification theory framework (see Figure 6.1), recurrent encounters of sexual objectification encourage a form of self-consciousness whereby women's thoughts and actions are "interrupted by images of how their bodies appear"

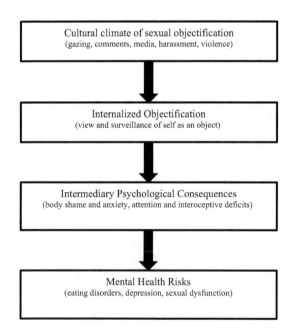

FIGURE 6.1 Objectification Theory Model

and a standpoint on the self whereby women regard their bodies as belonging "less to them and more to others" (Fredrickson and Roberts 1997). This self-perspective is dubbed *self-objectification*, a term that reflects incorporation of sexual objectification into one's own mental sphere, as articulated by the co-author of objectification theory, Tomi-Ann Roberts:

> That is, socialization of subordinates in a dominant culture achieves a kind of colonization of the mind that ensures self-imposed powerlessness. So too socialization of girls and women in a sexually objectifying culture achieves self-objectification—a perspective on oneself as an object to be looked at and evaluated.
>
> *(2002, 326)*

Girls and women who experience higher levels of self-objectification tend to regard appearance as central to their self-concept, anticipate others' reactions to their appearance, and chronically monitor how they ought to look to others, understanding that how they appear to others will determine how they will be treated (Berger 1972; Calogero 2011; Calogero and Watson 2009; McKinley and Hyde 1996).

When objectification theory was originally proposed, the primary aim was to explain why girls and women experience depression, sexual dysfunction, and eating disorders at disproportionately higher rates than men. What was it about being a woman that puts someone at greater risk for these specific mental health risks? The authors put forward the thesis that being female-bodied in a culture that accepts and perpetuates sexual objectification and engenders self-objectification is the key to understanding this gendered pattern. Specifically, self-objectification increases opportunities for a specific set of subjective experiences, including body shame, appearance anxiety, disrupted flow, and reduced sensitivity to internal bodily cues. This set of experiences then predicts more symptoms of depression, sexual dysfunction, and eating disorders. For over two decades scholars have garnered extensive empirical support for the objectification model of women's mental health risk (Moradi and Huang 2008; Tiggemann and Williams 2011).

The objectification theory literature has also linked self-objectification to consequences well beyond mental health (see Table 6.1). Some consequences remain situated in the realm of health and physicality (e.g., cosmetic surgery attitudes, substance abuse), whereas others represent more general motivational (e.g., self-efficacy, self-esteem) or behavioral (e.g., math performance, dysfunctional exercise) domains. Still other consequences are associated with perceptions of one's social environment (e.g., fear of rape, hostility toward women).

The burgeoning evidence suggests this self-perspective may govern and disrupt more aspects of women's lives than previously conceived. It is imperative to take

TABLE 6.1 Sampling of Correlates and Consequences Associated with Self-Objectification in Girls and Women Beyond the Original Theory

Health and Physicality	Motivational and Affective	Cognitive and Behavioral	Social & Environmental Perceptions
Reproductive functioning attitudes (Roberts 2004)	Negative affectivity (Miner-Rubino et al. 2002)	Appearance-driven exercise (Strelan et al. 2003)	Hostility toward women (Loya et al. 2006)
Self-injury (Muehlenkamp et al. 2005)	Intrinsic motivation and efficacy (Gapinksi et al. 2003)	Physical performance (Fredrickson and Harrison 2005)	Fear and perceived risk of rape (Fairchild and Rudman 2008)
Smoking (Harrell et al. 2006)	Life satisfaction (Mercurio and Landry 2008)	Avoid objectifying media (Aubrey 2006)	Proenvironmental attitudes (Scott 2010)
Use of sexual protection (Impett et al. 2006)	Real-ought self-discrepancy (Calogero and Watson 2009)	Prolonged body thoughts (Quinn et al. 2006)	Reasons for pubic hair removal (Smolak and Murnen 2011)
Management of urinary incontinence (Hines et al. 2007)	Body-based social comparisons (Tylka and Sabik 2010)	Self-silencing (Saguy et al. 2010)	Partner-objectification (Zurbriggen et al. 2011)
Substance abuse (Carr and Szymanski 2011)	Self-esteem (Choma et al. 2010)	Cognitive processing (Gay and Castano 2010)	Sex as personal source of power (Erchull and Liss 2013)
Trauma symptoms (Erchull et al. 2013)	Body guilt (Calogero and Pina 2011)	Clothing choices (Tiggemann and Andrew 2012)	Authenticity in interactions (Garcia, Earnshaw, and Quinn 2015)
Cosmetic surgery attitudes (Calogero and Tylka 2014)	Body esteem and satisfaction (Fitzsimmons-Craft et al. 2012)	Self-sexualization (Liss, Erchull, and Ramsey 2011)	Rape myth acceptance (Fox et al. 2015)

note of what women *lose* when this self-view is activated. The collective costs of self-objectification create deficits for women, requiring them to operate with fewer resources, more insecurity, and a narrowed self-image on a day-to-day basis. Under these limiting conditions, women are unlikely to investigate or even be conscious of the injustice of these conditions. My developing program of research on self-objectification is driven by this possibility, focused on the broader system-based implications of self-objectification, and examines this self-perspective in the context of women's political consciousness and activism to change the social arrangements and environments that disproportionately scrutinize and treat them unfairly.

Self-Objectification Obstructs Political Consciousness and Activism

To recap, the consequences of self-objectification accumulate for women, ulti-mately costing them subjectivity and personhood, cognitive capacity, confidence, voice, and physical and social presence. I contend these deficits to self require compensation and suggest that self-objectification might direct women's attention toward areas that will produce tangible rewards, avoid social penalties, and pre-sumably offset some of the costs (Calogero 2013a; Rudman and Fairchild 2004). In order to better understand this cost–benefit ratio of self-objectification, and how it relates to political consciousness and activism, my research draws upon system justification theory (Jost and Banaji 1994; Jost, Banaji, and Nosek 2004)—a framework that explains why people are more likely to comply with a societal status quo that disadvantages them instead of pushing for social change and progress.

From the perspective of system justification theory, people are motivated to rationalize, defend, and bolster the status quo because it makes them feel safer, happier, and more in control of their life and surroundings (Jost and van der Toorn 2012). For members of disadvantaged social groups where the status quo does not support their actual welfare or interests, this justification might be a bit trickier. Of course people can and do reject unfair social arrangements, but more often than not "members of disadvantaged groups not only pretend to accept their station in life, but actually do see themselves through the dominant cultural lens" (Jost, Pelham, and Carvallo 2002). Put differently, members of disadvantaged groups come to see their status in society as deserved and even natural, and thus are less likely to protest against it (Jost et al. 2011).

Integrating objectification and system justification theories, the program of research described here conceives of self-objectification as one way women come to view themselves through the dominant cultural lens, aligning their self-concept and pursuits with their (unequal) status in the gender social hierarchy (Calogero and Jost 2011), inevitably at the expense of alternative self-perspectives and other pursuits. The series of studies summarized below provide preliminary evidence that women who self-objectify are more likely to view existing social arrange-ments between women and men (i.e., the gender status quo) as fair and just, and are less likely to engage in actions that aim to alter those social arrangements.

Snapshots of the Evidence: Objects Don't Object

This section provides a current summary of the evidence for the role of self-objectification in women's political consciousness and activism. The measures of self-objectification used in these studies were drawn from the objectification theory literature and focus on valuing and viewing oneself as merely a body. The measures of gender-based political consciousness were drawn from the system justification literature and capture the perceived fairness of gender relations in society. The primary outcomes of interest pertain to prior or future engagement in gender-based activism and were drawn from feminist and social psychological literatures on collective action and protest. Notably, because self-objectification emphasizes women's gender status and experience of sexual objectification, this self-view was expected to impact perceptions, beliefs, and behaviors related to *gender* status and the *gender* system specifically. It is plausible that self-objectification might be linked to other domains of political consciousness and activism outside of the gender arena, and this should be explored in future research.

One set of experiments tested the idea that self-objectification would disrupt gender-based activism by increasing ideological support for the status quo (Calogero 2013b). A cross-sectional test of this possibility demonstrated that self-objectification was positively associated with support for the gender status quo and negatively associated with engagement in gender-based social activism in the previous six months (e.g., attended a meeting about gender equality issues, signed a petition related to gender equality). A second study activated a state of self-objectification to test this possibility experimentally with female undergraduates. Participants recalled a time when they were sexually objectified and wrote about it for a few minutes to activate a state of self-objectification, compared to control group participants who wrote about what they would do with a gift card. Results from this experiment revealed more support for the gender status quo and less willingness to engage in gender-based activism among women for whom self-objectification was activated. Moreover, in both studies, women's support for the gender status quo fully explained the relationship between self-objectification and their tendencies to agitate for justice on their own behalf. Put differently, objects don't object.

Another experimental study tested the self-objectification-activism link with an online community sample of adult women (Calogero, Harris, and Donnelly

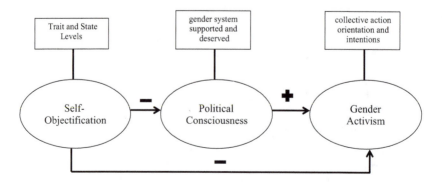

FIGURE 6.2 Self-Objectification—Activism Patterns Revealed in Three Experiments

2016). In this study, state self-objectification was activated using the same method described above and then participants completed relevant measures of political consciousness and activism. Here, we focused on the specific belief that social status and differential treatment on the basis of gender is deserved (e.g., "Society is set up so men and women usually get what they deserve") to capture the degree to which women were conscious of systemic gender inequality. Activism was measured as two separate dependent variables: collective active orientation (e.g., "Only if women organize and work together can anything really be done about discrimination") and activism intentions (e.g., "sign a petition related to gender equality issues"). After completion of filler tasks, participants also completed a short battery of questionnaires, including an individual difference measure of sexist beliefs.

Results from this experiment further confirmed the role of self-objectification in women's political consciousness and activism. First, when self-objectification was activated, women were more likely to believe the gender system was deserved, less likely to view collective action with other women as effective, and less likely to engage in gender-based activism. Second, two meditational models were conducted to test the collective action orientation and activism variables separately in relation to self-objectification and deservingness. In both models, self-objectification predicted deservingness beliefs and weaker collective action orientation and activism intentions. Support for the gender status quo fully explained the relationship between self-objectification and collective action orientation, and partially explained the link between self-objectification and activism intentions.

In addition, we performed both meditational models controlling for benevolent sexism, a set of beliefs that encompass subjectively positive (but patronizing) attitudes toward women in traditional roles (Glick and Fiske 1996). According to Glick et al. (2000), benevolent sexism is a deeply engrained belief system, more comparable to medieval chivalry than egalitarianism. Three components of benevolently sexist ideology have been identified: protective paternalism (e.g., women ought to be rescued first in emergencies), heterosexual intimacy (e.g., every man ought to have a woman he adores), and gender differentiation (e.g., women are purer than men).

Many people have difficulty labeling this benevolence as sexism, especially when compared to the more openly antagonistic attitudes toward women most people readily recognize as prejudice. Yet, these benevolent beliefs are sexist because they prescribe rigid gender roles to women, position women as subordinate to men, and portray women as unsuitable for "men's" work. Driving home this point, in an examination of gender equality across 19 nations, Glick et al. (2000) found that greater endorsement of benevolent and hostile sexism at the individual level predicted fewer women in high-powered roles in government and industry at the national level. That is, the more strongly people believed a woman's place was on her pedestal where she can be cherished and protected by men, the less likely women in these nations were to hold positions of power and status.

We included benevolent sexism in our study because these beliefs are associated with higher self-objectification (Calogero and Jost 2011), more system justification (Glick and Fiske 2001; Jost and Kay 2005), and less collective action (Becker and Wright 2011). Further, separate examination of the three components of benevolent sexism may isolate the particular sexist beliefs relevant to women's gender-based activism. This analysis produced several key results. Self-objectification was still a significant independent predictor of activism, after accounting for sexist beliefs. We also found that sexist beliefs around heterosexual intimacy (i.e., romantic views of women as the objects of men's affections) was the only component of benevolent sexism significantly associated with collective action orientation and activism, with stronger sexist beliefs linked to weaker collective action orientation and activism intentions. This pattern for heterosexual intimacy underscores the importance of the sexually objectified lens for abating political consciousness and deterring activism in women.

A parallel line of research investigates other mechanisms through which self-objectification may disrupt gender-based activism pursuits. A core ideological feature of self-objectification is valuing and investing in appearance over other attributes. Appearance investment is reflective of the gendered lens through which many women have come to view themselves when they self-objectify. One form of appearance investment is the endorsement of feminine beauty ideology, which refers to the socially constructed notion that compliance with Western standards, ideals, and practices around beauty and appearance is an imperative for women, achievable, and requires continuous effort. Ultimately, feminine beauty ideology sets 'beauty work' as the ultimate social currency for women. When beauty ideology is part of one's worldview, and especially if beauty is viewed as the primary social currency for women, we would expect more justification of the gender system that sustains this ideology and less inclination to change it—a proposition we refer to as the *beauty as currency hypothesis*.

We conducted a preliminary test of our hypothesis in a cross-sectional study with female undergraduates (Calogero et al. 2016). To do so, we created a composite measure of the belief that beauty is the most effective currency for women (i.e., "In most situations, a woman will get further by being attractive than by being competent"), drawing from prior work (Forbes et al. 2007), along with measures of self-objectification, support for the gender status quo, and engagement in activism. We also included items to assess the belief that beauty is the most effective currency for women (i.e., "In most situations, a woman will get further by being attractive than by being competent"), along with measures of support for the gender status quo and engagement in activism.

We relied on a series of regression analyses to test our theorized pathways linking the variables of interest in this study. The results supported the beauty as currency hypothesis, with most theorized pathways confirmed and other pathways revealed. Endorsement of feminine beauty as social currency for women predicted self-objectification, thus providing the first empirical link between this particular self-perspective and feminine beauty ideology. In turn, self-objectification predicted more support for the gender status quo, and both self-objectification and support for the gender status quo predicted less gender activism. Importantly, these pathways held when controlling for general levels of self-esteem and self-efficacy. These findings suggest that belief in the notion that women will reap more benefits from their bodies than their skills or other attributes and pursuits may be a particularly insidious feature of feminine beauty ideology that works with self-objectification and against gender social change for those women who adopt it.

Anticipating the Next Steps

Self-objectification undermines social change on behalf of women by dampening motivation to challenge an unfair gender status quo, which is needed in order to rally support and produce a tangible difference in women's social standing. The literature on self-objectification demonstrates a variety of ways women narrow their presence in physical, mental, and social domains. Women's presence in the socio-political sphere has also been narrowed historically, a sphere where women need to take up more space, not less. If self-objectification discourages them from doing so, it needs to be rooted out.

One line of research should further uncover the features of self-objectification that operate in a system-justifying way. In particular, researchers should examine which self-objectification deficits discourage women from challenging the gender hierarchy. Also, it is important to examine women with lower self-objectification, and how this personalized self-view relates to their motivation for and participation in gender-based collective action. Relatedly, can self-objectification be undone—that is, can the minds of girls and women be decolonized? If so, how so? What is the impact on political consciousness and action? Clearly both collective-level and individual-level solutions are needed to target sexual and self-objectification directly (see Calogero and Tylka 2014), but scholars should also examine whether participation in collective action and increased political consciousness lessen the tendency to self-objectify. The interplay of these variables to bolster or weaken the other is a ripe area of research.

A second line of research should explore other socio-political variables impacted by self-objectification. For example, the cognitive and subjectivity deficits incurred from self-objectification may decrease women's awareness of unjust circumstances that affect their lives, narrowing the limits of their political consciousness while expanding appearance consciousness, and thereby increase support for the gender status quo. I also suspect confidence deficits incurred from self-objectification may stifle political and civic efficacy and interest. We are currently exploring these possibilities with crowdsourcing and laboratory-based designs, as well as possible mediators of the self-objectification-activism link shown to be influential in other models of collective action, such as group-based anger and feminist identity (Liss, Crawford, and Popp 2004; van Zomeren, Postmes, and Spears 2008). The more general question of human agency (individual, proxy, and/or collective) in relation to self-objectification also requires attention (Bandura 2006).

A third line of research should investigate more closely the developmental trajectory of these patterns. How early in the gender socialization process does self-objectification undermine the political will and pursuits of girls? We know the sexualization of female children and young girls is fast and thorough (American Psychological Association 2007; Murnen et al. 2016; Zurbriggen and Roberts 2012). Research shows young girls are denied the same mind and moral status as observed with adult women when sexually objectified, and less concern is expressed over harming them (Holland and Haslam 2015). Girls between the ages of 6 and 11 already demonstrate features of self-objectification (Jongenelis, Byrne, and Pettigrew 2014). The impact of this self-perspective on the development of young girls is not yet well-understood, but surely the deficits that accrue at such an early stage will not be inconsequential.

Notably, Lawless and Fox (2013) pointed to a lack of encouragement by parents to pursue a political career, and less exposure to political content across various social contexts, as contributing factors to the ambition gender gap. Indeed, these factors underscore that the political gender gap is a problem of gendered socialization. Yet, the ubiquitous sexual objectification of women in Western cultures operates itself as a powerful gender socialization agent, along with family, peers, educators, and media. Combined with the depressed political focus is the heightened appearance focus and the communication of gender appropriate pursuits for girls. Part of the socialization process for girls that should be incorporated into future research on the gender differences in political ambition is their grooming as sex objects. A surfeit of body consciousness cues and a dearth of political consciousness cues during an early developmental period may be a particularly toxic gendered formula that warrants more scholarly attention.

Concluding Remarks

Three hundred years later, we have gathered evidence that confirm Mary Wollstonecraft's observations. Women's potential and power are thwarted as a result of the beauty socialization and sexual objectification endured by girls and women in everyday life. Although the extent to which sexually objectifying environments influence the self-concept and worldview of girls and women will vary, girls and women cannot completely escape or live outside of these environments. The UN Convention to Eliminate Discrimination Against Women (CEDAW) has made repeated calls to states and nations to end the sexual objectification of girls and women in light of the evidence for the widespread negative impact on them—calls that remain largely unanswered. Women's political consciousness and activism take a hard hit in this cultural climate, and the gender gap in political ambition and participation potentially widens, as appearance pressures and investment can overshadow other life domains.

Ultimately, at the heart of any democracy is the active participation of the citizens and equality for the citizens. Democratic societies are socially and economically impoverished where practices and policies exist that disadvantage women and sustain gender inequality. In my view, what is lost and gained through self-objectification come together in one perfect storm to shift women's attention away from the very social action necessary to change unfair social conditions and improve women's social standing and interests. On the whole, the empirical literature on the objectification of women stresses this is not a storm that women should continue to weather.

References

American Psychological Association. 2007. *Report of the APA Task Force on the Sexualization of Girls*. Washington, DC: American Psychological Association. https://www.apa. org/pi/women/programs/girls/report-full.pdf.

Aubrey, Jennifer S. 2006. "Effects of Sexually Objectifying Media on Self-Objectification and Body Surveillance in Undergraduates: Results of a 2-year Panel Study." *Journal of Communication* 56 (2): 366–386.

Aubrey, Jennifer Stevens, and Cynthia M. Frisby. 2011. "Sexual Objectification in Music Videos: A Content Analysis Comparing Gender and Genre." *Mass Communication and Society* 14 (4): 475–501, doi:10.1080/15205436.2010.513468.

Aubrey, Jennifer Stevens, K. Megan Hopper, and Wanjiru G. Mbure. 2011. "Check That Body! The Effects of Sexually Objectifying Music Videos on College Men's Sexual Beliefs." *Journal of Broadcasting & Electronic Media* 55 (3): 360–379, doi:10.1080/0883 8151.2011.597469.

Bandura, Albert. 2006. "Toward a Psychology of Human Agency." *Perspectives on Psychological Science* 1 (2): 164–180, doi:10.1111/j.1745-6916.2006.00011.x.

Bartky, Sandra Lee. 1990. *Femininity and Domination*. New York: Routledge.

Becker, Julia C., and Stephen C. Wright. 2011. "Yet Another Dark Side of Chivalry: Benevolent Sexism Undermines and Hostile Sexism Motivates Collective Action for Social Change." *Journal of Personality and Social Psychology* 101 (1): 62–77, doi:10.1037/ a0022615.

Berger, John. 1972. *Ways of Seeing*. London: Penguin.

Bernard, Philippe., Sarah J. Gervais, Jill Allen, Sophie Campomizzi, and Olivier Klein. 2012. "Integrating Sexual Objectification with Object Versus Person Recognition: The Sexualized-Body-Inversion Hypothesis." *Psychological Science* 23 (5): 469–471, doi:10.1177/0956797611434748.

Calogero, Rachel M. 2011. "Operationalizing Self-Objectification: Assessment and Related Methodological Issues." In *Self-Objectification in Women: Causes, Consequences, and Counteractions*, edited by Rachel M. Calogero, Stacey Tantleff-Dunn, and J. Kevin Thompson, 23–49. Washington, DC: American Psychological Association.

Calogero, Rachel M. 2013a. "On Objects and Actions: Situating Self-Objectification in a System Justification Context." In *Nebraska Motivation Symposium: Vol. 60. Perspectives on Motivation*, edited by Sarah Gervais, 97–126. Lincoln: University of Nebraska Press.

Calogero, Rachel M. 2013b. "Objects Don't Object: Evidence That Self-Objectification Disrupts Women's Social Activism." *Psychological Science* 24 (3): 312–318, doi:10.1177/0956797612452574.

Calogero, Rachel M., Stephanie A. Harris, and Lois C. Donnelly. 2016. "Deserved So Deterred: Self-Objectification Increases Perceptions of System Deservingness and Weakens Collective Action Orientation and Intentions." Manuscript under review.

Calogero, Rachel M., and John T. Jost. 2011. "Self-Subjugation among Women: Exposure to Sexist Ideology, Self-Objectification, and the Protective Function of the Need to Avoid Closure." *Journal of Personality and Social Psychology* 100 (2): 211–228, doi:10.1037/a0021864.

Calogero, Rachel M., and Afroditi Pina. 2011. "Body Guilt: Preliminary Evidence for a Further Subjective Experience of Self-Objectification." *Psychology of Women Quarterly* 35 (3): 428–440.

Calogero, Rachel M., Stacey Tantleff-Dunn, and J. Kevin Thompson. 2011. *Self-Objectification in Women.* Washington, DC: American Psychological Association.

Calogero, Rachel M., and Tracy L. Tylka. 2014. "Sanctioning Resistance to Sexual Objectification: An Integrative System Justification Perspective." *Journal of Social Issues* 70 (4): 763–778, doi:10.1111/josi.12090.

Calogero, Rachel M., Tracy L. Tylka, Lois C. Donnelly, Amber McGetrick, and Andrea Medrano Leger. 2016. "The Trappings of Femininity: Self-Objectification, Beauty Ideology, and the Shaping of Gender Collective Action." Manuscript under review.

Calogero, Rachel M., and Neill Watson. 2009. "Self-Discrepancy and Chronic Social Self-Consciousness: Unique and Interactive Effects of Gender and Real-Ought Discrepancy." *Personality and Individual Differences* 46 (5–6): 642–647, doi:10.1016/j.paid.2009.01.008.

Carr, Erika R., and Dawn R. Szymanski. 2011. "Sexual Objectification and Substance Abuse in Young Adult Women." *The Counseling Psychologist* 39 (1): 39–66.

Choma, Becky L., Beth A. Visser, Julia A. Pozzebon, Anthony F. Bogaert, Michael A. Busseri, and Stanley W. Sadava. 2010. "Self-Objectification, Self-Esteem, and Gender: Testing a Moderated Mediation Model." *Sex Roles* 63 (9): 645–656.

Cikara, Mina, Jennifer L. Eberhardt, and Susan T. Fiske. 2011. "From Agents to Objects: Sexist Attitudes and Neural Responses to Sexualized Targets." *Journal of Cognitive Neuroscience* 23 (3): 540–551, doi:10.1162/jocn.2010.21497.

Dworkin, Andrea. 1997. *Intercourse.* New York: Free Press Paperbacks.

Erchull, Mindy J., and Miriam Liss. 2013. "Exploring the Concept of Perceived Female Sexual Empowerment: Development and Validation of the Sex is Power Scale." *Gender Issues* 30 (1–4): 39–53.

Erchull, Mindy J., Miriam Liss, and Stephanie Lichiello. 2013. "Extending the Negative Consequences of Media Internalization and Self-Objectification to Dissociation and Self-Harm." *Sex Roles* 69 (11): 583–593.

Etcoff, Nancy, Susie Orbach, Jennifer Scott, and Heidi D'Agostino. 2006. *Beyond Stereotypes: Rebuilding the Foundation of Beauty Beliefs: Findings of the 2005 Dove Global Study.* Dove: Unilever. Accessed September 10, 2016. http://www.beperkthoudbaar.info/upload/documents/dove/DoveBeyondStereotypesWhitePaper.pdf.

Fairchild, Kimberly, and Laurie Rudman. 2008. "Everyday Stranger Harassment and Women's Objectification." *Social Justice Research* 21 (3): 338–357.

Faludi, Susan. 1991. *Backlash.* New York: Crown.

Fitzsimmons-Craft, Ellen E., Megan B. Harney, Laura G. Koehler, Lauren E. Danzi, Margaret K. Riddell, and Anna M. Bardone-Cone. 2012. "Explaining the Relation Between

Thin Ideal Internalization and Body Dissatisfaction Among College Women: The Roles of Social Comparison and Body Surveillance." *Body Image* 9 (1): 43–49.

Forbes, Gordon B., Linda L. Collinsworth, Rebecca L. Jobe, Kristen D. Braun, and Leslie M. Wise. 2007. "Sexism, Hostility toward Women, and Endorsement of Beauty Ideals and Practices: Are Beauty Ideals Associated with Oppressive Beliefs?" *Sex Roles* 56 (5–6): 265–273, doi:10.1007/s11199-006-9161-5.

Fox, Jesse, Rachel A. Ralston, Cody K. Cooper, and Kaitlyn A. Jones. 2015. "Sexualized Avatars Lead to Women's Self-Objectification and Acceptance of Rape Myths." *Psychology of Women Quarterly* 39 (3): 349–362.

Fredrickson, Barbara L., and Kristen Harrison. 2005. "Throwing Like a Girl: Self-Objectification Predicts Adolescent Girls' Motor Performance." *Journal of Sport & Social Issues* 29 (1): 79–101.

Fredrickson, Barbara L., and Tomi-Ann Roberts. 1997. "Objectification Theory." *Psychology of Women Quarterly* 21 (2): 173–206, doi:10.1111/j.1471-6402.1997.tb00108.x.

Garcia, Randi L., Valarie A. Earnshaw, and Diane M. Quinn. 2015. "Objectification in Action: Self- and Other-Objectification in Mixed-Sex Interpersonal Interactions." *Psychology of Women Quarterly* 40 (2): 213–228.

Gardner, Carol Brooks. 1980. "Passing by: Street Remarks, Address Rights, and the Urban Female." *Sociological Inquiry* 50 (3–4): 328–356, doi:10.1111/j.1475-682x.1980.tb00026.x.

Gay, Robin K., and Emanuele Castano. 2010. "My Body or My Mind: The Impact of State and Trait Objectification on Women's Cognitive Resources." *European Journal of Social Psychology* 40 (5): 695–703.

Gervais, Sarah J., Theresa K. Vescio, and Jill Allen. 2012. "When Are People Interchangeable Sexual Objects? The Effect of Gender and Body Type on Sexual Fungibility." *British Journal of Social Psychology* 51 (4): 499–513, doi:10.1111/j.2044-8309.2010.02016.x.

Glick, Peter, and Susan T. Fiske. 1996. "The Ambivalent Sexism Inventory: Differentiating Hostile and Benevolent Sexism." *Journal of Personality and Social Psychology* 70 (3): 491–512, doi:10.1037//0022-3514.70.3.491.

Glick, Peter, and Susan T. Fiske. 2001. "An Ambivalent Alliance: Hostile and Benevolent Sexism as Complementary Justifications for Gender Inequality." *American Psychologist* 56 (2): 109–118, doi:10.1037/0003-066x.56.2.109.

Glick, Peter, Susan T. Fiske, Antonio Mladinic, José L. Saiz, Dominic Abrams, Barbara Masser, and Bolanle Adetoun. 2000. "Beyond Prejudice as Simple Antipathy: Hostile and Benevolent Sexism across Cultures." *Journal of Personality and Social Psychology* 79 (5): 763–775, doi:10.1037/0022-3514.79.5.763.

Harrell, Zaje A., Barbara L. Fredrickson, Cynthia S. Pomerleau, and Susan Nolen-Hoeksema. 2006. "The Role of Trait Self-Objectification in Smoking Among College Women." *Sex Roles* 54 (11–12): 735–743.

Haslam, Nick. 2006. "Dehumanization: An Integrative Review." *Personality and Social Psychology Review* 10 (3): 252–264, doi:10.1207/s15327957pspr1003_4.

Heflick, Nathan A., and Jamie L. Goldenberg. 2009. "Objectifying Sarah Palin: Evidence That Objectification Causes Women to Be Perceived as Less Competent and Less Fully Human." *Journal of Experimental Social Psychology* 45 (3): 598–601, doi:10.1016/j.jesp.2009.02.008.

Heflick, Nathan A., Jamie L. Goldenberg, Douglas P. Cooper, and Elisa Puvia. 2011. "From Women to Objects: Appearance Focus, Target Gender, and Perceptions of Warmth,

Morality and Competence." *Journal of Experimental Social Psychology* 47 (3): 572–581, doi:10.1016/j.jesp.2010.12.020.

Hines, Sandra H., Carolyn M. Sampselle, David L. Ronis, SeonAe Yeo, Barbara L. Fredrickson, and Carol J. Boyd. 2007. "Women's Self-Care Agency to Manage Urinary Incontinence." *Advances in Nursing Science* 30 (2): 175–188.

Holland, E., and N. Haslam. 2015. "Cute Little Things: The Objectification of Prepubescent Girls." *Psychology of Women Quarterly* 40 (1): 108–119, doi:10.1177/0361684315602887.

Impett, Emily A., Deborah Schooler, and Deborah L. Tolman. 2006. "To Be Seen and Not Heard: Femininity Ideology and Adolescent Girls' Sexual Health." *Archives of Sexual Behavior* 35 (2): 131–144.

Jeffreys, Sheila. 2005. *Beauty and Misogyny*. London: Routledge.

Jongenelis, Michelle I., Susan M. Byrne, and Simone Pettigrew. 2014. "Self-Objectification, Body Image Disturbance, and Eating Disorder Symptoms in Young Australian Children." *Body Image* 11 (3): 290–302, doi:10.1016/j.bodyim.2014.04.002.

Jost, John T., and Mahzarin R. Banaji. 1994. "The Role of Stereotyping in System-Justification and the Production of False Consciousness." *British Journal of Social Psychology* 33 (1): 1–27, doi:10.1111/j.2044-8309.1994.tb01008.x.

Jost, John T., Mahzarin R. Banaji, and Brian A. Nosek. 2004. "A Decade of System Justification Theory: Accumulated Evidence of Conscious and Unconscious Bolstering of the Status Quo." *Political Psychology* 25 (6): 881–919, doi:10.1111/j.1467-9221.2004.00402.x.

Jost, John T., Vagelis Chaikalis-Petritsis, Dominic Abrams, Jim Sidanius, Jojanneke van der Toorn, and Christopher Bratt. 2011. "Why Men (and Women) Do and Don't Rebel: Effects of System Justification on Willingness to Protest." *Personality and Social Psychology Bulletin* 38 (2): 197–208, doi:10.1177/0146167211422544.

Jost, John T., and Aaron C. Kay. 2005. "Exposure to Benevolent Sexism and Complementary Gender Stereotypes: Consequences for Specific and Diffuse Forms of System Justification." *Journal of Personality and Social Psychology* 88: 498–509, doi:10.2139/ssrn.386981.

Jost, John T., Brett W. Pelham, and Mauricio R. Carvallo. 2002. "Non-Conscious Forms of System Justification: Implicit and Behavioral Preferences for Higher Status Groups." *Journal of Experimental Social Psychology* 38 (6): 586–602, doi:10.1016/s0022-1031(02)00505-x.

Jost, John T., and Jojanneke van der Toorn. 2012. "System Justification Theory." In *Handbook of Theories of Social Psychology*, edited by P. A. M. van Lange, A. W. Kruglanski, and E. T. Higgins, 313–343. London: Sage.

Langton, Rae. 2009. *Sexual Solipsism*. Oxford: Oxford University Press.

Lawless, Jennifer L., and Richard L. Fox. 2013. *Girls Just Wanna Not Run: The Gender Gap in Young Americans' Political Ambition*. Washington, DC: Women & Politics Institute.

LeMoncheck, Linda. 1985. *Dehumanizing Women*. Totowa, NJ: Rowman & Allanheld.

Liss, Miriam, Mary Crawford, and Danielle Popp. 2004. "Predictors and Correlates of Collective Action." *Sex Roles* 50 (11–12): 771–779.

Liss, Miriam, Mindy J. Erchull, and Laura R. Ramsey. 2011. "Empowering or Oppressing? Development and Exploration of the Enjoyment of Sexualization Scale." *Personality and Social Psychology Bulletin* 37 (1): 55–68, doi:10.1177/0146167210386119.

Loughnan, Steve, Silvia Fernandez-Campos, Jeroen Vaes, Gulnaz Anjum, Mudassar Aziz, Chika Harada, Elise Holland, Indramani Singh, Elisa Puvia, and Koji Tsuchiya. 2015.

"Exploring the Role of Culture in Sexual Objectification: A Seven Nations Study." *Revue Internationale De Psychologie Sociale* 28 (1): 125–152.

Loughnan, Steve, Nick Haslam, Tess Murnane, Jeroen Vaes, Catherine Reynolds, and Caterina Suitner. 2010. "Objectification Leads to Depersonalization: The Denial of Mind and Moral Concern to Objectified Others." *European Journal of Social Psychology* 40 (5): 709–717, doi:10.1002/ejsp.755.

Loya, Bianca N., Gloria Cowan, and Christine Walters. 2006. "The Role of Social Comparison and Body Consciousness in Women's Hostility Toward Women." *Sex Roles* 54 (7): 575–583.

MacKinnon, Catharine A. 1989. *Towards a Feminist Theory of the State.* Cambridge, MA: Harvard University Press.

Macmillan, Ross, Annette Nierobisz, and Sandy Welsh. 2000. "Experiencing the Streets: Harassment and Perceptions of Safety among Women." *Journal of Research in Crime and Delinquency* 37 (3): 306–322, doi:10.1177/0022427800037003003.

McKinley, Nita Mary, and Janet Shibley Hyde. 1996. "The Objectified Body Consciousness Scale: Development and Validation." *Psychology of Women Quarterly* 20 (2): 181–215, doi:10.1111/j.1471-6402.1996.tb00467.x.

Mercurio, Andrea E., and Laura J. Landry. 2008. "Self-Objectification and Well-Being: The Impact of Self-Objectification on Women's Overall Sense of Self-Worth and Life Satisfaction." *Sex Roles* 58 (7): 458–466.

Miner-Rubino, Kathi, Jean M. Twenge, and Barbara L. Fredrickson. 2002. "Trait Self-Objectification in Women: Affective and Personality Correlates." *Journal of Research in Personality* 36 (2): 147–172.

Moradi, Bonnie, and Yu-Ping Huang. 2008. "Objectification Theory and Psychology of Women: A Decade of Advances and Future Directions." *Psychology of Women Quarterly* 32 (4): 377–398, doi:10.1111/j.1471-6402.2008.00452.x.

Muehlenkamp, Jennifer J., Jenny D. Swanson, and Amy M. Brausch. 2005. "Self-Objectification, Risk Taking, and Self-Harm in College Women." *Psychology of Women Quarterly* 29 (1): 24–32.

Murnen, Sarah K., Claire Greenfield, Abigail Younger, and Hope Boyd. 2016. "Boys Act and Girls Appear: A Content Analysis of Gender Stereotypes Associated with Characters in Children's Popular Culture." *Sex Roles* 74 (1–2): 78–91, doi:10.1007/s11199-015-0558-x.

Nussbaum, Martha C. 1995. "Objectification." *Philosophy and Public Affairs* 24 (4): 249–291. Accessed March 15, 2016, doi:10.1111/j.1088-4963.1995.tb00032.x.

Quinn, Diane M., Rachel W. Kallen, and Cristie Cathey. 2006. "Body On My Mind: The Lingering Effect of State Self-Objectification." *Sex Roles* 55 (11): 869–874.

Reichert, T., and C. Carpenter. 2004. "An Update on Sex in Magazine Advertising: 1983 to 2003." *Journalism & Mass Communication Quarterly* 81 (4): 823–837, doi:10.1177/107769900408100407.

Roberts, Tomi-Ann. 2002. "The Woman in the Body." *Feminism & Psychology* 12: 324–329.

Roberts, Tomi-Ann. 2004. "Female Trouble: The Menstrual Self-Evaluation Scale and Women's Self-Objectification." *Psychology of Women Quarterly* 28 (1): 22–26, doi:10.1111/j.1471-6402.2004.00119.x.

Rudman, Laurie A., and Kimberly Fairchild. 2004. "Reactions to Counterstereotypic Behavior: The Role of Backlash in Cultural Stereotype Maintenance." *Journal of Personality and Social Psychology* 87 (2): 157–176, doi:10.1037/0022-3514.87.2.157.

Rudman, Laurie A., and Kris Mescher. 2012. "Of Animals and Objects: Men's Implicit Dehumanization of Women and Likelihood of Sexual Aggression." *Personality and Social Psychology Bulletin* 38 (6): 734–746, doi:10.1177/0146167212436401.

Saguy, Tamar, Diane M. Quinn, John F. Dovidio, and Felicia Pratto. 2010. "Interacting like a Body: Objectification Can Lead Women to Narrow Their Presence in Social Interactions." *Psychological Science* 21 (2): 178–182.

Scott, Britain A. 2010. "Babes and the Woods: Women's Objectification and the Feminine Beauty Ideal as Ecological Hazards." *Ecopsychology* 2 (3): 147–158.

Smolak, Linda, and Sarah K. Murnen. 2011. "Gender, Self-Objectification and Pubic Hair Removal." *Sex Roles* 65 (7): 506–517.

Strelan, Peter, Sarah J. Mehaffey, and Marika Tiggemann. 2003. "Self-Objectification and Esteem in Young Women: The Mediating Role of Reasons for Exercise." *Sex Roles* 48 (1): 89–95.

Swim, Janet K., Lauri L. Hyers, Laurie L. Cohen, and Melissa J. Ferguson. 2001. "Everyday Sexism: Evidence for Its Incidence, Nature, and Psychological Impact from Three Daily Diary Studies." *Journal of Social Issues* 57 (1): 31–53, doi:10.1111/0022-4537.00200.

Tiggemann, Marika, and Rachel Andrew. 2012. "Clothing Choices, Weight, and Trait Self-Objectification." *Body Image* 9 (3): 409–412.

Tiggemann, Marika, and Elyse Williams. 2011. "The Role of Self-Objectification in Disordered Eating, Depressed Mood, and Sexual Functioning among Women: A Comprehensive Test of Objectification Theory." *Psychology of Women Quarterly* 36 (1): 66–75, doi:10.1177/0361684311420250.

Tylka, Tracy. L., and Natalie J. Sabik. 2010. "Integrating Social Comparison Theory and Self-Esteem Within Objectification Theory to Predict Women's Disordered Eating." *Sex Roles* 63 (1): 18–31.

Vaes, Jeroen, Paola Paladino, and Elisa Puvia. 2011. "Are Sexualized Women Complete Human Beings? Why Men and Women Dehumanize Sexually Objectified Women." *European Journal of Social Psychology* 41 (6): 774–785, doi:10.1002/ejsp.824.

van Zomeren, Martijn, Tom Postmes, and Russell Spears. 2008. "Toward an Integrative Social Identity Model of Collective Action: A Quantitative Research Synthesis of Three Socio-Psychological Perspectives." *Psychological Bulletin* 134 (4): 504–535, doi:10.1037/0033-2909.134.4.504.

Wolf, Naomi. 1991. *The Beauty Myth.* New York: W. Morrow.

Wollstonecraft, Mary. 1792/2004. *A Vindication of the Rights of Woman.* New York: Barnes and Noble Publishing.

Zurbriggen, Eileen L., Laura R. Ramsey, and Beth K. Jaworski. 2011. "Self- and Partner-Objectification in Romantic Relationships: Associations with Media Consumption and Relationship Satisfaction." *Sex Roles* 64 (7-8): 449–462.

Zurbriggen, Eileen L., and Tomi-Ann Roberts. 2012. *The Sexualization of Girls and Girlhood.* New York: Oxford University Press.

7

NEW DIRECTIONS AT THE INTERSECTION OF RACE, ETHNICITY, AND GENDER

Christina E. Bejarano

The diverse political landscape of the most recent elections, with both racial/ethnic minorities and women as viable major party presidential candidates, bring up important questions concerning the impact of race/ethnicity and gender of candidates and voters alike. This chapter addresses the need to more fully incorporate race/ethnicity and gender to our studies of political psychology by highlighting research that shows how intersectionality can be used as a tool to our emerging studies of political psychology. This chapter bridges the discussions of women as citizens and women as political candidates by providing an overview of the recent work on intersectionality in these overarching areas.

Racial/ethnic minority women voters are critical to our discussions of campaign dynamics. In 2008, racial/ethnic minority women (especially African American women) were questioned about their cross-cutting identities; which would prove more salient for minority women, their gender or racial identity? Where would their allegiances lie when asked to choose between two different candidates with whom they share racial, ethnic, or gender identities? We might usually assume that one identity will prove more salient than, or "trump," another in shaping minority women's political priorities or behavior. However, some researchers (which I highlight in this chapter) are tackling a more complex analysis that challenges the idea that any one identity "trumps" others; instead, the intersections of multiple identities can create a new and distinct identity dynamic to acknowledge.

This chapter reviews a key question regarding intersectionality and women as citizens: How does intersecting identity impact our political attitudes and political participation? This section serves as a particular complement to the Lizotte chapter on the gender differences in public opinion, by adding the influence of race/ethnicity on gender gaps in public policy.

Moreover, we have moved past a time when candidates were only White males, and now the growing complexity of the race, gender, and ethnicity of political candidates requires the media and political researchers to question the very essence of identity, especially for the 2016 campaign top presidential contenders and their supporters. In 2016, the Republicans had two Latino males (Cruz and Rubio are both Cuban) and one Black male as their top presidential candidates, while the Democrats had a White woman as one of their top candidates. This primary contributed to growing debates over the importance and influence of identity politics. We asked if identity matters to the voters as much as it did in 2008, when the top two Democratic candidates challenged the status quo of a White male president. Questions arose concerning the predicted level of voter support for women, racial/ethnic minority, and racial/ethnic minority women political candidates. In other words, how do multiple identities impact our support or bias towards other groups? In particular, how does identity, of both the candidate and voter, impact the level of support for diverse political candidates? Are diverse candidates facing racial and gender bias from potential voters?

The chapter includes a discussion of intersectionality and support for diverse political candidates, asking how does intersecting identity impact level of support for political candidates? It serves as a particular complement to Bauer's chapter on gender stereotypes and voter evaluations of female candidates, by extending the discussion of intersecting identities and stereotypes.

The recent political examples complicate the study of gender in American politics by reminding us that it is essential to further explore the influence of intersecting identities of gender and race/ethnicity on electoral support and participation, as well as between voters and candidates. The chapter will conclude with a discussion of the future direction of political psychology work at the intersection of race/ethnicity and gender, which moves beyond questions of whether race or gender matters most and incorporates more identity categories and experiences. Even though researchers have increasingly acknowledged the call for intersectionality, "the idea that social identities such as race, gender, and class interact to form qualitative different meanings and experiences" (Warner 2008, 454), there are still very few studies that employ this concept in their research. Several authors in this volume recognize the importance of intersectionality theory for their work, however many do not further investigate or utilize the concept as a tool in their own chapters. For example, Lizotte examines the gender gap in public opinion, but only includes race as required control (with a variable for White). Authors often mention the significance of different subgroups of women, including women of color, in their conclusion or their thoughts on future research, but they generally do not investigate the influence of intersecting racial and ethnic identities for their specific study. As a result, this chapter can serve as a complement to the other existing chapters in this volume, by drawing on the additional intersectional perspectives of women in politics.

Emerging Studies of Race, Ethnicity, and Gender in Political Psychology

Obstacles for Studying Intersection of Race/Ethnicity and Gender

In political psychology work, researchers discuss the role of identity on the public's political attitudes and political behavior. Identity is a social category and "identity in psychological terms relates to awareness of self, self-image, self-reflection, and self-esteem" (Shields 2008, 301). Our identity can include various demographic identifiers, including gender, race, and ethnicity. This identity can influence how we situate ourselves in the political environment, both in terms of the groups we identify with and those that we mobilize.

However, "despite an abundance of theories on social identity within psychology, the prevailing view of social identities is one of uni-dimensionality and independence, rather than intersection" (Bowleg 2008, 313). The concept of intersectionality, developed by feminists and critical race theorists, is increasingly utilized by social scientists. Researchers are now continually being challenged to incorporate expanding categorizations of identities. The previous challenges were to include an analysis of identity characteristics like gender and race, as well as their intersection. Now the current research challenge is to think beyond gender and race to include multiple intersecting identity characteristics like sexuality, physical ability, and immigrant status.

In the last 10 years, there have been several special journal issues published on intersectionality for psychological and political science research. However, these journal issues tend to focus on their discipline specific work and generally fail to provide an interdisciplinary perspective. In terms of psychology, guides have recently been published to fill a gap in previous research that largely focuses on studying either gender or race separately and not the intersection of the constructs (Cole 2009; Silverstein 2006). Suggestions on the best practices for intersectional approaches to psychological research include pushing researchers to reconceptualize "the meaning and consequences of social categories," which can have important implications for all stages of the research process (Cole 2009, 176).

Political scientists have also published guides for intersectionality research, which include recommendations to treat intersectionality as "a normative and empirical research paradigm" that will enable understanding and articulation of the "multiple oppressions that all marginalized groups face" (Hancock 2007, 250 and 230). Recommendations also include that scholars clarify the relationship among categories of identity, which includes acknowledgement of within-group diversity (2007, 231).

In addition, interdisciplinary journals have also published best practices guides to intersectional approaches in psychological research. The suggestions include careful consideration of which particular intersections to examine, keeping in mind the rationale for the choice and the acknowledgement that some identities, such as race/ethnicity and gender, are largely invisible to researchers (e.g., Purdie-Vaughns and Eibach 2008; Warner 2008). When choosing intersections, it becomes more complicated to determine the comparison group, which often serves as the baseline to which the higher social status group is compared (456). Overall, the use of intersectionality work across psychology and political science research generally includes a both/and strategy to compare "individual identities to each other as well as considering intersections and their emergent properties" (2008, 307).

Intersecting Identities: Political Attitudes and Participation

The intersecting racial and gender identities can relate to unique psychological and political outcomes for women of color. For example, "it appears that holding multiple roles or identities may provide both advantages and disadvantages" (Settles 2006, 591), both in terms of psychological well-being and political outcomes, such as access to voter support and motivation for political participation. This section reviews a key question regarding intersectionality and women as citizens: How does intersecting identity impact our different political attitudes (intergroup attitudes and public policies) and our political participation?

Intergroup Attitudes

Few studies incorporate an intersectional analysis of the impact of voters' multiple identities on their political attitudes. The emerging studies of race/ethnicity and gender bias push to address the broader research questions on the impact of identity, as well as move our research beyond the sole examination of White attitudes about different racial/ethnic groups.

Previous studies have examined gender differences in attitudes, typically among Whites, toward other racial/ethnic groups (e.g. Hughes and Tuch 2003; Johnson and Marini 1998; Schnittker 2000), in terms of views of policies that benefit one particular racial group. Researchers extended the group justification theories to explore gender differences in racial attitudes and policy, which led to assumptions that there would be a hierarchy of identities where racial/ethnic groups would prioritize the group position of their own race or ethnicity. Based on this hierarchy, it was expected that there would be few gender differences in racial groups' political attitudes.

In particular, several studies generally found that race or ethnicity, rather than gender, was the primary factor influencing the significant differences between groups' political attitudes (Burns et al. 2001; Conway 2008; Lien 1998). This work cautioned that gender differences in racial attitudes would be "small, inconsistent, and limited mostly to attitudes on racial policy" (Hughes and Tuch 2003, 384). Findings demonstrated that White women's and White men's racial attitudes were similar and therefore more of a function of their shared sense of group position, which includes the view that other racial groups may pose a threat to their White privileged status. Therefore, the gender differences in socialization were expected to only play a negligible role in the formation of racial attitudes among Whites (Hughes and Tuch 2003).

However, when this research extended the analysis toward multiple identities, it usually resulted in an either/or identity battle that would demonstrate whether racial/ethnic minority women prioritized their gender or their racial identity. This either/or identity battle can result in a potential 'double-bind' where the position of minority women is conflicting among the multiple identities and therefore they are expected to decide between these dual identities (Gay and Tate 1998, 171; Reid 1984). Often this identity battle results in mixed findings, however it usually ends with the racial or ethnic identity proving to be more important than the gender identity. In particular, previous research found that ethnicity generally trumped gender as an important influence on the trends in political attitudes among Asian Americans and Hispanics (Almquist 1986; Chow 1987), as well as African Americans (Gay and Tate 1998; Joseph and Lewis 1981; Marshall and Read 2003). Scholars proposed this is because "minority women experience intense pressure to demonstrate primary loyalty to their ethnic group at the expense of gender interests" (Marshall and Read 2003, 877). For example, during the 2008 democratic primary campaign, Black women were pressured to decide between their apparent dual identities of gender and race, when they had to show electoral support for either Hillary Clinton or Barack Obama.

However, this identity battle depends on the racial/ethnic group being examined, as well as the distinction between voters or elites. For example, Gay and Tate studied this multiple identity issue among Black women and found that "their identification with their race more powerfully affected their political attitudes than did their identification on the basis of gender, except in instances where the interests of Blacks directly conflict with the interests of women" such as the issue of the women's movement, where gender remains politically relevant (1998, 169).

An alternative proposal to the either/or identity battle is the contagion hypothesis, where "experiences of racial discrimination facilitate heightened political consciousness and mobilization among minority women to remedy both forms of inequality" (Marshall and Read 2003, 877). The contagion hypothesis presents a different twist to the traditional group justification theories, since the new assumption is that some identity groups may share a sense of linked fate with other groups rather than a prioritization solely for their own racial group. For example, researchers have demonstrated significant gender differences in Whites' progressive racial attitudes with women expressing more favorable attitudes toward other racial groups than White men (Bejarano 2013; Johnson and Marini 1998; Schnittker 2000). This finding was also extended to examine the differences in minority group attitudes on gender with the assumption that racial/ethnic minorities will relate to experiencing comparable forms of inequality with women.

In addition, there can be distinction between attitudes toward specific public policies, such as race-related affirmative action and gender-related affirmative action, with research finding that women and Blacks were more likely to support gender-related affirmative action (Kane and Whipkey 2009). Most of this previous work still focused on either racial attitudes or gender attitudes, without an acknowledgement that they can intersect. For example, Kane and Whipkey in their previous work on race and gender-related affirmative action only briefly mentioned the further analysis of racial/ethnic minority women (2008). They noted that "not only women of color, but Black and Latino men as well, are more supportive of gender-based affirmative action than White men" (246).

Political Attitudes

A different take on group justification theories includes an intersecting analysis of the importance of multiple identities for individuals and their policy attitudes. In previous research on specific policy preferences, there were few gender differences within racial/ethnic minority groups from 1990–2000 (Bejarano 2014; Conway 2008), however more recent research highlights growing gender differences across racial/ethnic minority attitudes on public policy. For example, Carter, Corra, and Carter (2009) examined the interactive impact of race and gender on attitudes toward the changing roles of women. The results showed "that black women generally hold less traditional attitudes toward the changing roles of women than their white male, white female, and black male counterparts regardless of how attitudes are measured" (2009, 209). In addition, Clyde Wilcox (1990) examined the development of Black consciousness and suggested that it can facilitate the development of feminist consciousness (Gay and Tate 1998, 171) so that, "black women who strongly identified with their race were more likely to support a black feminist strategy because they more readily recognize and identify with the disadvantaged and discriminated in society" (1998, 171).

In terms of Latino gender differences in policy attitudes, there is growing evidence since the late 1990s that Latinas report significantly different attitudes on some public policy compared to Latino males (Bejarano 2014; Montoya 1996). Previous work by Lien (1998) argued that gender was not viewed as a useful predictor for the political attitudes of Latinos. However, there has been a small growth in the gender gap across public opinion attitudes, for example on attitudes toward 'women's roles' (Latinas slightly more progressive) (Montoya 1996) and on the policy of the death penalty (Latinas less supportive) (Garcia-Bedolla et al. 2007). The size and significance of the Latino gender policy gaps differ based on key factors like national origin group and generational differences, which highlight the unique role of immigrant experiences for groups such as Latinos and Asians.

Therefore, it is important to further investigate the additional identity intersections for racial/ethnic immigrant based groups, such as Latinos and Asians, which will help provide a closer analysis of gender differences on public policy. This further analysis will also help guard against relying on stereotypes of immigrant groups. For example, Latinos generally support more liberal public policies and even the more recent Latino "immigrants seem to arrive in the United States with egalitarian gender values relatively similar to those in the American society" (Bejarano, Manzano, and Montoya 2011, 541).

In addition, the dominant focus of previous research on group consciousness was also focused on either race or gender consciousness (Simien and Clawson 2004). To further push the concept of political consciousness, researchers have demonstrated how the concept can be "expanded to include not only a singular, but also an intersectional, dimension" (Greenwood and Christian 2008, 415). When White female participants are primed with intersectional consciousness, they reported more accepting attitudes toward Muslim women and their covering practices (the effect was moderated by participants' political orientation) (Greenwood and Christian 2008). Researchers have also examined whether multiple identities can be mutually supportive, such as ethnic or religious identities and gender. For example, a previous study examined whether ethnic and religious identities can be compatible with feminist attitudes, such as feminism among Arab-American women (Marshall and Read 2003). Marshall and Read found that "the cultural dimension of ethnic identity is far less important than the political dimension for predicting feminist" orientations among Arab-American women (2003, 886). In addition, similar to Bejarano, Manzano, and Montoya's (2011) findings on the similar attitudes of Latino immigrants and native born Americans, Marshall and Read found that "foreign-born women are no less feminist than are native-born Arab Americans" (886).

Political Participation

Researchers have often examined whether racial or gender identity is more important with regard to motivating political participation. This work demonstrated that socioeconomic status accounted for most differences in political participation across racial/ethnic groups (Lien 1998), finding that gender differences in political participation were less distinct than the racial/ethnic distinctions (Burns et al. 2001; Lien 1998). However, the previous expectations and research focus was on the 'either/or' scenario of multiple identities, for both voter and elite political participation and attitudes (Marshall and Read 2003). Emerging research is now updating the previous expectations to provide a more thorough examination of the growing gender gap in political participation for racial/ethnic minority women, with particular attention on evidence that racial/ethnic minority women participate at *higher* rates than their male counterparts.

Since 1996, the gender gap is evident in voter turnout rates across all racial and ethnic groups, with women voting at higher rates than the men. Figure 7.1 demonstrates this gender gap in voting from 2004–2012. In the 2012 election, this gender voting gap ranged from about 9 percent for Blacks and 2.5 percent for Asians (File 2013). In addition to turning out at higher rates than men (Black women have the highest rate of turnout), minority women are also more likely than their male counterparts to support the Democratic presidential candidate, as they did decisively for President Obama in 2012. Table 7.1 highlights the changing gender gap in presidential support across racial/ethnic groups for 2004–2012, which demonstrates how the modern partisan gender gap is now more perceptible for racial/ethnic minority groups than White voters (Bejarano 2014).

To understand the changing rates of political participation, intersectional scholars argue it is often necessary to further untangle intersecting identities. For example, Jaramillo (2010) introduced a typology of intersecting identities that acknowledge the intersectionality of gender and ethnic identity that is disaggregated along individualistic (personal needs) and collectivistic dimensions (collective or group needs). The collectivistic versus individualistic orientations of gender and ethnic identity can either mobilize or demobilize political behavior. For example, a collectivistic orientation of intersecting identities served to mobilize Latina political activism and the individualistic orientation of gender or ethnic identity demobilized (or redirected) Latina political activism (2010, 193).

We can also broaden our study of gender, race, and ethnicity by further interrogating our analysis of immigrant based groups in political psychology, like Latinos and Asians. In further studying Latino political behavior, for example, it

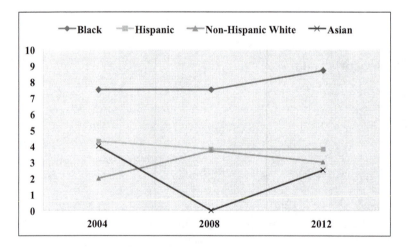

FIGURE 7.1 Gender Voting Gap, by Race and Hispanic Origin (2004–2012)

Note: Female voting rates in comparison to male voting rates, by percentage points.
Source: File, Thom (2013). Current Population Survey Reports.

TABLE 7.1 Gender and Racial/Ethnic Gap in U.S. Presidential Elections (2004–2012)

	2004 Election		2008 Election		2012 Election	
	Kerry (DEM)	Bush (GOP)	Obama (DEM)	McCain (GOP)	Obama (DEM)	Romney (GOP)
Men	44%	55%	49%	48%	45%	52%
Women	51%	48%	56%	43%	55%	44%
White Men	37%	62%	41%	57%	35%	62%
White Women	44%	55%	46%	53%	42%	56%
Black Men	—	—	95%	5%	87%	11%
Black Women	—	—	96%	3%	96%	3%
Latino Men	—	—	64%	33%	65%	33%
Latina (Women)	—	—	68%	30%	76%	23%
Non-White Men	67%	30%	—	—	—	—
Non-White Women	75%	24%	—	—	—	—
All Other Races	—	—	64%	32%	66%	31%

Source: CNN Exit Poll Data
www.cnn.com/ELECTION/2004/pages/results/states/US/P/00/epolls.0.html
www.cnn.com/ELECTION/2008/results/polls/#USP00p1
www.cnn.com/election/2012/results/race/president#exit-polls

is imperative to unpack the intersections of Latino gender, national origin, foreign-born status, and generational status (Bejarano 2014). This type of research has demonstrated differences among gender and across generations for Latino political views and participation (2014). In terms of identity, Latinos undergo changes to their sense of national origin, American, and pan-ethnic Latino identities depending on their generational status and length of time spent in the United States. In addition, the rates of change are dramatically different across the immigrant male and female patterns of identity formation and rates of transnational contact with their home countries.

The explanations for the gender differences in Latino political behavior "come from the gendered experiences of immigrant incorporation and socialization, which include varied gender experiences with socio-economic change and changing political attitudes that are experienced by later generations" (Bejarano 2014, 14). For example, as Latina immigrants spend more time in the U.S. and potentially acculturate, they are more likely than Latino male immigrants to identify with a political ideology and political party identity (2014). Further, later generations of Latinas also hold more liberal political ideologies and higher levels of Democratic Party affiliation compared to first generation Latinas. This evidence highlights the important process of immigrant political incorporation for immigrant based groups like Latinos and Asians. The results demonstrated that by including additional Latino-specific factors in a study, there is evidence of Latina gender differences, which parallel the U.S. modern gender gap phenomenon.

Overall, this review of emerging work highlights how we can understand political attitudes and political participation better by broadening our analysis of intersecting identities and not relying on an "either/or" identity battle.

Intersecting Identities: Candidate Evaluation and Voter Support

In terms of women as political candidates and representatives, racial/ethnic minority women currently form a greater share of minority political representatives, compared to White women as a share of White political representatives in both the U.S. Congress and most state legislatures. For example, in 2016 the U.S. Congress included 71 White women (16 percent of their White delegation), 18 Black women (39 percent of their Black delegation), 9 Latinas (28 percent of their Latino delegation), and 6 Asian American/Pacific Islander women (a majority or 55 percent of their delegation) (CAWP 2016). This is evidence of the growing political presence of minority women as representatives in their respective racial/ethnic delegations, or in comparison to their male counterparts. However, this growth is in stark contrast to their overall low numbers of minority elected officials in the country; for example minority women are still only 6 percent of all Congressional members. How can researchers make sense of this contrast and explain how race/ethnicity can interact with gender to result in a variety of possible explanations for this political phenomenon, such as the intersecting identities providing an electoral advantage in terms of multiple sources of electoral support? In particular: How do intersecting identities of candidate and voters impact level of support for political candidates?

Intersecting Identities of Political Candidates

Closer analysis of multiple intersecting identities has now been applied to studies of support for diverse political candidates. Intersectional researchers have cautioned others not to assume multiple identities operate together as an additive phenomenon. In addition, Crenshaw (1989, 1995) provided additional distinctions to keep in mind to assess "three ways in which race and gender intersect for women of color: structurally, representationally, and politically" (Settles 2006, 590). For example, previous research highlighted a unique problem that people with multiple identities face, an intersectional marginalization (Crenshaw 1989; Strolovitch 2006), whereby opportunities for political representation are closely related to the relative status of the disadvantaged or advantaged subgroup.

As a result of the relative novelty of minority women candidates, they are likely to either face particular advantages or disadvantages in terms of their potential to face voter and media bias. For example, non-traditional political candidates attract more media and voter attention to their particular group membership, which is suggested by the social psychological solo status hypothesis

(Golebiowska 2001, 536; Taylor 1981). In addition, previous psychological research (Brewer 1996; Fiske and Neuberg 1990; Riggle et al. 1992) suggested "that candidates' group memberships are likely to function as heuristics in low-information races because group stereotypes are most influential in person perception when little or no other information is available about the individual" (Golebiowska 2001, 536–537).

The influence of subordinate or disadvantaged identities are also complicated by intersectionality perspectives. In a society that tends to define the prototypical person as male, White, and straight (Purdie-Vaughns and Eibach 2008), people with a subordinate identity, such as race or ethnicity, can also possess additional subordinate or dominant identities, such as gender (either dominant male or subordinate female identity). Therefore, people who possess more prototypical subordinate-group identities, such as a Black male, will likely experience more direct targets of oppression compared to people who possess less prototypical subordinate-group identities, such as a Black female. So, "from the perspective of intersectional invisibility, subordinate men will often be the victims of active forms of oppression directed at their groups because of their greater prototypicality compared to subordinate women" (383). However, this also results in historical, cultural, political, and legal invisibility for people with multiple subordinate identities (such as racial/ethnic minority females). The intersectional invisibility model pushes the study of social identity, prejudice, and discrimination in social psychology and political science to be more critical of the intersection of multiple social identities.

Communication studies of media coverage for women candidates and minority candidates highlight the continued use of gender and racial stereotypes, despite some progress. In particular, Major and Coleman (2008) used "a content analysis of newspaper articles and editorials to examine what changes, if any, occur in media coverage when a women and a minority run against each other without a White, male candidate," in the 2003 Louisiana gubernatorial runoff election (315). They found that, despite the candidates' previous political experience, journalists still stereotyped the woman candidate with the traditional female issues and the male candidate with the traditional male issues. In an intersectional extension of this dynamic, Gershon (2013) found evidence that the media also varies its coverage of women in Congress across race/ethnicity, where Anglo congresswomen received a higher proportion of coverage compared to the Latina and African American counterparts.

Voter Support

It is important to examine the evaluations of candidates as an influence of the demographic traits (or identity) of the voter matching up with a political candidate's demographic traits. The voters could demonstrate an in-group bias (Brewer and Brown 1998; Tajfel 1970) and prefer a candidate who shares one of their group identities (Abney and Hutcheson 1981; Barreto 2010; Bejarano 2013, 33; Sanbonmatsu 2002). In terms of racial/ethnic minority female candidates, earlier research "used a 'double jeopardy' (Beale 1979) or multiple jeopardy (King 1988) approach to argue that various disadvantages" provided from a gender or racial/ethnic identity would "accumulate and produce distinctive forms of oppression" (Bejarano 2013, 1). However, this previous assumption of double disadvantages does not explain the growing strides racial/ethnic minority women have made in attaining political office.

Intersectional work broadens the standard assumptions made about the political obstacles that women and minorities face in the political environment to argue that overlapping identities can create electoral opportunities for racial/ethnic-minority women. For example, Philpot and Walton (2007) examined voter support for Black female candidates and "demonstrate that candidates belonging to two marginalized groups need not be doubly disadvantaged" (49). Voters do not need to prioritize their identities when making political decisions, instead multiple identities can interact to create a separate distinct identity that can influence candidate evaluation. As a result, gender and race can interact to create a separate consciousness that surpasses the separate impact of gender and race. For example, Philpot and Walton found that Black women voters were the strongest supporters of Black female candidates (49).

Moreover, there is also evidence that female political candidates from other racial/ethnic groups can also benefit from their intersecting identities rather than be doubly disadvantaged. In particular, Latina political candidates benefit from the availability of more voting coalitions as a result of their multiple and intersecting identities (Bejarano 2013). The fact that the political incumbent/candidate and voters do not share descriptive characteristics like gender and race/ethnicity, or descriptive divergence, does not have to provoke or result in voter bias. Instead, gender can actually mitigate the potential for racial bias. In addition, descriptive congruence or the shared descriptive characteristics among voters and candidates can also lead to increased electoral support for both racial/ethnic minority and White candidates. Gershon and Monforti (2015) tested this theory of Latina political advantages (Bejarano 2013), or 'multiple identity advantage,' by utilizing original data from a survey experiment to "simulate political races where a Latina candidate runs against another Latina, as well as Latino, African American male and female, and Anglo male and female candidates" (2015, 4–5). They found support for the 'multiple identity advantage,' since they demonstrated that "Latinas with male and white opponents who run for office in racially diverse areas indeed benefit from the intersectional nature of their identities" (2015, 17). Moreover, they found support to broaden the theory beyond Latinas to African American women in their study. Overall, this intersectional work "challenges scholars to rethink the common assumptions that have been made about female political candidates and demonstrates that gender stereotypes or expectations do not apply equally to all females regardless of their race or ethnicity" (Bejarano 2013, 6).

However, multiple identities can also still result in 'intersectional stereotyping' or "stereotyping that is created by the combination of more than one stereotype that together produce something unique and distinct from any one form of stereotyping standing alone" (Doan and Haider-Markel 2010, 63). Goff, Thomas, and Jackson (2008, 401) suggested that scholars re-examine the process of cat-egorization, since association with one basic identity category (such as race) may obscure the perception of another basic category (such as gender). For example, people tend to associate "Blackness" with "maleness," which can lead the public to assume that Black men and women are both more masculine than their White counterparts (2008, 401).

Further, research has also demonstrated that voters have different stereotypes of Black politicians than they do of Blacks in general, which can result in another entirely different categorization for Black female politicians (Schneider and Bos 2011). As a result, Black women and other racial/ethnic minority women can face unique gendered harms due to their unique intersecting identities, which often results in a particular form of voter bias and stereotyping.

Work by Gershon and Monforti (2014) has explored the role of ethnorace and gender-based stereotypes, as well as the intersection of both, in shaping voter support for political candidates. Their analysis demonstrated "that the combination of gender, race and ethnicity results in unique trait stereotypes of women running for political office" (2014, 19), such as positive assessments of their agentic qualities like leadership abilities and experience, which is reflective of the previous intersectionality research by Ghavami and Peplau (2013). Their work also highlights how campaign context can introduce additional dynamics to acknowledge when racial/ethnic minority women run their political campaigns.

Future Directions and Conclusion

This review of intersecting identities in this chapter pushes our analysis of gender in American politics. Future studies can incorporate more identity categories and experiences, such as sexual orientation, class, religion, immigrant status, age, and disability. Research can move beyond asking whether one identity trumps the other by continuing to expand on an intersectional analysis of gender and race/ethnicity, which can incorporate other overlapping and competing interests like sexual orientation. For example, political science scholars have engaged in unique examinations of group stereotypes for openly gay political candidates, by utilizing surveys asking the candidates/officials about their experiences (Gole-biowska 2002) or by asking the public about their perception of the candidates (Doan and Haider-Markel 2010). This group stereotypes research can also be extended by analyzing the overlapping identity of race and ethnicity for openly LGBT political candidates and officials. In addition, Hunter's (2013) sociological research has utilized national surveys, cultural criticism, and personal interviews to examine how racial and gender bias can be heightened by darker skin tones, which introduces an additional complexity to address for future intersectional research.

Another example of pushing the identity boundaries includes further research endeavors that seek to highlight the intersectional work of scholars. For example, the 2016 edited volume in political science *Distinct Identities: Minority Women in U.S. Politics* is not focused on highlighting political psychology research per se, however it is still guided in working towards pushing the boundaries of traditional political questions of race and gender identity (Brown and Gershon 2016). The featured authors in this volume focus their analysis on racial/ethnic minority women for a broader examination of intersecting gender, race, and ethnicity to our questions of political participation, campaigning for political office, and political representation. Overall, the highlighted work throughout the chapter speaks to the benefits of broadening the psychological foundations of identity theories, expanding the traditional political science understandings of the political environment, and charting future political psychology research that can encompass more comprehensive examinations of multiple and unique intersecting identities.

In terms of what to look for in future elections, we can continue to examine the political influence of intersecting identities. We know multiple identities—of voters and candidates—will prove salient in future political campaigns. The 2016 presidential campaign has only renewed our questions about the political impact of multiple identities, of which race, ethnicity, and gender are only a select few. We can look forward to the potential for more diverse candidates to enter the political arena, as well as recognize the critical role of diverse voters in influencing their success.

References

Abney, F. Glenn, and John D. Hutcheson. 1981. "Race, Representation, and Trust: Changes in Attitudes after the Election of a Black Mayor." *Public Opinion Quarterly* 45: 91–101.

Barreto, Matt A. 2010. *Ethnic Cues: The Role of Shared Ethnicity in Latino Political Participation.* Ann Arbor: University of Michigan Press.

Beale, Frances. 1979. "Double Jeopardy: To Be Black and Female." In *The Black Woman*, edited by T. Cade, 90–100. New York: New American Library.

Bejarano, Christina E. 2013. *The Latina Advantage: Gender, Race, and Political Success.* Austin: University of Texas Press.

Bejarano, Christina E. 2014. *The Latino Gender Gap in U.S. Politics.* New York: Routledge Press.

Bejarano, Christina E., Sylvia Manzano, and Celeste Montoya. 2011. "Tracking the Latino Gender Gap: Gender Attitudes across Sex, Borders and Generations." *Politics & Gender* 7 (4): 521–549.

Bowleg, Lisa. 2008. "When Black + Lesbian + Woman ≠ Black Lesbian Woman: The Methodological Challenges of Qualitative and Quantitative Intersectionality Research." *Sex Roles* 59: 312–325.

Brewer, Marilynn B. 1996. "When Stereotypes Lead to Stereotyping: The Use of Stereotypes in Person Perception." In *Stereotypes and Stereotyping*, edited by C. N. Macrae,
C. Stangor, and M. Hewstone. New York: Guilford.

Brewer, M. B., and R. J. Brown. 1998. "Intergroup Relations." In *The Handbook of Social
Psychology* (Vol. 2, 4th ed.), edited by D. T. Gilbert and S. T. Fiske, 554–594. New
York: McGraw-Hill.

Brown, Nadia E., and Sarah Allen Gershon, eds. 2016. *Distinct Identities: Minority Women
in U.S. Politics.* New York: Routledge Press.

Burns, Nancy, Kay Lehman Schlozman, and Sidney Verba. 2001. *The Private Roots of Public Action.* Cambridge: Harvard University Press.

Carter, J. Scott, Mamadi Corra, and Shannon K. Carter. 2009. "Interaction of Race and
Gender: Changing Gender-Role Attitudes, 1974–2006." *Social Science Quarterly* 90 (1):
196–211.

Center for American Women in Politics (CAWP). 2016. "Women of Color in Elective
Office 2016." *Fact Sheet.* New Brunswick, NJ: Eagleton Institute of Politics, Rutgers
University.

Chow, Esther Ngan-Ling. 1987. "The Development of Feminist Consciousness Among
Asian American Women." *Gender & Society* 1: 284–299.

Cole, Elizabeth R. 2009. "Intersectionality and Research in Psychology." *American Psychologist* 64 (3): 170–180.

Conway, M. Margaret. 2008. "The Gender Gap: A Comparison across Racial and Ethnic
Groups." In *Voting the Gender Gap*, edited by Lois Duke Whitaker, 170–183. Urbana,
IL: University of Illinois Press.

Crenshaw, Kimberlé. 1989. "Demarginalizing the Intersection of Race and Sex." *University
of Chicago Legal Forum* 39: 139–167.

Crenshaw, Kimberlé. 1995. "The Intersection of Race and Gender." In *Critical Race
Theory: The Key Writings that Formed the Movement*, edited by Kimberlé Crenshaw, Neil
Gotanda, Gary Peller, and Kendall Thomas, 357–383. New York: New Press.

Doan, Alesha E., and Donald P. Haider-Markel. 2010. "The Role of Intersectional Stereotypes on Evaluations of Gay and Lesbian Political Candidates." *Politics & Gender* 6
(1): 63–91.

File, Thom. 2013. "The Diversifying Electorate—Voting Rates by Race and Hispanic
Origin in 2012 (and Other Recent Elections)." Current Population Survey Reports,
P20–569. U.S. Census Bureau, Washington, DC.

Fiske, Susan, and Neuberg, Steven. 1990. "A Continuum of Impression Formation, from
Category-Based to Individuating Processes: Influences of Information and Motivation
on Attention and Interpretation." *Advances in Experimental Social Psychology* 23: 1–74,
edited by M. Zanna. San Diego, CA: Academic.

Garcia-Bedolla, Lisa, Jessica Lavariega Monforti, and Adrian Pantoja. 2007. "A Second Look:
Is There a Latina/o Gender Gap?" *Journal of Women, Politics & Policy* 28: 147–171.

Gay, Claudine, and Katherine Tate. 1998. "Doubly Bound: The Impact of Gender and
Race on the Politics of Black Women." *Political Psychology* 19: 169–184.

Gershon, Sarah Allen. 2013. "Media Coverage of Minority Congresswomen and Voter
Evaluations: Evidence from an Online Experimental Study." *Political Research Quarterly*
66 (3): 702–714.

Gershon, Sarah Allen, and Jessica Lavariega Monforti. 2014. "Intersecting Campaigns:
The Impact of Race, Gender, and Ethnicity of Candidates on Congressional Elections."
Paper Presented at the Mentoring Conference for New Research on Gender in Politi-
cal Psychology. Wooster, Ohio.

Gershon, Sarah Allen, and Jessica Lavariega Monforti. 2015. "Una Ventaja? A Survey Experiment of the Viability of Latina Candidates." Paper Presented at the American Political Science Association Annual Conference. San Francisco, CA.

Ghavami, Negin, and Letitia Anne Peplau. 2013. "An Intersectional Analysis of Gender and Ethnic Stereotypes Testing Three Hypotheses." *Psychology of Women Quarterly* 37 (1): 113–127.

Goff, Phillip Atiba, Margaret A. Thomas, and Matthew Christian Jackson. 2008. "Ain't I a Woman? Towards an Intersectional Approach to Person Perception and Group-based Harms." *Sex Roles* 59: 392–403.

Golebiowska, Ewa A. 2001. "Group Stereotypes and Political Evaluation." *American Politics Research* 29 (6): 535–565.

Golebiowska, Ewa A. 2002. "Political Implications of Group Stereotypes: Campaign Experiences of Openly Gay Political Candidates." *Journal of Applied Social Psychology* 32 (3): 590–607.

Greenwood, Ronni Michelle, and Aidan Christian. 2008. "What Happens When We Unpack the Invisible Knapsack? Intersectional Political Consciousness and Inter-group Appraisals." *Sex Roles* 59: 404–417.

Hancock, Ange-Marie. 2007. "Intersectionality as a Normative and Empirical Paradigm." *Politics & Gender* 3: 229–280.

Hughes, Michael, and Steven A. Tuch. 2003. "Gender Differences in White's Racial Attitudes: Are Women's Attitudes Really More Favorable?" *Social Psychology Quarterly* 66 (4): 384–401.

Hunter, Margaret L. 2013. *Race, Gender, and the Politics of Skin Tone.* New York: Routledge Press.

Jaramillo, Patricia A. 2010. "Building a Theory, Measuring a Concept: Exploring Inter-sectionality and Latina Activism at the Individual Level." *Journal of Women, Politics & Policy* 31 (3): 193–216.

Johnson, Monica Kirkpatrick, and Margaret Mooney Marini. 1998. "Bridging the Racial Divide in the United States: The Effect of Gender." *Social Psychology Quarterly* 61: 247–258.

Joseph, Gloria, and Jill Lewis. 1981. *Common Differences: Conflicts in Black and White Feminist Perspectives.* New York: Avon.

Kane, Emily W., and Kimberly J. Whipkey. 2009. "Predictors of Public Support for Gender-Related Affirmative Action: Interests, Gender Attitudes, and Stratification Beliefs." *The Public Opinion Quarterly* 73 (2): 233–254.

King, Deborah K. 1988. "Multiple Jeopardy, Multiple Consciousness: The Context of a Black Feminist Ideology." *Signs* 15: 42–72.

Lien, Pei-te. 1998. "Does the Gender Gap in Political Attitudes and Behavior Vary across Racial Groups? *Political Research Quarterly* 51 (4): 869–894.

Major, L. H., and Coleman R. 2008. "The Intersection of Race and Gender in Election Coverage: What Happens When the Candidates Don't Fit the Stereotypes?" *The Howard Journal of Communications* 19 (4): 315–333.

Marshall, Susan E., and Jen'nan Ghazal Read. 2003. "Identity Politics among Arab-American Women." *Social Science Quarterly* 84 (4): 875–891.

Montoya, Lisa J. 1996. "Latino Gender Differences in Public Opinion." *Hispanic Journal of Behavioral Sciences* 18: 255–276.

Philpot, Tasha S., and Hanes Walton, Jr. 2007. "One of Our Own: Black Female Candidates and the Voters Who Support Them." *American Journal of Political Science* 51 (1): 49–62.

Purdie-Vaughns, Valerie, and Richard P. Eibach. 2008. "Intersectional Invisibility: The Distinctive Advantages and Disadvantages of Multiple Subordinate-Group Identities." *Sex Roles* 59: 377–391.

Reid, P. 1984. "Feminism versus Minority Group Identity: Not for Black Women Only." *Sex Roles* 10: 247–255.

Riggle, Ellen D., Victor C. Ottati, Robert S. Wyer, James Kuklinski, and Nobert Schwarz. 1992. "Bases of Political Judgments: The Role of Stereotypic and Nonstereotypic Information." *Political Behavior* 14: 67–87.

Sanbonmatsu, Kira. 2002. "Gender Stereotypes and Vote Choice." *American Journal of Political Science* 46: 20–34.

Schneider, Monica C., and Angela L. Bos. 2011. "An Exploration of the Content of Stereotypes of Black Politicians." *Political Psychology* 32 (2): 205–233.

Schnittker, Jason. 2000. "Gender and Reactions to Psychological Problems: An Examination of Social Tolerance and Perceived Dangerousness." *Journal of Health and Social Behavior* 41: 224–240.

Settles, Isis H. 2006. "Use of an Intersectional Framework to Understand Black Women's Racial and Gender Identities." *Sex Roles* 54: 589–601.

Shields, Stephanie A. 2008. "Gender: An Intersectionality Perspective." *Sex Roles* 59: 301–311.

Silverstein, L. B. 2006. "Integrating Feminism and Multiculturalism: Scientific Fact or Science Fiction?" *Professional Psychology: Research and Practice* 37: 21–28.

Simien, Evelyn M., and Rosalee A. Clawson. 2004. "Intersection of Race and Gender: An Examination of Black Feminist Consciousness, Race Consciousness, and Policy Attitudes." *Social Science Quarterly* 85 (3): 793–810.

Strolovitch, Dara. 2006. "Interest Group Advocacy at the Intersections of Race, Class, and Gender." *The Journal of Politics* 68 (4): 894–910.

Tajfel, H. 1970. "Experiments in Intergroup Discrimination." *Scientific American* 223 (5): 96–102.

Taylor, Shelley E. 1981. "A Categorization Approach to Stereotyping." In *Cognitive Processes in Stereotyping and Intergroup Behavior,* edited by D. L. Hamilton. Hillsdale, NJ: Lawrence Erlbaum: 83–114.

Warner, L. R. 2008. "A Best Practices Guide to Intersectional Approaches in Psychological Research." *Sex Roles* 59: 454–463.

Wilcox, Clyde. 1990. "Black Women and Feminism." *Women & Politics* 10: 65–84.

PART II
Women as Candidates

Gender and Political Ambition

8

GENDER DIFFERENCES IN POLITICAL AMBITION

Kristin Kanthak

Suppose that the average man has about a 0.001 probability of running for office, and the average woman has about a 0.0003 probability of running. These probabilities are just examples—the actual numbers are likely even lower. But these probabilities allow us to conceptualize the potential effects of a very small gender-based difference in political ambition, a paltry 0.0007. Assuming a state of 10,000,000 people equally divided between men and women, using those probabilities, we would expect to see 5,000 male candidates and 1,500 female candidates. If one-quarter of those candidates win, and we assume that gender does not affect the probability of winning, 1,250 male politicians and 375 female politicians would be elected. In other words, a gender difference in willingness to run that is so tiny it is likely to be immeasurable, save through the use of the most precise of tools, yields a set of politicians that is 77 percent male.

This example illustrates that infinitesimally tiny gender differences in political ambition can compound within a large population to yield political ranks that are highly skewed. This is worrisome for two reasons, one normative and the other methodological. Normatively, we see that gender differences need not be large to have sizeable effects in the population that dramatically affect political representation. Methodologically, we are searching at the individual level for tiny effects, exactly the kinds of effects that are difficult to pinpoint with traditional statistical methods. "False negatives," failing to find a relationship when one does exist, is not only possible, but likely.

Uncovering these small effects calls for an "all hands on deck" approach. Political scientists join social scientists from several cognate fields—including economics, sociology, and psychology—in adding to our knowledge to meet this challenge. This chapter seeks to place gender differences in political ambition within a larger context of a cross-disciplinary understanding of how gender differences affect individual decision-making and to apply that understanding to the specific context of elections.

Women are a majority of the population of the world, but represent a minority among winners of democratic elections in virtually every nation. This simple fact provides prima facie evidence that elections are "gendered institutions," in which "gender is present in the processes, practices, images and ideologies, and distributions of power in the various sectors of social life" (Acker 1992, 567). Elections are gendered if gender—meaning the gender of the candidates and/ or of the voters—matters in how elections play out.

An institution may be gendered in both personal and structural ways. *Personal* gender effects are what we can call gendered election aversion (Kanthak and Woon 2015). In this conception, there is something about the electoral environment that attracts men more than it does women. Gendered election aversion happens because women are less willing to run for office than are men, even if the structural "playing field" is completely level. *Structural* gender effects are the "playing field," and include how forces outside of an individual candidate—such as access to money or relevant experience, party rules, electoral rules, and voter preferences—affect the choices of whether or not to run. Of course, structural and personal effects are largely intertwined. Access to money, for example, may be lower for women because women in the workforce are systematically paid less than men (Hegewisch et al. 2010). Could these women have chosen different careers, with greater access to campaign funds? Certainly, and the fact that women make choices that lead them to have lower access to resources may suggest that this is a personal gender effect because it is based on an individual's choices. But those choices are themselves based in interactions with gendered institutions that result in jobs that are considered "women's work" and come with significantly lower pay (Hegewisch, Williams, and Henderson 2011). In this sense, women's access to money is also structural.

This chapter draws on lessons from cognate fields on how women and men differ in decision-making in general, and how these differences might be exacerbated in the electoral environment. More specifically, the chapter will address the following questions: What can we learn from our cognate fields in the social sciences on how men and women differ in their approaches to decision-making, particularly as it applies to running for office? And how does the electoral environment trigger and perhaps exacerbate those differences to create gender-based election aversion? I further consider the consequences for representation—both for women and for men—based on gender-based election aversion.

Gender and Individual Decision-Making: An Interdisciplinary Approach

Evidence from myriad social science disciplines point to the same conclusion: Men and women systematically differ in how they make decisions. Of course, these far-reaching studies consider contexts other than the electoral environment, but we can expect that gender differences in some venues may translate to differences in others.

We know that women and men differ in their attitudes toward taking risks. The overwhelming majority of evidence in both economics (e.g., Eckel and Grossman 2008) and psychology (e.g., Byrnes et al. 1999) indicate that women tend to be more risk averse than do men. Furthermore, as discussed in the next section, attitudes toward risk play an important role in determining who runs for office and who does not, according to a seminal political science study (Rohde 1979).

Similarly, in a novel study of willingness to compete, Niederle and Vesterlund (2007) asked subjects to complete a simple math task and paid them based on a piece rate, or providing a fixed amount of money for each sum they correctly solved. They then asked the participants if they would like to do the sums again for a piece rate or if they would rather enter a tournament where they could compete against other participants for a larger prize. Not only were women less willing to compete than were men, but women whose high ability would have been advantageous chose not to do so. Related, men whose task ability indicated they should stick with the piece rate instead entered the tournament, indicating that women are averse to competition, but men actually derive benefits from the act of engaging in competition itself.

In a very similar study that shows how these approaches can apply to an electoral setting, Kanthak and Woon (2015) invited subjects to do the same piece rate task as in Niederle and Vesterlund (2007), but then asked if subjects would be willing to perform the task as a representative for their group, either randomly selected or chosen via election. Women volunteered as a representative at the same rate as men, but were much less likely to run for election than were men. Something about the context of an election put women off. Notably, the Kanthak and Woon (2015) result controlled for competition aversion and risk aversion, indicating that election aversion is a separate phenomenon, related to but distinct from these other gender differences.

Evidence also shows that women tend to take into account what they know about other people and the actions of other people when making interactive decisions (Croson and Gneezy 2009), differences that may contribute both to their lack of willingness to run for office but also to differences in leadership style that could benefit legislative decision-making. For example, when engaging in experiments involving economics games, men tended to choose just one strategy and stick with it, whereas women's strategies were more context-dependent. Women think about who their partners are, whether or not they think the rules are "fair," and other factors that men tend to ignore as they choose the best strategy to achieve payoffs. Specifically, in ultimatum games (in which one player makes an offer of a division of some "pie" of goods, and a second player can either accept or reject that offer), women's behavior changed with the gender of their partner (Eckel and Grossman 2001) and in a trust game, women's behavior differed when experimenters provide them with a picture of their counterpart (Eckel and Wilson 2004). And indeed, these results mirror work in psychology that showed that women demonstrate greater sensitivity to social cues than do men (Kahn et al. 1971). In this volume, Sanbonmatsu and

Carroll argue that these "relational" considerations are key to explaining women's political candidacies as being very different from the candidacies of men.

Related, Costa, Terracciano, and McCrae (2001) found that women and men differed on the Big Five personality traits, a measure of long-standing human personality, including: 1) extraversion, or the tendency to enjoy crowds and derive energy from being around other people, 2) agreeableness, or the tendency to cooperate with others and trust them, 3) stability, or the tendency to remain emotionally stable rather than to be quick to change moods, 4) conscientiousness, or the tendency to be disciplined and organized, and 5) openness, or the tendency to enjoy new experiences and the use of imagination. Women tended to be more agreeable and less emotionally stable than men (Costa, Terracciano, and McCrae 2001). Furthermore, we know that personality traits, such as extraversion and stability, can predict willingness to run for higher office (Dietrich et al. 2012). Taken together, these results indicate that gender differences in political ambition may stem at least partially from gender differences in personality.

Similarly, several studies in psychology demonstrate that women and men have different leadership styles and that those styles most associated with women may be beneficial (Eagly and Carli 2003, 2007; Eagly, Johannesen-Schmidt, and van Engen 2003) in a legislative setting. For example, women may be more democratic in their leadership styles and more willing to allow others to participate in decision-making processes. Related, with the observation that women do not negotiate well (e.g., Babcock and Laschever 2009), sometimes missed is that women have different negotiating styles than men, and these differences may result in negative effects for women, such as lower salaries, but can also lead to better outcomes when they are negotiating on behalf of others.

One can place too fine a point on gender differences in decision-making between men and women, however. The laboratory—either in the psychology or economics tradition—allows us to study choices in a fictional "level playing field." But we know the playing field is, in fact, not level at all. Compared to men, women tend to spend more time caring for children and doing housework (Sayer 2005), systematically make less money (Hegwisch et al. 2010), and are segregated into "occupational ghettoes," or less attractive professions (Charles and Grusky 2004). These external factors are not specific to the electoral environment, but affect women's career decisions. To better understand how all of these factors intersect to affect the decision of whether or not to run for office, we now turn to the electoral environment itself.

Do Elections Exacerbate Gender Differences?

The extant literature is clear: Men and women tend to make decisions differently. But how do those differences affect the specific choice of whether or not to run for political office? Answering that question requires considering what political scientists already know about political ambition through the lens of gender. The seminal early work (Schlesinger 1966) found that political ambition was based largely on the "opportunity structure" of a particular politician. In other words, opportunities to run for office caused potential candidates' desire to run. This "opportunity structure" model hints at a potential explanation for gender differences in willingness to run for office. Specifically, do women and men face different opportunity structures?

An early consideration of opportunity structures found that those who followed their political ambition came from higher social classes and had more access to education and money (Matthews 1954a, 1954b), access that we know is gendered. Further, we know from Sayer (2005) that women have more familial obligations than do men. That said, there is mixed evidence on the role of family in women's opportunity structure. For example, in a survey of potential candidates for public office from political scientists, women were no more likely than men to cite family responsibilities as a reason to defer political ambition (Fox and Lawless 2004, 2005). But other studies indicated that among those women already holding office, child-care responsibilities tended to tamper progressive ambition (Fulton et al. 2006; Stalsburg 2012). And strikingly, young women were much more likely than young men to consider distance from home to the capital when deciding whether or not to run for political office (Silberman 2015). In this case, women chose to not engage in political life in deference to families that may not yet exist.

Yet perhaps the greatest barrier to female candidates—and the largest effect of gender on the opportunity structure—comes at the recruitment and retention stage. Much of women's relatively lower engagement in political activity is due to the fact that women have less access to resources than do men, differences stemming from women's greater role in the home (Burns, Schlozman, and Verba 2001). Even more important, women are not recruited to be candidates at the same rate as are men. Niven (1998) found that women's under-recruitment at the state level accounts for the dearth of women in state legislatures, and differences in recruitment account for much of the state-level differences in the proportion of candidates who are women, though few states even approach parity (Sanbonmatsu 2006). Furthermore, these differences in recruitment are magnified since women are much more likely to *need* to be asked before they are willing to run (Fox and Lawless 2004).

Black (1972) argued, slightly differently from Schlesinger's approach, that potential candidates consider the costs of running for an office, the benefits associated with that office, and the probability of being victorious when deciding whether or not to run. Many of the factors we have already considered could certainly affect this equation: Greater family obligations, for example, could make the costs of holding office systematically greater for women than for men. And lower levels of recruitment could increase the costs of running for female candidates vis-à-vis their male counterparts. If gender differentially affects the probability of winning for women and men, this would also lead women to make different calculations.

And indeed, political scientists have shown us—for example in Bauer's chapter in this volume—that voters may also act as a deterrent to female candidates. Huddy and Terkildsen (1993), for example, found that citizens thought women were more capable to handle compassion issues (e.g., helping the poor or the elderly), whereas men were competent to take on masculine issues (e.g., defense, security). Similarly, McDermott (1997) found that low-information voters thought women candidates were more liberal. Gender also played into the vote as a baseline preference for one gender over another (Sanbonmatsu 2002). So while voters do not reject female candidates outright (Dolan 2004), the evidence is clear that women and men do not traverse the same path from candidate to political office.

Of the early researchers on political ambition, Rohde (1979) constructed the most explicitly individualized argument, positing that attitudes toward risk were one factor that would differentiate candidates from non-candidates. Specifically, Rohde argued that those potential candidates who are what he called "risk-takers" were more likely to run for a particular office than those who were not. Furthermore, we saw in the previous section that women tend to be more risk averse than are men, which indicates that risk attitudes are correlated both with gender and willingness to run, although that relationship may not be causal.

Remarkably, in a psychology study, Finucane et al. (2000) showed that gender differences in risk aversion were significant only among White subjects—subjects of other races did not show this strong gender difference in attitudes toward risk. This is of particular note in the current context, because the same pattern seems to appear in willingness to run for office among women of color. More specifically, women of color were more likely than were White women to express confidence and self-direction when describing their stories of running for office (Frederick 2013) and subsequently, women of color held a larger proportion of seats vis-à-vis men of color than do their White women counterparts (Garcia Bedolla et al. 2005; Scola and Hardy-Fanta 2006). If risk attitudes drive political ambition, and gendered risk attitudes follow this pattern, we would expect to see relatively more women of color than White women running for office, and that is what we observe. That said, Sanbonmatsu and Carroll (this volume) argue that women may not fit into these traditional models of political ambition, and Windett (2014) provides evidence that women may actually be more risk accep-tant than men when it comes to running for office. The role women's generally lower risk tolerance plays in the electoral environment, then, remains an open question.

Gender differences in the Big Five personality traits, too, could affect political ambition: We already know that personality is tied to individual political choices. Drawing on in-depth one-on-one interviews, Lasswell (1930) attempted to describe how personality characteristics related to different political "types." Using surveys rather than interviews, McConaughy (1950) subjected 18 South Carolina legisla-tors to a series of psychological tests, and compared those results to those of similar nonpoliticians. Differences between the two groups included greater neuroticism (emotional stability) among the nonpoliticians, but more extroversion, self-sufficiency, and dominance among the politicians. Related, Browning and Jacob (1964) conducted a test of "power motivation," in which subjects were asked to tell stories about pictures they are given, and scored based on how much those stories relate to attempts to control others. By comparing politicians to a group of subjects from nonpolitical lines of work, they found that power motivation in politicians was conditional on the type of environment the politicians are in. Furthermore, Dietrich et al. (2012) found that those who scored highest on the Big Five's extraversion and stability scales may exhibit greater political ambition. Potentially, then, the electoral environment could interact with gender differences in personality traits to create or exacerbate differences in willingness to run.

These studies, though, compared politicians to nonpoliticians or progressively ambitious politicians to statically ambitious politicians, ignoring differences between those who run and those who are willing to run, but have not yet done so. More recent work in political science is meant to untangle causality in this question of political ambition, attempting to explain how (and if) the politically ambitious (whether or not that ambition has yet been realized) are different from those who prefer not to run. Coining the phrase "nascent political ambition," Fox and Lawless (2005, 642) found that those who were interested in politics felt a sense of efficacy as would-be candidates, and those who were raised in politically minded families were most likely to kindle those early flames of political ambition. Furthermore, and most important to the current question, Fox and Lawless (2005) drew on their survey of 3,800 citizens working in careers most likely to yield political candidates to show that those who were members of traditionally politically excluded groups, such as women, were less likely to show signs of nascent political ambition. Already, at the very early stages of considering a political life, women are selecting themselves out of full participation as candidates for representative office.

Some Consequences of Gender Differences in Political Ambition

What is the effect of all women making individual choices to opt out of candidacies for office? If winning elections is a central component of the qualifications for being a representative, we lose nothing: Those who opted out would have been poor representatives in any event. But this may not be so. Indeed, the skills used to win elections—raising money, giving speeches, meeting constituents, greeting a competitive environment with relish—are very different from the skills used to be a representative—engaging in service for constituents, writing legislation, garnering support for policy proposals, and finding areas of compromise with other legislators. Indeed, the job of elective representative may be entirely sui generis as a job in which the application procedure is almost completely divorced from the assessment of the qualifications to do the actual job. How this matters in the current context is that women may select out of representation because they feel ill-suited for the job interview, not for the job itself.

Osborn (2012) and Swers (2002, 2013) showed that women champion different issues than do men, illustrating a vital and enduring connection between Pitkin's (1972) definitions of descriptive and substantive representation (see also Frederick's chapter). Furthermore, diverse groups may lead to better outcomes than more homogeneous ones, meaning that legislatures that are largely male-dominated would solve problems better if they included more women. In work that traverses much of the social sciences, Page (2008) found that diverse groups operated better at solving complex problems than even groups comprised entirely of experts. This is because diverse groups can draw on several different ways to address a problem, whereas groups of experts think of a problem in only one way. Simply by virtue of the fact that men and women are different, women might provide new and different perspectives to help groups solve difficult problems. The women who are excluded from representing because they prefer not to run may bring with them skills and perspectives that are particularly useful for governing.

For example, Neiderle and Vesterlund (2008) indicated that decreasing the competitive environment may actually increase the objective ability of those who participate. Recall that in their experiment, under-qualified men entered a tournament when highly qualified women demurred. The researchers were able to erase that effect, however, by creating a "gender quota." When men and women knew that at least one tournament victor would be a woman, under-qualified men entered the tournament at a lower rate, but highly qualified women increased their level of participation. In this sense, then, increasing women's participation would not only increase diversity, but it would also increase legislators' objective abilities.

Equally worrisome, gender differences may mean that women simultaneously demonstrate characteristics that make them less likely to run, but at the same time better able to represent, were they to be given a chance. For example, in their book on gender differences in negotiation, Babcock and Laschever (2009) pointed to what they call "the mythical fixed pie bias," whereby negotiators wrongly believe that negotiations are zero-sum: Whatever one side wins, the other loses. Certainly, this type of negotiation might trigger women's competition aversion and leave them at a disadvantage. But the "mythical fixed pie bias" is just that—a myth. Babcock and Laschever pointed out that negotiation may not necessarily be zero-sum but may instead be an opportunity for diverse people to work together to find solutions to shared problems. Women are perhaps more likely to reconceptualize a negotiation as an opportunity for both sides to find a way to work together, thus allowing everyone to walk away from the negotiation having "won." Women, then, can use their different perspectives to change the landscape of the negotiation.

And indeed, work in political science echoes this notion of women having a more communal perspective. Schneider et al. (2016) showed experimentally that one can mitigate the gender gap in political ambition by asking subjects to consider a political position as an opportunity to fulfill communal, rather than power-related, goals. Similarly, women tended to consider their ability relative to others, not just their own ability, when deciding whether or not to run in a laboratory election (Kanthak and Woon 2016).

It is important to point out, however, that reaping these benefits of diversity may not be straightforward. Negotiating group status can be difficult in itself. Women seem to face problems associated with their token status when they are limited to a small minority (Kanthak and Krause 2010, 2011, 2013). Specifically, they receive benefits from their token status, such as special attention and mentoring opportunities from majority group members, but risk losing them if they speak out or otherwise indicate that they think differently from members of the majority group. Furthermore, they face new difficulties as their numbers increase because the transition to relying on members of their own (now larger) group may not be easy or straightforward.

Despite these difficulties, what women offer as representatives may be precisely what our government needs. Considering that gridlock in the U.S. Congress is at an all-time high (Binder 2014), perhaps breaking the myth of the mythical fixed pie bias and thinking about the perspectives of others is exactly what would break the gridlock. Working together to achieve mutual benefits is exactly the opposite of gridlock, and this more productive type of negotiation could become the norm in a woman-dominated legislature. Unfortunately, though, these salutatory benefits women could provide seem to be inextricably packaged with their greater election aversion. Women have perspectives and characteristics that might render them more likely than men to break the legislative gridlock, but those same perspectives and characteristics seem also to keep women off the ballot in the first place.

Steps for Future Research

The evidence presented here indicates that gendered election aversion is a complex and complicated phenomenon. Researchers in political science, psychology, and economics, all attempting to draw a clear picture of these related gender differences, have yet to succeed in doing so. We do know, however, that simply expecting gender differences in willingness to run to go away in time is a fool's errand. These differences persist, and they appear to be grounded in other, related but distinct, gender differences in decision-making. Women do not run both because of their relative lower levels of political ambition vis-à-vis men, and because of their (often correct) perceptions that the electoral playing field is not level. Of course, leveling the playing field is an important and valuable goal. At the same time, though, continuing interdisciplinary research into gendered election aversion and related phenomena may help to provide better answers for how to mitigate those differences in individual political ambition.

There are a number of potential pathways for continuing the study of women's political ambition. For example, properly designed experiments can take advantage of the control permitted in the social science laboratory. Generally, external validity (the relationship between what happens in the lab to naturally occurring phenomena) is taken to be a weakness of the experimental methods, because the sterility of the lab is so different from the complexity of the "real world." But in this case, that abstraction from reality is a feature, not a glitch. We know the electoral playing field is not level for men and women, but the laboratory allows us to explore what would be the case if it were, holding the "playing field" constant, thus allowing us to determine other causal factors.

Additionally, longer-term studies might help to determine the factors in early life that may best translate to willingness to run for office in the future. We have only anecdotal information about political ambition among young boys and girls. For example, we could implement the Kanthak and Woon (2015) protocol for young children, attempting to discern at what point boys and girls begin to show evidence of patterns of gendered election aversion. Furthermore, those studies ought to focus both on women *and* men. We know that men tend to overestimate their own intelligence (Furnham and Rawles 1995), are over-confident (Kling et al. 1999), and are much more willing to celebrate their victories than are women (Wigfield, Eccles, and Pintrich 1996). Perhaps, then, it is not women that are the problem. We could change the focus from trying to discover why women do not run to instead developing theories to explain why men—particularly those with low qualifications—run so much.

Last, we in political science ought to continue to look to methods and pro-cedures of studying women's political ambition that combine the knowledge gathered about gender differences in both economics and psychology. Both disciplines have long and well-developed literatures on how women and men differ from both a psychological and an economic standpoint. Of course, dif-ferences in research strategies persist. For example, economists shun the use of deception in experiments, whereas psychologists tend not to tie subject payments to performance. Those differences can make it difficult to find common ground in the interpretation and implementation of diverse research findings. Yet the entire business of studying gender differences in political ambition is predicated on the notion that increasing the number of women in politics is normatively good because diversity itself is good. We cannot, then, study diversity in a way that ignores the diversity in our own midst as researchers. Political science can learn a great deal by looking to how these different fields are asking similar questions about gender and getting strikingly similar answers, despite the inherent difficulties in navigating the very different approaches each field has to these questions.

Conclusions

Suppose for the sake of argument that a municipality decided to enact a rule stating that a candidate for election must submit their filing documents by placing them on a shelf that stood seven feet off the ground, and that the candidate must do so without any help from other people or tools like ladders. Such a rule would exclude a great many people running for office, and would in fact exclude more women than men, because men are, on average, taller than women. "That is unfair," we would argue. "Height has nothing to do with ability to represent a constituency." Indeed, the rule would be unfair, both to potential candidates who are talented but shorter, and to their potential constituents who would benefit from receiving representation from these diminutive, but otherwise highly qualified, candidates.

This chapter ends, then, with a provocative question: Does the willingness to enter an election have any more bearing on the ability to represent than height does? And even more provocative: If we think willingness to run *is* essential to being a good representative, how much of that belief is based in our own gendered notions of what it means to represent? For example, voters often equate "toughness" with the ability to be a good leader (Barbara Lee Family Foundation 2001), but we also know that there is much evidence— including in other chapters of this volume—that female candidates have a fraught relationship with the notion of "toughness." Toughness is gendered, but it also may not be the best characteristics to have in a representative. And even if we think toughness is desirable from a representative, it may not be a good idea for *all* representatives to be tough, at the expense of other desirable traits. Perhaps "able to negotiate on behalf of others"—something at which we know women excel—is as good of a, or an even better, characteristic for a representative to have. Indeed, representatives with less toughness and more negotiating on behalf of others may be the answer to leading us out of our current quagmire of deadlock and polarization. Even if that is not the case, Page (2008) indicates that simply having some diversity in characteristics might reap the benefits of new and fresh perspectives.

This chapter places diverse cross-disciplinary literature into the context of winner-take-all elections to make two important points. First, elections are gendered institutions, and not simply because electoral structures favor men over women. If this were the case, we could "level the playing field" and solve the problem. But gendered election aversion means that the electoral environment itself prevents women from entering the fray, as surely as would instituting a requirement of a seven-foot reach. Rather than high shelves, requirements that candidates exhibit high tolerance for risk, low competition aversion, and low election aversion preclude some potential candidates from running and for reasons that have little or nothing to do with their actual ability to represent.

And second, it matters that elections are gendered because elections can create harm that goes beyond selecting our people based on irrelevant criteria. Surely, good representatives would be forced out by a rule requiring a seven-foot reach, because we have no reason to believe that ability to represent is associated with height. But gendered elections are *actually worse* than height requirements because they actively de-select people with characteristics that might make them *better* representatives. The same selection mechanism that selects out the risk averse, the competition averse, and the election averse is also selecting out highly competent people, as we saw most explicitly from Kanthak and Woon's (2015) and Neiderle and Vesterlund's (2008) work. It selects out people who bring with them much-needed legitimacy for the legislatures in which they would serve (Schwindt-Bayer and Mishler 2005). It selects out people whose negotiation styles may, in fact, be better suited for coming up with holistic solutions that solve a greater number of problems for a greater number of people (Babcock and Laschever 2009). In sum, maintaining elections as gendered institutions unfairly stifles the opportunities for many women to serve. But more important, it limits the scope of what representatives can offer their constituents. Mitigating the effects of elections as gendered institutions is not only better for the women who otherwise get shut out of the democratic process, but it is better for the health of democracy as a whole.

References

Acker, Joan. 1992. "Gendering Organizational Theory." In *Gendering Organizational Theory*, edited by Albert J. Mills and Peta Tancredo, 420–426. London: Sage.

Babcock, Linda, and Sara Laschever. 2009. *Women Don't Ask: Negotiation and the Gender Divide*. Princeton: Princeton University Press.

Barbara Lee Family Foundation. 2001. *Keys to the Governor's Office, Unlock the Door: The Guide for Women Running for Governor*. Cambridge, MA: The Barbara Lee Family Foundation.

Binder, Sarah. 2014. *Polarized We Govern?* Washington, DC: The Brookings Institution.

Black, Gordon S. 1972. "A Theory of Political Ambition: Career Choices and the Role of Structural Incentives." *The American Political Science Review* 66: 144–159.

Browning, Rufus P., and Herbert Jacob. 1964. "Power Motivation and the Political Personality." *Public Opinion Quarterly* 28: 75–90.

Burns, Nancy, Kay Lehman Schlozman, and Sidney Verba. 2011. *The Private Roots of Public Action: Gender, Equality, and Political Participation*. Cambridge, MA: Harvard University Press.

Byrnes, James P., David C. Miller, and William D. Shafer. 1999. "Gender Differences in Risk Taking: A Meta–Analysis." *Psychological Bulletin* 125 (3): 367–383.

Charles, Maria, and David B. Grusky. 2004. *Occupational Ghettos: The Worldwide Segregation of Women and Men*. Stanford: Stanford University Press.

Costa Jr., Paul, Antonio Terracciano, and Robert R. McCrae. 2001. "Gender Differences in Personality Traits across Cultures: Robust and Surprising Findings." *Journal of Personality and Social Psychology* 81: 322–331.

Croson, Rachel, and Uri Gneezy. 2009. "Gender Differences in Preferences." *Journal of Economic Literature* 47 (2): 448–474.

Dietrich, B. J., S. Lasley, J. J. Mondak, M. L. Remmel, and J. Turner. 2012. "Personality and Legislative Politics: The Big Five Trait Dimensions among U.S. State Legislators." *Political Psychology* 33: 195–210.

Dolan, Kathleen. 2004. "The Impact of Candidate Sex on Evaluations of Candidates for the U.S. House of Representatives." *Social Science Quarterly* 85: 206–217.

Eagly, A. H., and Linda L. Carli. 2003. "The Female Leadership Advantage: Evaluating the Evidence." *The Leadership Quarterly* 14: 807–834.

Eagly, A. H., and Linda L. Carli. 2007. *Through the Labyrinth: The Truth about How Women Become Leaders*. Boston, MA: Harvard Business Review Press.

Eagly, A. H., M. C. Johannesen-Schmidt, and M. L. van Engen. 2003. "Transformational, Transactional, and Laissez-Faire Leadership Styles: A Meta-Analysis Comparing Men and Women." *Psychological Bulletin* 129: 569–591.

Eckel, Catherine C., and Philip J. Grossman. 2001. "Chivalry and Solidarity in Ultimatum Games." *Economic Inquiry* 39: 171–188.

Eckel, Catherine C., and Philip J. Grossman. 2008. "Men, Women and Risk Aversion: Experimental Evidence." In *Handbook of Experimental Economics Results*, Vol. 1, edited by Charles Plott and Vernon Smith, 1061–1073. New York: Elsevier.

Eckel, Catherine C., and Rick K. Wilson. 2004. "Whom to Trust? Choice of Partner in a Trust Game." Unpublished manuscript.

Finucane, Melissa L., Paul Slovic, C. K. Mertz, James Flynn, and Theresa A. Satterfield. 2000. "Gender, Race, and Perceived Risk: The 'White Male' Effect." *Health, Risk and Society* 2: 159–172.

Fox, Richard L., and Jennifer L. Lawless. 2004. "Entering the Arena? Gender and the Decision to Run for Office." *American Journal of Political Science* 48 (2): 264–280.

Fox, Richard L., and Jennifer L. Lawless. 2005. "To Run Or Not to Run for Office: Explaining Nascent Political Ambition." *American Journal of Political Science* 49: 642–659.

Frederick, Angela. 2013. "Bringing Narrative IN: Race-Gender Storytelling, Political Ambition, and Women's Paths to Public Office." *Journal of Women, Politics & Policy* 34: 113–137.

Fulton, S. A., C. D. Maestas, L. S. Maisel, and W. J. Stone. 2006. "The Sense of a Woman: Gender, Ambition, and the Decision to Run for Congress." *Political Research Quarterly* 59: 235–248.

Furnham, Adrian, and Richard Rawles. 1995. "Sex Differences in the Estimation of Intelligence." *Journal of Social Behavior and Personality* 10: 741–748.

Garcia Bedolla, Lisa, Katherine Tate, Janelle Wong, Sue Thomas, and Clyde Wilcox. 2005. "Indelible Effects: The Impact of Women of Color in the U.S. Congress." In *Women and Elective Office: Past, Present, and Future*, edited by Sue Thomas and Clyde Wilcox, 152–175. New York: Oxford University Press.

Hegewisch, Ariane, Hannah Liepmann, Jeffrey Hayes, and Heidi Hartmann. 2010. "Separate and Not Equal? Gender Segregation in the Labor Market and the Gender Wage Gap." In *IWPR Briefing Paper*. Washington, DC: Institute for Women's Policy Research.

Hegewisch, Ariane, Claudia Williams, and Amber Henderson. 2011. "The Gender Wage Gap by Occupation." *IWPR Fact Sheet*. Washington, DC: Institute for Women's Policy Research.

Huddy, Leonie, and Nayda Terkildsen. 1993. "Gender Stereotypes and the Perception of Male and Female Candidates." *American Journal of Political Science* 37: 119–147.

Kahn, Arnold, Joe Hottes, and William L. Davis. 1971. "Cooperation and Optimal Responding in the Prisoner's Dilemma Game: Effects of Sex and Physical Attractiveness." *Journal of Personality and Social Psychology* 17 (3): 267–279.

Kanthak, Kristin, and George A. Krause. 2010. "Valuing Diversity in Political Organizations: Gender and Token Minorities in the U.S. House of Representatives." *American Journal of Political Science* 54: 839–854.

Kanthak, Kristin, and George A. Krause. 2011. "Coordination Dilemmas and the Valuation of Women in the U.S. Senate: Reconsidering the Critical Mass Problem." *Journal of Theoretical Politics* 23: 180–214.

Kanthak, Kristin, and George A. Krause. 2013. *The Diversity Paradox: Political Parties, Legislatures, and the Organizational Foundations of Representation in America.* New York: Oxford University Press.

Kanthak, Kristin, and Jonathan Woon. 2015. "Women Don't Run? Election Aversion and Candidate Entry." *American Journal of Political Science* 59: 595–612.

Kanthak, Kristin, and Jonathan Woon. 2016. *Deconstructing the Ambition Gap: How Women and Men Approach Running for Office Differently.* Typescript: University of Pittsburgh.

Kling, Kristen C., Janet Shibley Hyde, Carolin J. Showers, and Brenda N. Buswell. 1999. "Gender Differences in Self-Esteem: A Meta-Analysis." *Psychological Bulletin* 125: 470–500.

Lasswell, Harold D. 1930. *Psychopathology and Politics.* Chicago: University of Chicago Press.

Matthews, Donald R. 1954a. *The Social Background of Political Decision-Makers.* New York: Random House.

Matthews, Donald R. 1954b. "United States Senators and the Class Structure." *Public Opinion Quarterly* 18: 5–22.

McConaughy, John B. 1950. "Certain Personality Factors of State Legislators in South Carolina." *American Political Science Review* 45: 897–903.

McDermott, Monika L. 1997. "Voting Cues in Low-information Elections: Candidate Gender as a Social Information Variable in Contemporary United States Elections." *American Journal of Political Science* 41: 270–283.

Niederle, Muriel, and Lise Vesterlund. 2007. "Do Women Shy Away from Competition? Do Men Compete Too Much." *Quarterly Journal of Economics* 122: 1067–1101.

Niederle, Muriel, and Lise Vesterlund. 2008. "Gender Differences in Competition." *Negotiation Journal* 24: 447–464.

Niven, David. 1998. *The Missing Majority: The Recruitment of Women as State Legislative Candidates.* Westport: Praeger.

Osborn, Tracy. 2012. *How Women Represent Women: Political Parties, Representation, and Gender in the State Legislatures.* New York: Oxford University Press.

Page, Scott E. 2008. *The Difference: How the Power of Diversity Creates Better Groups, Firms, Schools, and Societies.* Princeton: Princeton University Press.

Pitkin, Hanna. 1972. *The Concept of Representation.* Berkeley, CA: University of California Press.

Rohde, David W. 1979. "Risk-Bearing and Progressive Ambition: The Case of Members of the United States House of Representatives." *American Journal of Political Science* 23: 1–26.

Sanbonmatsu, Kira. 2002. "Gender Stereotypes and Vote Choice." *American Journal of Political Science* 46: 20–34.

Sanbonmatsu, Kira. 2006. *Where Women Run: Gender and Party in the American States.* Ann Arbor: University of Michigan.

Sayer, Liana C. 2005. "Gender, Time, and Inequality: Trends in Women's and Men's Paid Work, Unpaid Work, and Free Time." *Social Forces* 84: 285–303.

Schlesinger, Joseph. 1996. *Political Ambition*. Chicago: Rand McNally.

Schwindt-Bayer, Leslie A., and William Mishler. 2005. "An Integrated Model of Women's Representation." *The Journal of Politics* 67: 407–428.

Scola, Becki, and Carol Hardy-Fanta. 2006. "Women of Color in State Legislatures: Gender, Race, Ethnicity, and Legislative Officeholding." In *Intersectionality and Politics: Recent Research on Gender, Race, and Political Representation in the United States*, edited by Carol Hardy-Fanta, 43–70. Binghamton, NY: Haworth Press.

Silbermann, Rachel. 2015. "Gender Roles, Work-Life Balance, and Running for Office." *Quarterly Journal of Political Science* 10: 123–153.

Stalsburg, B. 2012. *Running with Strollers?: The Impact of Family Life on Political Ambition*. Ph.D. Dissertation, Rutgers University.

Swers, Michele L. 2002. *The Difference Women Make: The Policy Impact of Women in Congress*. Chicago: University of Chicago Press.

Swers, Michele L. 2013. *Women in the Club: Gender and Policy Making in the Senate*. Chicago: University of Chicago Press.

Wigfield, A., J. S. Eccles, and P. R. Pintrich. 1996. "Development between the Ages of 11 and 25." In *Handbook of Educational Psychology*, edited by D. C. Berliner and R. C. Calfee, 148–187. New York: Macmillan.

Windett, Jason. 2014. "Differing Paths to the Top: Gender, Ambition, and Running for Governor." *Journal of Women, Politics, and Policy* 35: 287–314.

9

WOMEN'S DECISIONS TO RUN FOR OFFICE

A Relationally Embedded Model

Kira Sanbonmatsu and Susan J. Carroll

When I graduated in '72, I got involved with a group, Young Democratic Women, in Ingham County. The county board of commissioners at the time was trying to close the local nursing home, and I ended up leading the effort to keep it open. I remember one county meeting where the county commissioner was ridiculing those of us who were concerned with low-income senior citizens, and it just made me mad. Everyone came up to me and asked me why I didn't run against him. I was 24. He was a very entrenched incumbent who referred to me as "that young broad." This made me have even more resolve. My tenacity kicked in.

Senator Debbie Stabenow, Democrat, Michigan (Kohen 2007)

I think women and men weigh considerations about children and spouses differently. And I also think it is much harder for women, and here is why. First of all, I believe most women view themselves as the primary parent. The husband or father may be very much involved, but it is the mom who replaces herself when she is not home at night. It is the mom who starts the dinner in the crockpot if she is not going to be home to make dinner. It is the mom who calls and says, "Did you do your homework?" . . . In the legislature we are running every other year. We are always running. So you are always attending a Boy Scout function or a fire company function or knocking on doors. . . . So if you are the primary parent, and most women are the primary parent, it is a harder decision to make and you need a lot of support.

State Legislator, 2008 (CAWP Recruitment Study)

As these quotes from female elected officials illustrate, the support and encouragement of other people are often critical to women's decisions to run for office. In fact, in the absence of support and encouragement—from spouses and children, friends and acquaintances, activists and practitioners—many women would never think of running for office themselves nor feel comfortable doing so.

Women's political presence has increased over the past several decades. As women's educational, occupational, and family roles have evolved, so too have their roles in politics. In some respects women's political progress is impressive. Today the proportion of women serving in some offices stands at an historic high (CAWP 2016). For example, a record 104 women serve in Congress in 2016 compared to 65 who served at the turn of the century. And Hillary Clinton's campaign for president in the 2016 election marks the first time a woman appears poised to capture a major party presidential nomination.

However, in other respects the political progress women have made is disappointing. For offices such as state legislative and statewide executive, the numbers of women serving have stagnated (CAWP 2016). The extent of gains that were initially expected to occur as women's roles modernized in the wake of the modern women's movement have not materialized; women's inequality in officeholding has simply been more persistent than expected by most scholars of women and politics (e.g., Darcy, Welch, and Clark 1994). Between 1985 and 2000, the proportion of state legislative offices held by women increased from 15.0 percent to 22.4 percent. Yet, in the subsequent 15 years, change in the percentage of female state legislators is barely perceptible. In 2016 women are just 24.5 percent of all state legislators.

Why has women's political progress failed to meet early expectations? Why have the numbers and proportions of women officeholders not increased more dramatically? One explanation with which most scholars and activists agree is that too few women become candidates. But why are more women not coming forward to seek office? As noted in the chapter by Kristin Kanthak, recent work on gender and candidate emergence has for the most part adopted the ambition framework that has traditionally guided campaigns and elections research, suggesting that women's lack of officeholding ambition is the primary factor accounting for the paucity of female candidates. However, our research findings indicate that this preoccupation with ambition has led researchers to overlook some of the major factors affecting women's decisions to seek public office. Rather than adopting a traditional ambition framework, we argue that a "relationally embedded" model, highlighting the importance of the reactions of and considerations of other people, better captures women's decision-making about officeholding (Carroll and Sanbonmatsu 2013). The relationally embedded model not only helps to account for the paucity of female candidates, but also reorients the agenda of practitioners interested in increasing the level of women's representation.

The Ambition Framework

Women's quest for equality in politics has been a struggle for inclusion and incorporation. Because the barriers women faced were enshrined in law, women had to secure formal rights to participate in politics including the right to stand for office. Perhaps because women sought inclusion in what was a male-dominated endeavor, research about women's struggle for political equality has often adopted the dominant framework employed in other studies of American politics. Scholars have typically assessed the status of women using the same models and assumptions that had been used to explain men's involvement in politics. For example, even though women's forms of engagement with politics historically have differed quite dramatically from men's (Matthews 1992), women's political participation has largely been analyzed in terms of the same electorally based categories (e.g., voting, working in a campaign, making a campaign contribution, contacting a government official) that have characterized most studies of (men's) political participation in American politics.

When it comes to studying candidacy for office, a framework about ambition has traditionally been employed. At the heart of this research is the rational individual (Schlesinger 1966). Studies examine the strategic calculations that ambitious politicians make around the costs and benefits of pursuing an office, taking into account the probability of winning (Abramson, Aldrich, and Rohde 1987; Black 1972; Brace 1984; Jacobson and Kernell 1981; Maisel et al. 1990; Rohde 1979; Stone, Maisel, and Maestas 2004).

Several recent studies have incorporated women into ambition models although the factors affecting the calculus might be weighed differently by gender (Palmer and Simon 2003). For example, Sarah Fulton et al. (2006) found that female and male state legislators differed in their decisions about pursuing a seat in the U.S. Congress with women being more responsive to the expected benefit of office-holding. Similarly, Kathryn Pearson and Eric McGhee (2013) have argued that female congressional candidates are more likely than men to be strategic because of the hurdles that women face in electoral politics.

Because ambition theory takes the ambitious politician as given, it is better suited to explaining the decisions of officeholders than first-time candidates (Fowler 1993). As a consequence, Lawless and Fox (2010) investigated the origins of political ambition. Their research on gender and ambition focuses not on candidates or officeholders, but rather citizens who have the occupational backgrounds typical of officeholders and are therefore potential candidates. In their view candidate emergence proceeds in two stages: In order to leave the pool of eligible candidates and run for office, potential candidates must first consider running for elective office and then, subsequently, weigh the costs and benefits of office-seeking (Fox and Lawless 2004, 267).

The lower rate of ambition that Fox and Lawless found among women in the eligibility pool is problematic for women's representation because, in their view, "nascent ambition—or the inclination to consider a candidacy" is a precursor to expressive ambition or interest in a specific electoral contest (2005, 644). The main challenge facing women's election to office in this account is the lower levels of ambition among female citizens compared with men (Fox and Lawless 2014; Lawless and Fox 2010). Other scholars, as well, have sought to analyze the origins and contours of ambition in women (Elder 2004; Greenlee, Holman, and VanSickle-Ward 2014; Holman and Schneider 2014; Schneider et al. Forthcoming).

Relationally Embedded Candidacy

We question the ability of ambition theory to provide a full understanding of women's election to office. To some extent, the adoption of the ambition framework in candidacy studies is similar to other areas of research (e.g., political participation, voting, leadership, legislative behavior) in which the existing framework is taken as a universal standard and women are held up to what is essentially a male norm for political behavior. Feminist scholars such as Susan C. Bourque and Jean Grossholtz (1974) have documented this tendency to measure women's political behavior against a male norm, the result of which is that women are usually found to be deficient. The application of an underlying male norm has similarly been critiqued in some previous work on women's ambition. For example, Burt-Way and Kelly (1992, 23) observed:

> The assumption has long been that women's different, and usually lower, socioeconomic status, different and less prestigious types of political experience, and different sex role attitudes are constraints not only in the development of ambition but also in deciding to run for higher office. Thus, the definition of what constitutes political ambition has typically been defined by male political career patterns and leads to the conclusion that women will be more ambitious and more successful when they attain the same characteristics as men.

At its core, the ambition framework is premised on the existence of an individual with a long-standing interest in politics. The right conditions enable that ambitious individual to seek office. But some extant research on gender and elections challenges the notion that there is a linear pathway to elective office in which nascent ambition necessarily precedes the decision to run for office. In some cases the act of recruitment by parties or other actors can itself lead to the development of ambition (Aldrich 1995; Fowler 1993; Fox and Lawless 2010; Sanbonmatsu 2006). Ambition and candidacy can occur more or less simultaneously: Ambition can develop when and because an individual is asked or encouraged to run for a specific office (Carroll and Sanbonmatsu 2013). Ambition, then, can be a result, rather than a precondition, of recruitment for an electoral contest.

An analysis by Gary Moncrief, Peverill Squire, and Malcolm Jewell (2001), likewise, offered a more complicated portrayal of women's candidacies than is embodied in the ambition account. Their study of nonincumbent state legislative candidates shows a gender gap in which women were much more likely than men to seek a state legislative seat after receiving the suggestion to run. Women were less likely than men to be "self-starters" who reached the decision to run for the legislature entirely on their own. In contrast, women were more likely than men to be "persuaded" candidates who ran after receiving the suggestion to run. And women were more likely than men to be "encouraged" candidates: those who said their candidacies reflected their own thinking in addition to the encouragement of others.

While we do not wish to argue that there are "male" and "female" ways of deciding to become a candidate, we do want to advance an alternative view of the decision to run for office that may more often characterize women's decision-making processes than men's (Carroll and Sanbonmatsu 2013). For women more often than for men, we argue that candidacy is a "relationally embedded decision." By this, we mean that women's decision-making about officeholding "is more likely to be influenced by the beliefs and reactions, both real and perceived, of other people and to involve considerations of how candidacy and office holding would affect the lives of others with whom the potential candidate has close relationships" (Carroll and Sanbonmatsu 2013, 45).

Our view of the relational aspects of women's decision-making is consistent with research on leadership and moral reasoning. Eagly and Johannesen-Schmidt (2001) concluded that female managers often have a more transformational leadership style that focuses on mentoring followers and attending to their individual needs. Judy B. Rosener (1990), as well, found female managers more likely to have an "interactive leadership" style. Alice Eagly and her colleagues have found that women are viewed as more communal in their qualities—as warm and selfless, for example—while men are seen as having more agentic qualities—as assertive and instrumental (Eagly and Carli 2003; Eagly, Makhijani, and Klonsky 1992). Pioneering work by Carol Gilligan (1993), a moral development theorist, is also relevant, given her argument that concepts of care and responsibility figured centrally in women's resolution of moral dilemmas. Gilligan's finding that relationships with others often weighed heavily in women's moral decisions is consistent with the focus on the concerns and interests of peers and subordinates apparent in the research on women's leadership.

This decision-making research has implications for the political domain. Running for office can be conceptualized as an act that takes place within a broader context, and so we would expect women's relationships to impact the candidate emergence process. Gender differences in the economy, society, and family have already been implicated in the gender gap in political participation. Gender roles are changing, but women are still disproportionately responsible for childcare and the household (Sayer 2005; Sayer et al. 2009). The traditional division of labor in the home affects the resources, education, and skills available to women for political participation (Burns, Schlozman, and Verba 2001). We believe, as well, that gender differences in social and economic roles and in the household division of labor will give rise to different patterns of decision-making about candidacy. Both the findings of research on women's leadership and moral reasoning and women's greater traditional responsibility for caregiving within the home lead us to expect women's decisions about running for office to be more likely than men's to be influenced by considerations about how other family members feel about the decision and how their lives might be affected.

The decision to run takes place in a political as well as a social context. It is common for gender scholars to privilege social factors such as changes in women's levels of education or patterns of work outside the home over political factors such as the role played by political parties and other actors in explaining changes in women's political status and participation. But we contend that gender is a political category as well as a social category. By treating gender as a political category, we argue that women's relationship to politics has been inherently shaped by the formal and informal exclusions that women have faced in politics. Moreover, the world of politics remains a highly masculinized space with women often still viewed as intruders whose presence disrupts the traditional order (Duerst-Lahti 2005; Puwar 2004). The public as well as political elites believe that women face inequalities in contemporary electoral politics (CBS 2008; Sanbonmatsu 2006). But while the public supports the idea of electing more women to public office, there is also some contentment with having men in the majority of elected positions (Dolan and Sanbonmatsu 2009).

Arguably, women have internalized the idea that they are outsiders to political life. Lawless and Fox (2005) argued that potential female candidates are less likely than men to view themselves as qualified for holding public office. Because women traditionally have not had an equal role in political life, we can expect that the candidate emergence process may work differently for women than for men. We show that a long-standing interest in running for office need not precede a political career.

The CAWP Recruitment Studies

Our research is focused on state legislators. State legislative office is an important office in its own right, and state legislative officeholding can be a credential for the pursuit of other offices including congressional office. Often, the state legislature marks the beginning of a political career. The large number of state legislators—more than 7,000 nationwide—also makes the legislatures an attractive site for research.

We demonstrate the utility of the relationally embedded model with data from the 2008 and 1981 Center for American Women and Politics (CAWP) Recruitment Studies. These studies provide the most comprehensive data ever collected about the backgrounds, prior officeholding experiences, and candidacy decisions of female state legislators. The surveys were conducted in the 50 states with nearly identical survey instruments in 1981 and 2008. All female state legislators were surveyed; male legislators were systematically sampled and surveyed based on the proportion of women in each chamber of the legislature in each state.[1] This sampling strategy was necessary since female legislators are distributed quite unevenly across the states and enables us to compare women with men who serve in similar political and legislative environments. To supplement and help us interpret the survey results, we conducted a small number of phone interviews in 2009 with women state legislators of both parties who were diverse in ideology and backgrounds and who served in different types of states and legislatures.

The Decision to Run

The CAWP Recruitment Studies offer a unique window into the decision-making processes of women and men who have successfully achieved state legislative office. We find substantial support for our relationally embedded model of candidacy based on an analysis of the legislators' backgrounds and decisions to run. This model stands in contrast to the traditional ambition model. While we are not able to compare all of the evidence over time because of some differences in survey questions between 1981 and 2008, we find similar gendered patterns in both time periods.

We queried 2008 legislators about the decision to seek their current state legislative office. We also asked about their initial decision to run if they sought an office prior to running for their current state legislative office. Our survey question is modeled on the candidate survey question used by Moncrief, Squire, and Jewell (2001).

While the ambition model is premised on the existence of an ambitious politician with a long-standing interest in holding office, we wanted to determine if there were individuals other than "self-starters" serving in the legislatures. Figure 9.1 reveals that conceptualizing candidacies as a long-standing, personal goal of individuals may obscure the reality of office-seeking behavior. Instead, we see that the idea of running for office often originates outside the individual. Importantly, there are significant gender differences on this question.

Our exact question was as follows: "In thinking about your initial decision to seek elective office the very first time, which of the following statements most accurately describes your decision?" A majority of female state legislators—just over 50 percent—said they "had not seriously thought about running until someone else suggested it" (see Figure 9.1). By comparison only 28.0 percent of men chose this response.[2]

In sharp contrast to the women, the modal response for men state legislators is the self-starter response option: "It was entirely my idea to run." Fully 42.7

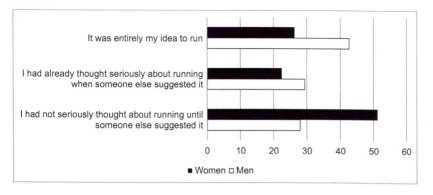

FIGURE 9.1 State Legislators' First Decision to Seek Elective Office

Source: 2008 CAWP Recruitment Study.

percent of men chose this option. Only 26.4 percent of women reported that they were self-starters.

As a third possibility, some women and men reported they had already thought seriously about running when someone else suggested it. These individuals are best described as having elements of both the relationally embedded and ambition models of candidacy. Among women, 29.4 percent chose this option as did 22.5 percent of men.

Although some men ran for office because of the encouragement they received from others, such encouragement was far more important for women's decisions. Women's decision-making, to a greater extent than men's, seems to take place in relationship with other people and to fit the embedded candidacy model. Men's decisions are more consistent with the self-initiated notion of candidacy and traditional ambition framework. As one female state legislator we interviewed explained:

> Men are more often likely to say, "I always wanted to be a state legislator; I am a good business person." And they step up and say, "I am going to run." They step up on their own whereas women very rarely do it on their own. It takes someone talking them into it.
>
> *(in Carroll and Sanbonmatsu 2013, 53)*

A separate, though related, survey question from 2008 also informs our understanding of how candidacies come about. Regardless of what office they first sought, we asked legislators the reason behind their bid for their current office.[3] Here, we posed a closed-ended question and asked legislators to choose the reason that best characterized their decision to seek their current state legislative position (Carroll and Sanbonmatsu 2013, 59). The results appear in Table 9.1.

Men's responses were notably more consistent with the assumptions of the political ambition literature. More than one-fourth of the male representatives

TABLE 9.1 Most Important Reason Legislator Sought Current Office

	Representatives		Senators	
	Women %	Men %	Women %	Men %
My long-standing desire to be involved in politics	16.2**	28.9	15.5*	26.1
A party leader or an elected official asked me to run or serve	23.8**	14.8	14.9	7.8
My concern about one or more specific public policy issues	35.9**	26.7	45.8	35.7
My desire to change the way government works	11.0*	16.6	12.5	20.0
Dissatisfaction with the incumbent	6.1	5.7	7.7	2.6
It seemed like a winnable race	1.9	1.6	0.6	2.6
Other	5.1	5.7	3.0	5.2
N =	526	439	168	115

Source: 2008 CAWP Recruitment Study.

* $p \leq .05$, ** $p \leq .01$

Question wording: "Other than your desire to serve the public, what was the single most important reason that you decided to seek the office you now hold?"

and senators, compared with only 16.2 percent of female representatives and 15.5 percent of female senators, cited a long-standing desire to be involved in politics as the most important reason for running for their current office (Table 9.1). Along with the finding that men were more likely than women to be self-starters, this gender difference suggests that self-initiation of candidacy is less likely to characterize women's bids for office.

Another finding from Table 9.1 is also consistent with our hypothesis that the ambition model is less likely, and the relationally embedded model more likely, to describe the decision-making of women than men. Female state legislators more often than men attributed their decision to run for their current office to the encouragement of another political figure. More women than men in both chambers sought their seats because a party leader or elected official asked them to run. This was especially true of female state representatives (23.8 percent). Relationships with others—in this case, party officials and elected leaders—were more consequential for women than men and help to explain how women's pathways to office take shape when self-initiation is not at work.

It is worth acknowledging that the most common response among women to our question about the most important factor affecting their decision-making about seeking office seems on the surface to fit neither the ambition nor the relationally embedded model. More than one-third of female representatives and more than two-fifths of female senators reported that the major factor affecting their decision was their concern about one or more specific public policy issues. As with the other motivations, gender differences were apparent: Women were more likely than men to run because of policy considerations. While deciding to run for office because of a concern over a particular policy does not explicitly involve interactions with other people, nevertheless most public policy does have a direct effect on people's lives. Consequently, an interest in improving people's lives may well underlie women's concerns about particular public policy issues, and thus there may perhaps be a more indirect relational component even in those cases where women responded that the major factor affecting their decision to run was policy-related.

What we have primarily seen thus far, then, is that a long-standing interest in holding office is not a prerequisite for becoming a candidate. This finding disrupts the conventional wisdom about political motivations and departs from the dominant narrative concerning the reasons for women's underrepresentation. The desire to run for office may first arise within the context of a specific electoral contest, implying that prior political ambition is not a prerequisite.

Familial, Organizational, and Political Factors

Much of the evidence thus far points away from motivations that are solely internal to individuals and directs our scholarly attention to the broader social, familial, and political environments in which potential candidates live and interact. If only a minority of state legislators can be characterized as self-propelled individuals who initiate candidacy on their own, then our accounts of candidacy and officeholding must be broadened to incorporate considerations and actors other than the candidate.

We probe further into the circumstances surrounding state legislators' decisions to run, finding that state legislators often took into account the perspectives of others and considered how their candidacy might affect other people. We view this as further evidence in support of a relationally embedded model of decision-making. To some degree this alternative model is applicable to men as well as women. But we find that this type of decision-making is more often characteristic of women's decisions.

Among the factors we examine are considerations about family. Some of the most dramatic gender-related social changes to occur in recent decades are related to marriage, family structure, and child-rearing. Fathers today are more involved in domestic responsibilities than in the past, mothers are much more likely to be combining paid work with motherhood, and women are more likely to be pursuing high-status occupations (Bureau of Labor Statistics 2013; Pew Research Center 2015; U.S. Census Bureau 2011). Despite significant changes in gender relations between our 1981 and 2008 points in time, however, combining familial

responsibilities with the pursuit of political office continues to pose a disproportionate challenge to women. This phenomenon is evident in our data.

First, female state legislators are less likely than their male colleagues to have
young children, suggesting that they less often than men are willing to run for
office while they have major child-rearing responsibilities. This was the case in
the early 1980s and remained so in 2008. For example, in 2008 female state
legislators less often than men had a child under age six (3.0 percent compared
with 8.2 percent) and also less often had a child under age 18 (14.5 percent
compared with 22.4 percent).[4]

Related to this difference is the weight that women ascribe to family in their
office-seeking decisions. A gender difference is evident in legislators' attitudes
about how candidacy would affect family members. We asked legislators: "Below
are various factors that have been suggested to be important in influencing
decisions to run for office. Please indicate how important each factor was in
affecting your decision to run the first time for the office you now hold." One
of these factors was: "My children being old enough for me to feel comfortable
not being home as much."

In both 1981 and 2008, women were much more likely than men to cite
the age of children as a "very important" factor in their decision to run (see
Table 9.2). Among state representatives, for example, a majority of women
compared with a minority of men (57.3 percent compared with 37.7 percent)
rated the age of their children as very important in 1981, and the same pattern
was apparent in 2008 (56.7 percent compared with 41.9 percent). In fact, it is
striking how consistent the gender differences were over time.

A second area where we see the significance of factors external to the individual candidate comes with respect to organizations. We asked legislators in

TABLE 9.2 Legislators' Age of Children as a Very Important Factor in the Decision to Run

	Representatives		Senators	
	Women %	Men %	Women %	Men %
2008	56.7**	41.9	50.9*	34.8
N =	526	437	171	115
1981	57.3**	37.7	69.4**	35.8
N =	426	191	72	67

Source: 2008 and 1981 CAWP Recruitment Studies.

* $p \leq .05$, ** $p \leq .01$

Question wording: "Below are various factors that have been suggested to be important in influencing
decisions to run for office. Please indicate how important each factor was in affecting your decision
to run the first time for the office you now hold. . . . My children being old enough for me to feel
comfortable not being home as much." Cell entries are percentage of legislators citing this factor as
"very important."

both 1981 and 2008 whether there was "an organization that played a particularly important role in getting you to run the first time" for the legislators'
current office. In both time periods, and in both legislative chambers, women
were more likely to benefit from such organizational encouragement. In 1981,
33.9 percent of female state representatives, compared with 16.3 percent of men,
reported that an organization played an important role in their decisions to
run. In 2008, 28.4 percent of female state representatives and 19.1 percent of
men reported the same.[5]

The encouragement of women's organizations seems to be part of the explanation for this gender difference in organizational encouragement. We also asked
female legislators (but not the men) if one or more women's organizations actively
encouraged the legislators to run when they first sought their current office. In
1981, 27.3 percent of female state representatives reported encouragement, compared with 21.4 percent in 2008. The proportion of female state senators receiving
encouragement was similar in 1981 but greater in 2008 (26.0 percent in 1981
and 30.2 percent in 2008).

The third area where we found differences in the significance of factors
external to the candidate involves political parties. Despite occasional concern
expressed about the decline of political party organizations, candidacy in the
United States still entails attracting support from one of the two major parties.
In our study, most legislators reported that "party leaders generally supported
my candidacy"; few legislators were able to reach the legislature with active
opposition from party leaders (Carroll and Sanbonmatsu 2013).

Our survey enables us to analyze in more detail the relationship that legislators have with their parties. We find evidence that women were slightly more
likely than men to have received encouragement from their party when they
first sought their current office. A narrow majority of 2008 female state representatives (54.9 percent) reported that the party encouraged them to run, compared with half (49.9 percent) of their male colleagues. Encouragement rates
were also somewhat higher among women than among men senators (56.6
percent of women compared with 43.5 percent of men).

We also asked 2008 state legislators to rate the importance of "party support"
as a factor in their decision to run, and again we find gender differences. Female
state representatives were more likely than their male colleagues to rate the party
as very important (34.9 percent compared with 25.3 percent) with a similar
gender difference evident among senators.[6]

All told, we contend that legislators often come to the decision to run through
interacting with other people and/or taking into account a series of relationships—
personal, organizational, and partisan. Family considerations and expressions of
support from organizations and parties can be critical. Moreover, the very idea
for the candidacy can be brought to the candidate by an external source even
in the absence of a prior interest in seeking elective office. For many people
who seek office the decision to run is thus embedded in relational considerations,

and women more often than men seem to follow a relationally embedded decision-making process.

Conclusion

We can all agree that men and women must decide to run for office in order to become candidates. But how they make that decision has been the topic of some debate. In this chapter, we have argued for an alternative way of conceptualizing the decision to run that recognizes the ways that candidacy decisions are embedded in relationships. We have also argued that this alternative framework is especially important in understanding women's election to office.

We found that women are much more likely than men to run for office because they were recruited. Their pathways to office are much less likely to be consistent with a traditional framework of candidacy that assumes a self-initiated individual with a long-standing interest in politics. Our alternative view recognizes that candidacies can be initiated through recruitment and encouragement by others in the context of a specific political opportunity. Undoubtedly, the pathways of some female legislators can be explained by an ambition framework. Indeed, a minority of the women in our study said that the decision to run was their own.

Our perspective also argues that candidacy may be equally, or even more, dependent on the consequences of candidacy for *others* than on the costs and benefits to the *candidate* personally. We have seen that women are more likely than men to take into account and to be encouraged by an array of actors, from the expected impact of a candidacy on the lives of their children to expressions of support by organizations and party leaders.

These findings hold significant implications for the study of gender and politics and for understanding the future of women's officeholding. As we discussed at the outset of this chapter, gains in women's representation have been much slower than anticipated and at some levels of office women's representation is stagnant today. Our research suggests that more research about the strength of recruitment mechanisms and support for female candidates is needed. While our studies have, understandably, often treated the individual as the unit of analysis, our research implies that future scholarship must think more broadly about the contexts in which women candidates emerge. In other words, we must look beyond women as individuals in order to understand women's representation.

Taking the relationally embedded model of decision-making into account, we argue for studies that seek to incorporate the relationships that are integral to the candidate emergence process. For example, we envision more studies that identify and assess the strength of organizational and party recruitment mechanisms that seem so integral to women's emergence as candidates. To what extent are organizations, parties, and political action committees (PACs) recruiting and supporting women candidates today? What makes these actors more likely to facilitate women's representation? When are they less likely to support women?

Measuring the strength of these recruitment mechanisms nationally, as well as in states and localities, can help explain variation in the level of women's representation. More research is needed on the receptivity of donors, groups, and parties to women's candidacies given that these factors may be better predictors of women's representation than the levels of ambition expressed in the general public. Consideration of which women are more likely to be encouraged and supported is also essential because of racial/ethnic and partisan differences evident in women's officeholding (Carroll and Sanbonmatsu 2013). Analysis of institutional barriers to female recruitment is critical given that women's opportunities for office are uneven across the United States and levels of office (Dittmar 2015).

More research could be conducted on the effectiveness of recruitment practices and messages (Preece and Stoddard 2015; Preece, Stoddard, and Fisher Forthcoming). Racial/ethnic differences could be analyzed in this area because recruitment may be more likely to occur—and may be more effective—if conducted among women with shared racial/ethnic backgrounds (Sanbonmatsu 2015). Scholarship that identifies the social, economic, political, and familial networks in which women potential candidates are situated could help to contextualize individual-analysis and link individual women to the relationships that are likely to inform their decision-making.

From a practical standpoint, our findings imply that improvements in women's descriptive representation can take place even in the absence of widespread cultural changes in socialization patterns. "Waiting on the world to change," in the words of recording artist John Mayer, is not likely to alter the current pattern of slow growth or stagnation in the number of female officeholders. Instead, our findings suggest that political practitioners can take steps now to improve women's representation by providing women with campaign infrastructure, encouragement, and support and by working to ensure that organizations and political parties provide the same. Although some women's organizations (e.g., EMILY's List, Emerge America, Ready to Run™) and advocates are already heavily engaged in efforts to recruit and support female candidates, much more needs to be done.

The mere removal of impediments to women's officeholding through cultural change and legal reform is insufficient. Women's greater reliance on a relationally embedded approach to making candidacy decisions suggests that support and encouragement must also be present in order for women to succeed (Carroll and Sanbonmatsu 2013).

Notes

1. State legislators were promised confidentiality. The surveys were primarily conducted online and by mail; a small number of telephone interviews were also conducted at the end of the field period. In 2008, a total of 1,268 legislators completed surveys; in 1981, 789 did so. The overall response rate was 36.5 percent in 2008 and 55.4 percent

in 1981. See Carroll and Sanbonmatsu (2013) for a full discussion of the methodology. The 2008 CAWP Recruitment Study was funded by the Barbara Lee Family Foundation, the Susie Tompkins Buell Foundation, Wendy McKenzie, and other donors. The 2008 data are available through the Inter-university Consortium for Political and Social Research (ICPSR Study Number 35244).

2. A chi-square test indicates that the relationship between gender and recruitment is statistically significant ($p \leq .01$).

3. The exact question wording was: "Other than your desire to serve the public, what was the single most important reason that you decided to seek the office you now hold?"

4. These gender differences are statistically significant ($p \leq .01$).

5. These gender differences are statistically significant ($p \leq .01$).

6. This gender difference is statistically significant ($p \leq .01$).

References

Abramson, P. R., J. H. Aldrich, and D. W. Rohde. 1987. "Progressive Ambition among United States Senators: 1972–1988." *Journal of Politics* 49 (February): 3–35.

Aldrich, J. H. 1995. *Why Parties? The Origin and Transformation of Political Parties in America.* Chicago: University of Chicago Press.

Black, G. 1972. "A Theory of Political Ambition: Career Choices and the Role of Structural Incentives." *American Political Science Review* 66 (March): 144–159.

Bourque, S. C., and J. Grossholtz. 1974. "Politics an Unnatural Practice: Political Science Looks at Female Participation." *Politics and Society* 4 (Winter): 225–266.

Brace, P. 1984. "Progressive Ambition in the House: A Probabilistic Approach." *Journal of Politics* 46: 556–571.

Bureau of Labor Statistics, U.S. Department of Labor. 2013. TED: The Economics Daily. "Women's Earnings, 1979–2012." Accessed December 4, 2015. http://www.bls.gov/opub/ted/2013/ted_20131104.htm.

Burns, N., K. L. Schlozman, and S. Verba. 2001. *The Private Roots of Public Action: Gender, Equality, and Political Participation.* Cambridge: Harvard University Press.

Burt-Way, B. J. B., and R. M. Kelly. 1992. "Gender and Sustaining Political Ambition: A Study of Arizona Elected Officials." *The Western Political Quarterly* 45 (1): 11–25.

Carroll, S. J., and K. Sanbonmatsu. 2013. *More Women Can Run: Gender and Pathways to the State Legislatures.* New York: Oxford University Press.

CBS News Poll. 2008. "Breaking the Glass Ceiling: A Woman Presidential Candidate." May 30 to June 2. Press Release.

Center for American Women and Politics (CAWP). 2016. "Women in Elective Office 2016." *Fact Sheet.* New Brunswick, NJ: Center for American Women and Politics, Rutgers University.

Darcy, R., S. Welch, and J. Clark. 1994. *Women, Elections and Representation* (2nd ed.). Lincoln, Nebraska: University of Nebraska Press.

Dittmar, K. 2015. "Encouragement Is Not Enough: Addressing Social and Structural Barriers to Female Recruitment." *Politics & Gender* 11 (4): 759–765.

Dolan, K., and K. Sanbonmatsu. 2009. "Gender Stereotypes and Attitudes toward Gender Balance in Government." *American Politics Research* 37 (3): 409–428.

Duerst-Lahti, G. 2005. "Institutional Gendering: Theoretical Insights into the Environment of Women Officeholders." In *Women and Elective Office: Past, Present, and Future*

(2nd ed.), edited by Sue Thomas and Clyde Wilcox, 230–243. New York: Oxford University Press.

Eagly, A. H., and L. L. Carli. 2003. "The Female Leadership Advantage: An Evaluation of the Evidence." *Leadership Quarterly* 14: 807–834.

Eagly, A. H., and M. C. Johannesen-Schmidt. 2001. "The Leadership Styles of Women and Men." *Journal of Social Issues* 57: 781–797.

Eagly, A. H., M. G. Makhijani, and B. G. Klonsky. 1992. "Gender and the Evaluation of Leaders: A Meta-Analysis." *Psychological Bulletin* 111 (1): 3–22.

Elder, L. 2004. "Why Women Don't Run." *Women & Politics* 26 (2): 27–56.

Fowler, L. L. 1993. *Candidates, Congress, and the American Democracy*. Ann Arbor: University of Michigan Press.

Fox, Richard L. and Jennifer L. Lawless. 2004. "Entering the Arena? Gender and the Decision to Run for Office." *American Journal of Political Science* 48 (2): 264–280.

Fox, Richard L., and Jennifer L. Lawless. 2005. "To Run or Not to Run for Office: Explaining Nascent Political Ambition." *American Journal of Political Science* 49 (3): 642–659.

Fox, Richard L., and Jennifer L. Lawless. 2010. "If Only They'd Ask: Gender, Recruitment, and Political Ambition." *Journal of Politics* 72 (2): 310–326.

Fox, Richard L., and Jennifer L. Lawless. 2014. "Uncovering the Origins of the Gender Gap in Political Ambition." *American Political Science Review* 108 (3): 499–519.

Fulton, S. A., C. D. Maestas, L. S. Maisel, and W. J. Stone. 2006. "The Sense of a Woman: Gender, Ambition, and the Decision to Run for Congress." *Political Research Quarterly* 59 (2): 235–248.

Gilligan, C. 1993. *In a Different Voice: Psychological Theory and Women's Development*. Cambridge: Harvard University Press.

Greenlee, J. S., M. Holman, and R. VanSickle-Ward. 2014. "Making It Personal: Assessing the Impact of In-Class Exercises on Closing the Gender Gap in Political Ambition." *Journal of Political Science Education* 10 (1): 48–61.

Holman, M. R., and M. Schneider. 2014. "Experimental Investigations of the Gendered Political Ambition Gap." Paper Presented at the American Political Science Association, Washington, DC.

Jacobson, G. C., and S. Kernell. 1981. *Strategy and Choice in Congressional Elections*. New Haven: Yale University Press.

Kohen. Yael. 2007. "Why I Ran for Office." *Marie Claire*, December 9. Accessed February 16, 2016. http://www.marieclaire.com/politics/news/a1048/politics-women-run-for-office/.

Lawless, J. L., and R. L. Fox. 2005. *It Takes a Candidate: Why Women Don't Run for Office*. New York: Cambridge University Press.

Lawless, J. L., and R. L. Fox. 2010. *It Still Takes a Candidate: Why Women Don't Run for Office* (revised ed.). New York: Cambridge University Press.

Maisel, L. S., L. L. Fowler, R. S. Jones, and W. J. Stone. 1990. "The Naming of Candidates: Recruitment or Emergence?" In *The Parties Respond: Changes in the American Party System*, edited by Mark D. Brewer and L. Sandy Maisel, 137–159. Boulder: Westview Press.

Matthews, Glenna. 1992. *The Rise of Public Woman*. New York: Oxford University Press.

Moncrief, G. F., P. Squire, and M. E. Jewell. 2001. *Who Runs for the Legislature?* Upper Saddle River, NJ: Prentice Hall.

Palmer, B., and D. M. Simon. 2003. "Political Ambition and Women in the U.S. House of Representatives, 1916–2000." *Political Research Quarterly* 56 (2): 127–138.

Pearson, K., and E. McGhee. 2013. "What It Takes to Win: Questioning Gender Neutral Outcomes in U.S. House Elections." *Politics & Gender* 9 (4): 439–462.

Pew Research Center. 2015. "Raising Kids and Running a Household: How Working Parents Share the Load." November 4. Accessed February 14, 2016. http://www. pewsocialtrends.org/2015/11/04/raising-kids-and-running-a-household-how-working-parents-share-the-load/.

Preece, J. R., and O. B. Stoddard. 2015. "Does the Message Matter? A Field Experiment on Political Party Recruitment." *Journal of Experimental Political Science* 2 (1): 26–35.

Preece, J. R., O. B. Stoddard, and R. Fisher. Forthcoming. "Run, Jane, Run! Gendered Responses to Political Party Recruitment." *Political Behavior*, doi:10.1007/s11109-015-9327-3.

Puwar, N. 2004. *Space Invaders: Race, Gender and Bodies Out of Place*. Oxford: Oxford University Press.

Rohde, D. W. 1979. "Risk-Bearing and Progressive Ambition: The Case of Members of the United States House of Representatives." *American Journal of Political Science* 23 (February): 1–26.

Rosener, J. B. 1990. "Ways Women Lead." *Harvard Business Review* 68: 119–125.

Sanbonmatsu, K. 2006. *Where Women Run: Gender and Party in the American States*. Ann Arbor: University of Michigan Press.

Sanbonmatsu, K. 2015. "Electing Women of Color: The Role of Campaign Trainings." *Journal of Women, Politics, & Policy* 36 (2): 137–160.

Sayer, L. C. 2005. "Gender, Time, and Inequality: Trends in Women's and Men's Paid Work, Unpaid Work, and Free Time." *Social Forces* 84 (1): 285–303.

Sayer, L. C., P. England, M. Bittman, and S. M. Bianchi. 2009. "How Long is the Second (Plus First) Shift? Gender Differences in Paid, Unpaid, and Total Work Time in Australia and the United States." *Journal of Comparative Family Studies* 40 (4): 523–545.

Schlesinger, J. A. 1966. *Ambition and Politics: Political Careers in the United States*. Chicago: Rand McNally.

Schneider, M. C., M. R. Holman, A. B. Diekman, and T. McAndrew. Forthcoming. "Power, Conflict, and Community: How Gendered Views of Political Power Influence Women's Political Ambition." *Political Psychology*, doi:10.1111/pops.12268.

Stone, W. J., L. S. Maisel, and C. D. Maestas. 2004. "Quality Counts: Extending the Strategic Politician Model of Incumbent Deterrence." *American Journal of Political Science* 48: 479–495.

U.S. Census Bureau. 2011. "Statistical Abstract of the United States: 2012." Accessed December 4, 2015. http://www.census.gov/library/publications/2011/compendia/statab/131ed.html.

Gender Stereotypes
and Group Identity

10

GENDER STEREOTYPES AND VOTER EVALUATIONS OF FEMALE CANDIDATES

Nichole M. Bauer

Each election cycle increasing numbers of women run for political office at the local, state, and even the national level. These female candidates adopt a variety of campaign strategies from Iowa Senate candidate Joni Ernst who touted her credentials as a soldier and a mother with unique "pork-cutting" skills to Texas gubernatorial candidate Wendy Davis who emphasized her background as a single, working mother. These divergent strategies reflect the diversity of women running for political office, but also different ways candidates can talk about their gender. Ernst's strategy focused on downplaying feminine stereotypes while Davis embraced her gender as a benefit. The extent to which feminine stereotypes helped Ernst's victory or contributed to Davis's defeat is unclear. These strategies do reflect the lack of consensus on whether female candidates do best by avoiding or embracing feminine stereotypes on the campaign trail.

Feminine stereotypes characterize women as warm, nurturing, and sensitive; and these qualities contrast with voter expectations that political candidates emphasize traits that fit with leadership roles such as being outspoken, decisive, and assertive (Eagly and Karau 2002). Scholars disagree about whether voters rely on feminine stereotypes in decision-making. One perspective argues the incongruity between feminine stereotypes and leadership roles leads voters to form negative impressions of female candidates (Huddy and Terkildsen 1993). Another approach suggests that feminine stereotypes can benefit female candidates because they include positive traits valued in leaders, such as honesty and empathy. Additionally, voters consider female candidates competent on critical issues such as education and reproductive rights (Sanbonmatsu 2002).[1] Finally, the no stereotype approach contends that voters do not rely on feminine stereotypes to make evaluations of female candidates (Brooks 2013; Dolan 2014). Overall, existing research offers three competing conclusions about whether and how feminine stereotypes affect voter impressions of female candidates.

Resolving this debate requires answering two separate though related questions. First, when do voters use feminine stereotypes to evaluate female candidates? Second, do feminine stereotypes help, hurt, or have no effect on voter impressions of female candidates? I start by reviewing the current literature, and I then identify the psychological conditions that will affect stereotype reliance among voters. The latter half of the chapter presents the results of an experiment and outlines a set of priorities for future research.

Feminine Stereotypes and Voter Evaluations

Feminine stereotypes reflect beliefs about the characteristics women are expected to embody, and include being "affectionate, helpful, kind, sympathetic, interpersonally sensitive, nurturant, and gentle" (Eagly and Karau 2002). These traits align with the communal roles women historically filled such as being a mother or a homemaker. Contrasting communal roles are agentic roles, such as being an economic provider or a political leader, and traits such as aggressiveness and dominance define these roles. For men, being male, filling agentic roles, and possessing masculine traits all reinforce each other.

Voters often think about holding political office as a "masculine" position, and value masculine traits in political leaders (Holman, Merolla, and Zechmeister 2016; Huddy and Terkildsen 1993). The alignment between women and communality may lead to the perception that women lack the qualifications required for leadership roles (Eagly and Karau 2002). Not all leadership traits are masculine as voters do value some feminine traits in leaders, such as honesty and empathy; but voters attribute negative feminine qualities with female politicians, such as lacking knowledge or experience, and not positive feminine qualities, such as empathy or honesty (Schneider and Bos 2014).

At a baseline level, voters use candidate gender to make political inferences about the issue competencies and ideological leanings of candidates. First, voters associate communal issues with female politicians such as education, health care, and social welfare policy (Schneider 2014). Conversely, voters associate agentic issues such as national security, military policy, and foreign affairs with male politicians (Holman, Merolla, and Zechmeister 2016). These issue inferences come from the communal and agentic traits assigned separately to women and men. Female politicians receive high competency ratings on child welfare issues because caring for children requires communal traits and fits the conventional communal roles of women. Voters make this same type of association about male politicians who are perceived as competent on issues requiring agentic traits such as national security and defense (Huddy and Terkildsen 1993).

Second, voters infer female candidates in both parties as more ideologically liberal compared to their male counterparts (McDermott 1998) because candidate gender leads to the inference that female candidates are competent on issues that reflect communality and these issues reflect a more liberal ideology (Koch 2000). The issues associated with female politicians are also Democratic issues (Petrocik 1996); and this association could also come from the Democratic partisanship of most female candidates (Bauer 2015b). These ideological associations suggest that candidate gender affects voter evaluations, but they do not directly speak as to whether feminine stereotypes affect perceptions of female candidate qualifications.

Research on the effects of feminine stereotypes offers ambiguous conclusions about whether these concepts help, hurt, or have no effect on candidate evaluations. The feminine stereotypes as helpful approach argues that voters see female candidates as bringing a fresh perspective to politics with a unique set of skills differentiating them from their male counterparts (Brown, Diekman, and Schneider 2011). At the state and local level, feminine stereotypes align with the issues that dominate this level of office, such as education or social welfare policy, and these issues match women's stereotypic strengths, suggesting feminine stereotypes can be particularly advantageous (Windett 2014). Feminine stereotypes also motivate the gender affinity effect where female voters are more likely to support female politicians based on the belief these politicians will represent the interests of women. As voters, women support issues that benefit the interests of other women such as reproductive rights, equal pay, and childcare policies (Sanbonmatsu 2002). These issues fit into the perceived issue strengths of female politicians—an inference that ties back to feminine stereotypes.

The negative feminine stereotypes approach argues the incongruity between being a woman and being a leader leads to the perception that female candidates lack the traits needed to serve in leadership roles (Eagly and Karau 2002). Higher levels of political office, such as gubernatorial seats, the Senate, and the Presidency, place a strong emphasis on masculine traits and masculine issues, and this can disadvantage female candidates (Holman, Merolla, and Zechmeister 2016).[2] For instance, one study found that voters are more likely to search for competency related information about female candidates in a mock presidential primary compared to male candidates (Ditonto, Hamilton, and Redlawsk 2014). This information searching behavior suggests that voters assume that female candidates lack critical traits necessary for leadership roles.

Finally, the no effects perspective suggests that feminine stereotypes have little bearing on how voters evaluate female candidates. While feminine stereotypes are abstract ideas people have about women in general, these abstract ideas do not necessarily influence how voters think about specific female candidates (Dolan 2014). The ideas and expectations voters have about the traits, behaviors, and abilities of female candidates and politicians differ from the expectations voters have about women in general (Schneider and Bos 2014). Much of this research argues that partisanship overwhelms gender in vote choice decisions (Dolan 2014). Brooks (2013) goes further and makes the argument that voters evaluate female and male candidates equitably as leaders. For example, Brooks finds that female candidates who cry or act tough on the campaign trail receive ratings comparable to male candidates who also cry or act tough. The logic is that an absence of gender differences means that voters evaluate women as leaders, but the underlying assumption is that voters *always* evaluate male candidates as leaders.

To resolve this theoretical and empirical conflict, I argue that voter reliance on feminine stereotypes might be more conditional then previously considered. Much of the extant scholarship assumes that feminine stereotypes always or never affect voter evaluations, but I suggest that a female candidate's gender might not always trigger feminine stereotyping. I outline several theoretical premises drawn from psychology research to identify the conditions under which feminine stereotypes are most likely to affect voter decision-making.

The Conditions of Feminine Stereotype Reliance in Campaigns

Psychology research argues that stereotyping is a conditional process and not an automatic process (Bargh 1994; Blair 2002). Automatic processes occur with little conscious awareness (Bargh 1994). For example, automatic stereotyping occurs if a person sees a woman and then, based only on the observation of the woman's gender, assumes she is going to be sensitive or emotional. Conditional processes, on the other hand, involve more thought behind the associations made between a woman and broader stereotypes about women (Bargh 1994). An employer interviewing a woman for a job might initially assume the woman is passive but might re-evaluate this assessment if the woman offers no evidence of passivity. This more deliberate and thoughtful processing of information is a controlled and conditional process.

Treating stereotype reliance as a conditional process requires identifying the conditions under which feminine stereotypes become cognitively salient to voters, and when these stereotypes affect electoral assessments of female candidates. Kunda and Spencer (2003) describe these two distinct stages: "stereotype activation is the extent to which a stereotype is accessible in one's mind, and stereotype application is the extent to which one uses a stereotype to judge a member of a stereotyped group" (522). Stereotype activation is critical, because this is when the concepts associated with a stereotype move from being dormant information in the back of someone's mind to being salient information ready for use in decision-making (Kunda and Spencer 2003).

The Psychology of Stereotype Activation

Stereotype activation distinguishes between "a person's awareness of a stereotype . . . and the actual influence of the construct on the person's judgment" (Bargh 1994, 13). Individuals know the content of feminine stereotypes because these are ubiquitous concepts; but knowledge of a stereotype does not always lead to stereotype reliance. Under automatic stereotyping, a voter might see a female candidate is running for political office and associate the female candidate with feminine qualities such as sensitivity and emotionality. The automaticity in this process is that the association between the female candidate and feminine traits occurs rapidly based on only the candidate's gender. However, a number of recent studies found that knowing only the gender and partisanship of a female candidate does *not* lead voters to automatically attribute feminine stereotypes with female candidates (Bauer 2015a, b).[3]

Stereotype activation occurs when an external stimulus increases the salience or accessibility of feminine stereotypes in a voter's mind (Blair 2002). This external stimulus can be information that directly connects a woman to concepts associated with feminine stereotypes (Kunda and Spencer 2003). For example, Sarah Palin famously made motherhood a major component of her 2008 vice presidential narrative describing herself as a "Mama Grizzly" and a "Hockey Mom." This type of information could activate feminine stereotypes. One study found that feminine stereotype activation occurred after voters read information that described a female candidate as having feminine traits—an effect that did not occur for male candidates (Bauer 2015a).

Candidate partisanship is an accessible source of information but existing research is at odds on whether partisanship suppresses or activates feminine stereotypes. As a stereotype suppression tool, partisan labels can limit the activation of feminine stereotypes because voters will use party information to make inferences rather than candidate gender (Bauer 2015b; Dolan 2014). Partisanship could also activate feminine stereotypes. Partisan and gender stereotypes overlap as voters stereotype Democrats as being feminine and Republicans as being masculine (Winter 2010). The connection between feminine stereotypes and Democratic partisanship can lead voters to simultaneously process these cues. This simultaneous, or parallel, processing leads voters to attribute more feminine traits to Democratic female candidates compared to Democratic male candidates and Republican female candidates (Bauer forthcoming; Schneider and Bos 2016). Thus, partisanship may activate feminine stereotypes for Democratic female candidates, but it is not clear how partisanship affects Republican female candidates.

Other types of information that might affect stereotype activation include candidate characteristics such as race, ethnicity, gender identity, or sexual orientation. Candidate race, for instance, may limit the activation of feminine stereotypes or the intersection of race and gender may create a new stereotype category against which voters evaluate female candidates. The way voters stereotype a Black female candidate will likely differ from how voters stereotype a White female candidate and a Black male candidate. Few studies to date consider these intersections (for exceptions see Bejarano 2013; Philpot and Walton 2007).

The Psychology of Stereotype Application

Stereotype activation must occur before stereotype application, though stereotype activation does not always lead to application (Kunda and Spencer 2003). For example, feminine stereotype activation might occur when a voter hears a female candidate describe herself as caring, which leads the voter to think that she will also be weak and emotional. If the voter does not use feminine stereotypes to evaluate the female candidate's abilities as a political leader then the activated stereotype is not applied. In a campaign context, for example, when stereotypes are not activated voters express relatively equal levels of support for a female candidate and a male candidate who is of the voter's political party (Bauer 2015b). But, when feminine stereotype activation occurs vote support for a female candidate decreases, and feminine stereotypes drive this decline (Bauer 2015a). Psychology research identifies several factors that affect stereotype application including a voter's comprehension goals, the relevance of the stereotypic information, characteristics of the perceiver, and the availability of counter-stereotypic information (Blair 2002). I consider each of these factors.

Comprehension Goals

Comprehension goals refer to the "need to understand events, reduce the complexity of the environment, gain clarity, and form coherent impressions" (Kunda and Spencer 2003). Applied to a voter, comprehension goals can refer to a voter's need to make a decision, form an evaluation about a candidate, or have more information about a candidate. Comprehensions goals can be operationalized as the strength of a voter's partisanship, levels of political sophistication, or the extent to which voters follow political news (Bauer 2015b). These characteristics reflect how much information a voter is likely to have about a candidate and how much information a voter might seek during a campaign. For example, a voter might be ambivalent about supporting a female candidate and have little information about a specific female candidate. Ambivalence and low information can interact to increase a voter's comprehension needs thus motivating the voter to seek out additional information. Under these conditions, voters will turn to easily accessible information to quickly make inferences about a female candidate. In this case, candidate gender can be a useful and powerful cue. When information is low and the need for comprehension is high, voters will be more likely to apply activated feminine stereotypes—though the effect of this stereotype application could be either negative or positive.

Comprehension goals may be high, for example, when party heuristics are not useful such as in the case of a primary election or for an Independent voter. Bauer (2015b) found that Democratic and Republican voters, even those who identified as strong partisans, were unlikely to use feminine stereotypes to evaluate female candidates when a partisan cue was available; but that Independent voters were more likely to use feminine stereotypes. This need for information increases the likelihood a voter will apply feminine stereotypes to a particular female candidate. For example, voters might use feminine stereotypes to infer a female candidate is strong on issues such as education and health care. When a voter's need for information is high, stereotype reliance is likely to increase; and a voter will have a high need for information when other candidate heuristics, such as partisanship, are not helpful information sources.

Different electoral contexts can also affect a voter's comprehension goals. An open-seat election with two unknown candidates or a primary election where partisanship is constant can increase the need for comprehension and therefore increase stereotype reliance. Additionally, races for lower levels of office or offices that are not very visible, such as non-partisan judicial elections, may be contexts that increase the use of gender as a heuristic (Mo 2015). Judicial races, for example, are not high-profile contests, and this means that voters may not learn about a candidate's policies or judicial philosophy through the course of a campaign. In this type of low-profile race, feminine stereotypes can help voters acquire more information about a candidate.

Stereotype Relevance

Relevance refers to how well the information provided by feminine stereotypes fits the type of decision an individual is trying to make (Blair 2002; Kunda and Spencer 2003). For example, feminine stereotype activation might occur when an individual sees a woman caring for a small child. If the individual must form an evaluation of whether the woman would be a good lawyer, activated feminine stereotypes may not be very helpful tools. In this example, feminine stereotypes are not directly relevant to the decision-making task, and stereotype application is unlikely to occur.

The separate assignment of feminine traits and communal roles to women and masculine traits and agentic roles to men means that feminine traits are incongruent with leadership roles and masculine traits are congruent with leadership roles. There are two possibilities for how stereotype relevance might affect stereotype application, based on this incongruence (Eagly and Karau 2002). This incongruence can lead voters to either reject feminine stereotypes as irrelevant to evaluating the leadership ability of a female candidate or the incongruence could lead voters to see the female candidate as lacking the relevant qualities necessary for office. For example, a voter may see an ad aired in support of a female candidate that describes how her background as a homemaker prepares her to serve in political office—a strategy that can activate feminine stereotypes (Bauer 2015a). The voter might dismiss this information as not very relevant to evaluating the female candidate's ability to legislate on defense policy or perform other leadership tasks. Alternatively, the voter could use the information about the female candidate as a homemaker to infer that the female candidate lacks masculine qualities.

Feminine stereotypes may not always be congruent with leadership roles, and they may not always have a negative effect on evaluations of female candidates (Bos, Schneider, and Utz forthcoming). Feminine stereotypes include traits that are positive qualities voters value in political leaders (Funk 1999). Female politicians also engage in desirable leadership behaviors such as promoting consensus and building compromise among colleagues (Barnes 2016). When the political climate calls for leaders with compassion, female candidates may have an electoral edge. Conversely, when a political climate calls for leaders with strengths voters may use feminine stereotypes to form negative judgments of female candidates (Holman, Merolla, and Zechmeister 2016).

In lower races, feminine stereotypes are more directly relevant to the issues at stake and may have a positive effect on female candidates—though the research offers unclear conclusions on this point. Issues that reflect women's stereotypical strengths dominate state and local offices (Windett 2014). One reason why voters associate female candidates with issues such as education and health care is that female candidates are thought to have the traits needed to legislate on these issues (Huddy and Terkildsen 1993). Many studies find, however, that regardless of the level of office at stake, female candidates do not do well with feminine traits (Bauer 2015a). But, other studies find that female candidates receive positive ratings when they emphasize feminine issues at lower levels of office, but only when doing so in response to an opponent's criticism (Windett 2014).

These divergent findings about feminine stereotypes in local races may have to do with the difference in feminine stereotypic strategies that emphasize traits versus strategies that emphasize issues. Issues have broad political relevance, and voters expect candidates to talk about issues widely in their campaign. And, research shows that when female candidates emphasize women's issues voters respond positively (Herrnson, Lay, and Stokes 2003). Traits, on the other hand, may lead voters to focus more on the personal qualities of a candidate and less on substantive policies. This focus on a candidate's personal qualities can lead voters to more closely scrutinize the qualifications of a candidate or search for more competency related information about the candidate (Ditonto, Hamilton, and Redlawsk 2014). Essentially, feminine traits may lead voters to question the ability of a female candidate to fill leadership roles while feminine issues do not. In sum, whether feminine stereotypes are relevant depends on the characteristics of the broader decision-making context such as the level of office at stake, and when relevant voters can use feminine stereotypes to make either positive or negative assessments of female candidates.

Voter Characteristics

In addition to comprehension and relevance, voter characteristics can affect stereotype application. Individuals with high levels of prejudice are more likely to see stereotypes as relevant and use stereotypes to form negative judgments compared to those with low levels of prejudice (Brewer 1988). The extent to which outright gender prejudice poses a problem for female candidates is not entirely clear. Sanbonmatsu (2002) found that most male voters have a baseline preference for male candidates—suggesting bias against female candidates. Mainstream public opinion surveys, however, regularly find that voters express a willingness to vote for a female presidential candidate—though this could be a social desirability effect (Krupnikov, Piston, and Bauer 2016). These ambiguous findings come, in part, from the lack of a clear method to measure prejudice against female candidates. Most scholars simply use vote choice against a female candidate. The logic being that a vote against a female candidate offers evidence of gender bias. This approach does not account for the reasons a voter may have beyond gender bias to vote against a female candidate.

As a voter characteristic, partisanship can affect stereotype application. Motivated stereotype theory argues that individuals will be more likely to apply stereotypes when motivated to form a negative impression of a woman (Kunda and Spencer 2003). This motivation increases when there is a perceived disagreement or conflict between a woman and an individual. For example, a student who receives a bad grade from a female professor will be more motivated to use feminine stereotypes to negatively judge the female professor—essentially, the student is motivated to punish the female professor for not being warm and kind. Had the student received a good grade, there would be no motivation to use stereotypes. Being on opposite sides of the political aisle in a highly polarized political environment can be a source of conflict that motivates feminine stereotyping among out-partisans (Bauer forthcoming; Krupnikov and Bauer 2014). Among opposing partisans, female candidates may face higher levels of stereotype application.

Once activated, stereotype application might occur under several conditions including an individual's comprehension goals, stereotype relevance, and a voter's characteristics. The next section outlines the conditions of stereotype suppression.

The Psychology of Stereotype Suppression

A variety of factors related to a voter's decision-making environment and a voter's individual characteristics can affect how voters apply activated feminine stereotypes, but it is also possible that external stimuli can suppress the use of feminine stereotypes. Psychology research suggests that priming voters to have counter-stereotypic expectations decreases the accessibility of feminine stereotypes, and increases the accessibility of masculine stereotypes (Blair 2002). Voters expect candidates and leaders, in general, to emphasize masculine stereotypes (Huddy and Terkildsen 1993). However, voters do not seem to have these same masculine expectations for female candidates (Schneider and Bos 2014). Counter-stereotypic messages can lead voters to evaluate female candidates as having masculine qualities that match the expectations voters have for leadership. For example, a female candidate who describes herself as willing to fight for her constituents is evoking a masculine trait with the use of the verb fight. Describing a female candidate as tough and asser-tive can increase vote support for a female candidate (Huddy and Terkildsen 1993). These counter-stereotypic messages can activate masculine stereotypes and lead individuals to associate a female candidate with counter-stereotypic, or in this case masculine, qualities (Holman, Merolla, and Zechmeister 2016).

Female candidates often emphasize both feminine and masculine characteristics in campaign communication (Schneider 2014); but, news coverage focuses more on masculine stereotypes (Hayes and Lawless 2015). One reason why female can-didates emphasize a mix of counter-stereotypic and stereotypic messages may be the fear of a backlash from being too tough and not nice enough (Rudman and Glick 1999). Brooks (2013), however, in an experimental study did not find that voters disproportionately punished female congressional candidates compared to male candidates who displayed toughness or anger during a campaign, two counter-stereotypic behaviors for women. But, Krupnikov and Bauer (2014) found that female candidates who aired negative ads, another counter-stereotypic behavior for women, only faced a feminine stereotype motivated backlash from voters of the opposite political party. The literature offers mixed results on the extent to which a female candidate will face a backlash effect for being counter-stereotypic, and it is not clear how much a loss on likability harms female candidates at the polls.

Summary

The process of stereotype reliance can be broken down into three phases: activa-tion, application, and suppression. Stereotype activation is a necessary first step that must occur before the stage of stereotype application; and stereotype sup-pression offers insight into how female candidates can strategically shape their images to avoid any negative repercussions from feminine stereotypes. The next section offers a preliminary experimental test of the processes of stereotyping.

Experimental Design

The experiment presented here tests three hypotheses. First, I hypothesize that individuals will only associate female candidates with feminine stereotypes when they have information that connects a female candidate to feminine stereotypes. Second, individuals will only apply feminine stereotypes after stereotype activa-tion occurs. Finally, when individuals have masculine information, which is counter-stereotypic for female candidates, feminine stereotype activation will not occur. Important to note is that this study only tests some of the conditions of stereotyping that might occur in a political context, and future research should expand on these analyses.

The study manipulated candidate gender (male or female) and gender ste-reotypes (feminine, masculine, or no stereotypes). The study also randomized candidate partisanship (Democratic or Republican). I collapsed the Democratic and Republican candidate conditions in the analyses as there are no differences across candidate partisanship. The experimental sample comes from the 2014 Cooperative Congressional Election Study (CCES). The sample size is N = 850 with approximately n = 135 participants in each of the six conditions.

Each participant only saw information about one candidate. The names Karen Bailey and Kevin Bailey along with photos cued candidate gender (Brooks 2013), and additional pre-tests of the names and photos show no significant differences. I used traits to manipulate feminine and masculine stereotypes (Kunda and Spencer 2003). The feminine stereotype condition used the traits *caring* and *sensitive* to describe the candidates and the masculine stereotype condition used the traits *tough* and *assertive*. The control groups removed the stereotypic adjectives. I embedded these manipulations in a screenshot of the candidate's campaign homepage. All the candidates were running for a U.S. Senate race, and there was no information about their previous political experience.

Measures

I measure feminine stereotypes with a scale from social psychology research designed to measure implicit stereotyping along power and warmth dimensions. Participants placed the candidates on a series of scales ranging from 1–7 with the ends defined as strong–weak, harsh–lenient, and hard–soft (Rudman, Greenwald, and McGhee 2001). The final measure is the average of these items. Higher values on this measure indicate stronger feminine stereotyping and lower values indicate stronger masculine stereotyping. This scale is appropriate here because it measures "the automatic concept-attribute associations that are thought to underlie implicit stereotypes" (Rudman, Greenwald, and McGhee 2001, p. 1165). Additionally, scholars have found it to be comparable to other measures of stereotyping such as an implicit association test (Brooks 2013; Krupnikov and Bauer 2014).

To investigate the substantive effects of feminine and masculine stereotypes on candidate evaluations, I asked participants to indicate the extent to which they thought the phrases *good representative of constituent opinion* and *experienced* described the candidate. These questions provide an approximation of how participants rate the abilities and qualifications of the candidates. I also asked participants to rate how qualified they thought the candidate was to move onto *higher levels of political office*. I rescaled each of these variables to range from 0–1 and recoded them so that higher values indicate a more positive evaluation.

Testing the Conditions of Stereotype Reliance

In the following section, I show how information about candidate traits affects the activation, application, and suppression of feminine stereotypes. I use a series of t-tests to make relevant comparisons across candidate gender between the female and male candidates. I also make comparisons within each candidate type comparing the control condition ratings to the treatment condition for the female and male candidate.

Feminine Stereotype Activation

If a female candidate's gender does not activate feminine stereotypes, there should be no differences in the stereotype ratings of the female and male candidates across the control conditions. A two-tailed t-test shows there are no statistically significant differences in the stereotype ratings of female ($M = 0.50$, $SD = 0.14$) and male ($M = 0.51$, $SD = 0.17$) candidates, $p = 0.6771$ in the control conditions. Next, I test whether feminine traits activate corresponding feminine stereotypes. In the feminine condition, the female candidate's stereotype rating increases from 0.50 ($SD = 0.14$) to 0.53 ($SD = 0.14$), and this is statistically significant, $p = 0.0386$. There is no significant increase in the salience of feminine stereotypes for the male candidate in the feminine ($M = 0.52$, $SD = 0.14$) compared to the control condition ($M = 0.51$, $SD = 0.17$), $p = 0.4107$. Voters do not automatically turn to feminine stereotypes to judge female candidates, but linking female candidates to feminine traits activates these concepts.

Feminine Stereotype Application

If feminine stereotypes directly affect candidate evaluations, there should be a significant difference in the female candidate's ratings in the feminine compared to the control condition on the outcome measures.[4] Figure 10.1 shows the difference in the female and male candidate ratings in the feminine condition compared to the control condition on the three outcome variables. Several patterns emerge from these comparisons. First, the female candidate's ratings do not significantly change on being a good representative ($p = 0.2039$) or on experience ($p = 0.6302$). The male candidate benefits from feminine stereotypes on both good representative ($p < 0.001$) and experience ($p = 0.0252$). On the higher office variable, the effects of feminine stereotypes are significant for the female

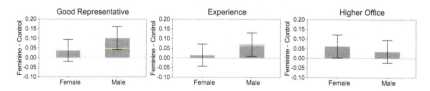

FIGURE 10.1 Effects of Feminine Traits on Candidate Evaluations

Note: Each bar shows the difference in the candidate's average rating in the feminine condition—the control condition. Ninety-five percent confidence intervals included.

candidate, and positive with a 0.06 increase on the 0 to 1 scale, $p = 0.0428$. The male candidate's rating on qualifications for higher office do not significantly change compared to the control condition, $p = 0.2417$.

Activated feminine stereotypes may not always directly shift how voters evaluate female candidates. An indirect mediation effect could occur if the feminine condition activates feminine stereotypes, and the activated feminine stereotypes subsequently affect candidate evaluations. I conducted a mediation analysis by calculating the average causal mediated effect (ACME) of the ratings on the stereotype scale on candidate evaluations in the feminine condition. On each of the three outcome variables, feminine stereotypes have a statistically significant negative mediating effect on the female candidate's ratings. Most critically, this significant mediation effect does not occur for male candidates.

Counter-Stereotype Suppression Strategies

Emphasizing masculine stereotypes should decrease the salience of feminine stereotypes. The female candidate's stereotype evaluation decreases by 0.04 points, and this is a marginally significant effect, $p = 0.0923$ (one-tailed test, $p = 0.0462$). Feminine stereotype suppression also occurs for the male candidate whose ratings decrease by 0.05 points, $p = 0.0044$. Figure 10.2 shows the effects of masculine stereotypes on the three substantive outcome measures. Starting with the female candidate's ratings on being a good representative, the change from the masculine ($M = 0.41$, $SD = 0.24$) to the control ($M = 0.45$, $SD = 0.46$) condition does not quite reach significance, $p = 0.1535$. The female candidate receives a 0.10 boost on experience, $p = 0.0009$, and a 0.11 boost on higher office, $p = 0.0006$. The male candidate's ratings also significantly improve in the masculine conditions for each of the three outcome measures.

Results Summary

These findings suggest several trends in the process of feminine stereotype reliance. First, feminine stereotype activation is not automatic. Second, voters can use activated feminine stereotypes to negatively evaluate female candidates along

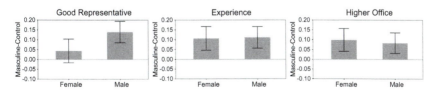

FIGURE 10.2 The Effects of Masculine Traits on Candidate Evaluations

Note: Each bar shows the difference in the candidate's average rating in the masculine condition—the control condition. Ninety-five percent confidence intervals included.

critical leadership characteristics. Finally, counter-stereotypes, or in this case masculine trait associations, benefit both female and male candidates. While this study does not test all the conditions under which feminine stereotypes activation might occur, it provides a useful starting point for future research on how voters use stereotypes to form impressions of female candidates.

Avenues for Future Research

Treating feminine stereotype reliance as a conditional process not only reconciles the conflicts in existing literature about the role of feminine stereotypes in voter decision-making, but also opens up new avenues for future scholarship. Several areas for future research include the role of information in stereotype activation, stereotype intersectionality, expanding the set of outcome measures used in research, and examining the effects of feminine stereotypes at different stages in the political process.

The results of the experiment presented here suggest that written feminine trait information activates feminine stereotypes—but other types of information might also activate feminine stereotypes. For example, feminine information can come from cues about a candidate's appearance (Carpinella et al. 2016). There may also be differences in the ability of traits and issues to activate feminine stereotypes. Additionally, the source of feminine information, whether it is directly from the candidate, the media, or an opponent, may not always activate feminine stereotypes. Voters may be more likely to dismiss information that does not directly come from the candidate such as negative criticisms from an opponent.

To date, extant research focuses on the role of stereotypes for White female candidates, and some research examines the intersection of party and gender (Bauer forthcoming; Schneider and Bos 2016). Most research, however, overlooks how feminine stereotypes interact with other candidate characteristics. Stereotypes about women intersect with stereotypes about race, ethnicity, and social class background among other characteristics. Each of these intersections may change the way voters process information about feminine stereotypes. For example, stereotypes about race and gender are likely to intersect in ways that create a new stereotype category for Black or Latina women that differs from the stereotypes voters have about White women (Bejarano 2013).[5] A next step is to clarify these intersectional relationships, and how they affect candidate evaluations.

Much of the past research focuses on vote choice as the key dependent variable to show evidence of gender bias. Recent literature finds that gender bias can affect evaluations of female candidates at other stages of the voter evaluation process. Activated feminine stereotypes can affect the trait attributions to female candidates, evaluations of candidate viability, assessments of candidate ability, and issue competencies. Future research should develop outcome measures that can more accurately assess how and when stereotypes affect candidate evaluations. These include not only qualification assessments but also measures of stereotype and prejudice. Schneider and Bos (2014), for example, convincingly showed that voters stereotype female politicians as neither leaders nor ladies suggesting the need for developing a new set of measures for capturing stereotype activation.

Campaigns are not the only stage of the political process where feminine stereotypes can affect female politicians. Evidence suggests that candidate recruitment strategies at the state and local level can affect how voters think about the viability of female candidates (Bos 2015). Moreover, feminine stereotypes may affect how voters respond to the behaviors of female politicians once elected to office (Barnes 2016). Voter responses to legislative behaviors may involve feminine stereotypes, and may be important to understanding the dynamics female incumbents face in re-elections.

Conclusion

The process of feminine stereotype reliance in vote choice is not a question of whether voters ever use these concepts to form impressions of female candidates, but a question of when and how feminine stereotypes are most likely to affect impression formation. The conditional nature of feminine stereotypes means that female candidates may have more control over their images than indicated by previous research. The downside is that female candidates often need to prove their qualification through campaign messages that highlight their leadership abilities. By strategically emphasizing qualities that align most strongly with leadership roles, female candidates can limit the influence of feminine stereotypes and maximize their electoral prospects. Increasing women's representation requires understanding how voters think about female candidates, including the role of stereotypes in the voter evaluation process. After all, improving women's representation requires first electing more women to Congress.

Notes

1. See the Greenlee et al. chapter of this volume for insights about candidate parental status.
2. See the Frederick chapter of this volume for more on women in local office.
3. Schneider and Bos (2014) find that while voters do not associate female politicians with conventional feminine traits voters do associate female politicians with negative feminine qualities such as being inexperienced and unknowledgeable.
4. Control group comparisons of the female and male candidate's ratings show no statistically significant differences on being a good representative of constituent opinion ($p = 0.1570$), experience ($p = 0.2330$), and being qualified to move up to a higher office ($p = 0.9504$).
5. See the Bejarano chapter of this volume for a discussion of the intersection of ethnicity and gender.

References

Bargh, John A. 1994. "The Four Horsemen of Automacity: Awareness, Intention, Efficiency, and Control in Social Cogniton." In *Handbook of Social Cognition*, edited by R. S. Wyer, Jr. and T. K. Skrull, 1–40. Hillsdale, NJ: Erlbaum.

Barnes, Tiffany D. 2016. *Gendering Legislative Behavior*. New York: Cambridge University Press.

Bauer, Nichole M. 2015a. "Emotional, Sensitive, and Unfit for Office: Gender Stereotype Activation and Support for Female Candidates." *Political Psychology* 36 (6): 691–708.

Bauer, Nichole M. 2015b. "Who Stereotypes Female Candidates? Identifying Individual Differences in Feminine Stereotype Reliance." *Politics, Groups, and Identities* 3 (1): 94–110.

Bauer, Nichole M. forthcoming. "Untangling the Relationship between Partisanship, Gender Stereotypes, and Support for Female Candidates." *Journal of Women, Politics & Policy* forthcoming.

Bejarano, Christina. 2013. *The Latina Advantage: Gender, Race, and Political Success*. Austin, TX: University of Texas Press.

Blair, Irene V. 2002. "The Malleability of Automatic Stereotypes and Prejudice." *Journal of Personality and Social Psychology Review* 6 (3): 242–261.

Bos, Angela L. 2015. "The Unintended Effects of Political Party Affirmative Action Politics on Female Canddiate's Nomination Chances." *Politics, Groups, and Identities* 3 (1): 73–93.

Bos, Angela L., Monica C. Schneider, and Brittany L. Utz. forthcoming. "Gender Stereotypes and Prejudice in U.S. Elections." In *APA Handbook of the Psychology of Women*, edited by Cheryl Travis and Jackie White.

Brewer, Marily. 1988. "A Dual Process Model of Impression Formation." In *Advances in Social Cognition* (vol. 1), edited by Robert S. Wyer and Thomas Srull, 1–36. Hillsdale, NJ: Lawrence Erlbaum Associates.

Brooks, Deborah Jordan. 2013. *He Runs, She Runs*. Princeton: Princeton University Press.

Brown, Elizabeth R., Amanda B. Diekman, and Monica C. Schneider. 2011. "A Change Will Do Us Good: Threats Diminish Typical Preferences for Male Leaders." *Personality and Social Psychology Bulletin* 37 (7): 930–941.

Carpinella, Colleen M., Eric Hehman, Jonathan B. Freeman, and Kerri L. Johnson. 2016. "The Gendered Face of Partisan Politics: Consequences of Facial Sex Typicality for Vote Choice." *Political Communication* 33 (1): 21–38.

Ditonto, Tessa M., Allison J. Hamilton, and David P. Redlawsk. 2014. "Gender Stereotypes, Information Search, and Voting Behavior in Political Campaigns." *Political Behavior* 36 (2): 335–358.

Dolan, Kathleen. 2014. *When Does Gender Matter? Women Candidates and Gender Stereotypes in American Elections*. New York: Oxford University Press.

Eagly, Alice H., and Steve J. Karau. 2002. "Role Congruity Theory of Prejudice toward Female Leaders." *Psychological Review* 109 (3): 573–594.

Funk, Carolyn L. 1999. "Bringing the Candidate into Models of Candidate Evaluation." *Journal of Politics* 61 (3): 700–720.

Hayes, Danny, and Jennifer L. Lawless. 2015. "A Non-Gendered Lens: The Absence of Stereotyping in Contemporary Congressional Elections." *Perspectives on Politics* 13 (1): 95–118.

Herrnson, Paul S., J. Celeste Lay, and Atiya Kai Stokes. 2003. "Women Running as 'Women': Candidate Gender, Campaign Issues, and Voter Targeting Strategies." *The Journal of Politics* 65 (1): 244–255.

Holman, Mirya R., Jennifer L. Merolla, and Elizabeth J. Zechmeister. 2016. "Terrorist Threat, Male Stereotypes, and Candidate Evaluations." *Political Research Quarterly* 69 (1): 134–147.

Huddy, Leonie, and Nayda Terkildsen. 1993. "Gender Stereotypes and the Perception of Male and Female Candidates." *American Journal of Political Science* 37 (1): 119–147.

Koch, Jeffrey W. 2000. "Do Citizens Apply Gender Stereotypes to Infer Candidates' Ideological Orientations?" *The Journal of Politics* 62 (2): 414–429.

Krupnikov, Yanna, and Nichole M. Bauer. 2014. "The Relationship between Campaign Negativity, Gender and Campaign Context." *Political Behavior* 36 (1): 167–188.

Krupnikov, Yanna, Spencer Piston, and Nichole M. Bauer. 2016. "Saving Face: Identifying Voter Responses to Black and Female Candidates." *Political Psychology* 37 (2): 253–273.

Kunda, Ziva, and Steven J. Spencer. 2003. "When Do Stereotypes Come to Mind and When Do They Color Judgment: A Goal-Based Theoretical Framework for Stereotype Activation and Application." *Psychological Bulletin* 129 (4): 522–544.

McDermott, Monika L. 1998. "Race and Gender Cues in Low-Information Elections." *Political Research Quarterly* 51 (4): 895–918.

Mo, Hyunjung Cecilia. 2015. "The Consequences of Explicit and Implicit Gender Attitudes and Candidate Quality in the Calculations of Voters." *Political Behavior* 37 (2): 357–395.

Petrocik, John R. 1996. "Issue Ownership in Presidential Elections, with a 1980 Case Study." *American Journal of Political Science* 40 (3): 825–850.

Philpot, Tasha S., and Hanes Walton, Jr. 2007. "One of Our Own: Black Female Candidates and the Voters Who Support Them." *American Journal of Political Science* 51 (1): 49–62.

Rudman, Laurie A., and Peter Glick. 1999. "Feminized Management and Backlash toward Agentic Women: The Hidden Costs to Women of a Kinder, Gentler Image of Middle Managers." *Journal of Personality and Social Psychology* 77 (5): 1004–1010.

Rudman, Laurie A., Anthony G. Greenwald, and Debbie E. McGhee. 2001. "Implicit Self-Concept and Evaluative Implicit Gender Stereotypes: Self and Ingroup Share Desirable Traits." *Personality and Social Psychology Bulletin* 27 (9): 1164–1178.

Sanbonmatsu, Kira. 2002. "Gender Stereotypes and Vote Choice." *American Journal of Political Science* 46 (1): 20–34.

Schneider, Monica C. 2014. "Gender-Based Strategies on Candidate Websites." *Journal of Political Marketing* 13 (4): 264–290.

Schneider, Monica C., and Angela L. Bos. 2014. "Measuring Stereotypes of Female Politicians." *Political Psychology* 35 (2): 245–266.

Schneider, Monica C., and Angela L. Bos. 2016. "The Intersection of Party and Gender Stereotypes in Evaluating Political Candidates." *Journal of Women, Politics & Policy* 37 (3): 274–294.

Windett, Jason. 2014. "Gendered Campaign Strategies in U.S. Elections." *American Politics Research* 42 (4): 628–655.

Winter, Nicholas J. G. 2010. "Masculine Republicans and Feminine Democrats: Gender and Americans' Explicit and Implicit Images of the Political Parties." *Political Behavior* 32 (4): 587–618.

11

THE IMPACT OF MOTHERHOOD AND MATERNAL MESSAGES ON POLITICAL CANDIDACIES

Jill Greenlee, Grace Deason, and Carrie Langner

At the 2008 Republican national convention, Alaska Governor Sarah Palin accepted the vice presidential nomination for her party. In her fiery speech, she conveyed that she was tough as nails but also a loving mother. She noted that her path to politics began with the PTA when she was "just your average hockey mom." In one of her most notable lines from the election, she declared, "You know . . . the difference between a hockey mom and a pit bull? Lipstick" (Palin 2008). Palin's focus on motherhood stood in contrast with that of the Democratic Party vice presidential candidate in 1984, Geraldine Ferraro. Palin spent her first moments in the national spotlight talking about her children and her role as a mother, whereas Ferraro mentioned her family only briefly in the final lines of her nomination speech (Ferraro 1984). Though many factors distinguished Palin and Ferraro as vice presidential candidates, the contrasting ways in which they invoked motherhood can be seen as an illustration of how the dynamics among gender, motherhood, and politics may have changed over the past several decades. Once a necessary qualification in order to fit with social expectations of what a woman "should be," but antithetical to strong leadership, motherhood has been portrayed in recent years as an asset by some female candidates: evidence of both selflessness and toughness. This trend raises some key questions that we explore in this chapter. Does the evolving focus on motherhood by female candidates mark a shift in how women are evaluated when they run for office? Is there evidence that mothers are viewed more favorably by voters than women without children who run for office? How do voters respond to maternal appeals by female candidates (and male candidates as well)? And are women well-positioned to frame their candidacies around "fighting for families"? Our discussion offers new directions for researchers to explore as we move toward a clearer under-standing of how motherhood fits into the gender stereotype literature.

To answer these questions, we review research on the possible effects that motherhood—broadly construed as both candidates' parental status and the use of familial or maternal appeals in campaigns—may have on women's political candidacies. We also discuss how men may be affected by a recent political context in which families and motherhood are politicized (Deason, Greenlee, and Langner 2015; Elder and Greene 2013; Greenlee 2014). To do this, we explore how divergent findings in the gender stereotyping literature may mask the impact of motherhood on women's political candidacies. We review how motherhood and maternal messages are used in electoral politics and then discuss the effects of those appeals, introducing some new findings on the use of family advocacy messages and how they affect evaluations of candidates. Taking stock of the current research, we show that there is a lack of congruence among research on motherhood, maternal messages, and candidate evaluations. We argue that these inconsistencies may be due to contemporary politicization of motherhood that exists in the public sphere and political discourse. In order to fully understand the complex dynamics of gender on the campaign trail, we must understand how gender stereotypes may be in flux in this contemporary period.

Gender Stereotypes and the Role of Motherhood

As Bauer discusses in the previous chapter, women running for public office can face disadvantages because their perceived traits and expertise do not match with the demands of a masculine job; yet, some voters may *not* rely on gender stereotypes when evaluating candidates. Similarly, some electoral contexts may activate gender stereotypes, whereas other contexts may not. In some cases, gender stereotypes may serve as an advantage to female candidates, particularly when they tap into notions about women as feminists or mothers and activate traits and issue expertise that some voters value (Bell and Kaufmann 2015; Herrnson et al. 2003; Plutzer and Zipp 1996; Stalsburg 2010).

One optimistic interpretation of research on gender stereotypes is that barriers to women in the minds of the electorate are beginning to fall, or that the impact of gender stereotypes is quite limited. Another possibility is that we are unable to fully understand the contemporary impact of gender stereotypes on the campaign trail because the research arises from different methodological approaches and is developing during a time in which women's status in the political sphere is in flux. As we have argued elsewhere (Deason, Greenlee, and Langner 2015), the role of motherhood in the political sphere and in public discourse is changing such that motherhood has become more politicized in recent years. These three variables—methodological approaches, women's political status, and the politicization of motherhood—require that we refrain from making any concrete conclusions about whether and how gender stereotypes shape evaluations of women candidates.

In this chapter, we argue that the politicization of motherhood can explain some of the inconsistencies in the literature on gender stereotypes. In short,

voters may now see motherhood, once the embodiment of feminine characteristics that were incompatible with leadership roles, as a positive component of
female candidacies. Thus, the tender and tough associations that candidates such
as Sarah Palin have tied to motherhood might be driving—and responding to—a
shifting perspective on the competencies and leadership traits associated with
motherhood.

The Meanings of Motherhood

Scholars have conceptualized and operationalized motherhood in the campaign
and candidate literature in three different ways. First, scholars have conceptualized
motherhood as the parental status of female candidates and/or the degree of
emphasis that women place on their children. This has been operationalized as
candidate profiles mentioning that the candidate has children and offering visual
presentations with their children. The second way in which traits connected to
motherhood are present in this research is through the maternal nature of candidates' political appeals. Maternal appeals are the campaign images and words used
to emphasize a candidate's commitment to maternal values (a morality grounded
in love within the home, connections to others, an ethic of care) or to show that
the candidate possesses traits that are stereotypically associated with mothers (e.g.,
warmth, kindness, selflessness; Deason 2011). Female and male candidates can make
these appeals; thus, this representation of maternal characteristics is not tethered to
women. Candidates without children can also make these appeals, thereby separat-
ing out a maternal self-presentation from a candidate's parental status. The final
way that ideas connected to motherhood and maternity are represented is through
the invocation of family themes on the campaign trail. Specifically, we consider
candidate claims that she or he will advocate for families (Greenlee and Langner
2013). This third presentation is an assertion of policy concerns and expertise
separate from a candidate's own parental status and gender.

I'm a Mom: Women and Parental Status on the Campaign Trail

In the past decade, several female candidates and officeholders have brought discussion of their children into the public light through campaign ads (former
Senator Blanche Lincoln, D-AR, ran television ads in her 1998 campaign that
featured her husband caring for her young children), press coverage (Senator
Kirsten Gillbrand, D-NY, talked about her pregnancies in a Vogue magazine piece
and posed for a photo with her young sons, reading to them on her Senate office
floor), and in national speeches (Representative Cathy McMorris-Rodgers, R-WA,
gave the GOP response to State of the Union in 2014 and in doing so, spoke of
her children, including her baby who she gave birth to just eight weeks earlier;
McMorris-Rodgers 2014; Van Meter 2010). These women in the political spotlight

with their young children contrast with research that shows women who enter into politics are less likely to have children than men who enter politics (Carroll 1989; Thomas 2002). When mothers do run for office, they tend to do so when their children are older, whereas men often have young children (Carroll 1989; Dodson 1997; Thomas 2002). For example, when Representative Paul Ryan (R-WI) accepted the Speaker of the House position on the condition that he would be able to return home on the weekends to spend time with his family, it was his insistence on having time with his young children—not his status as a father—that was noteworthy (Terkel 2015).

The question of whether one's status as a mother will help or hurt a political candidate has been addressed in experimental studies using fictional candidates. Stalsburg (2010) found that female candidates who are mothers attract higher levels of support than female candidates without children. Stalsburg (2010) also found that mother candidates were seen as particularly competent on issues related to children. Despite the expertise that they are seen to bring to some policy areas, mother candidates were also seen as having less time to devote to the job than were female candidates without children. Interestingly, for male candidates, having children lowered voters' evaluations, such that men without children were seen as stronger candidates than men with children. However, much like female candidates with children, men with children were seen as being better equipped to legislate on childcare and children's issues.

Bell and Kaufmann (2015) found similar results in another survey experiment. A fictional unmarried female candidate without children was disadvantaged relative to a married mother. The bias against the unmarried, childless female candidate, who violated traditional expectations for women, was particularly pronounced among respondents with a more traditional gender ideology. The authors argued that because her family situation violated social norms, the single and childless female candidate primed gender ideologies that may otherwise be inconsequential. Campbell, Childs, and Cowley (2015) similarly found that women without children were viewed less favorably than men with children, although their design did not allow them to compare evaluations of women with children to those of women without children.

Taken together, these studies suggest that female candidates should no longer feel compelled to hide their children on the campaign trail. But, two factors may moderate the relationship between parental status and candidate evaluation; these include respondents' level of support for traditional motherhood and respondent partisan identification. Bell and Kaufman (2015) found that the greater the support that individuals had for traditional motherhood the lower the level of support for mother candidates. They measured motherhood beliefs with statements about whether men should be "the achiever" while women should manage the home and children, and whether working mothers can have warm and secure relationships with their children (8). They found that respondents with traditional views of motherhood had much more negative evaluations of a female candidate who was described as single and childless compared to an identical candidate for whom there was no information about her marital or parental status. The reverse was true for respondents who held very progressive views of gender and motherhood. This study concludes that instead of a "mommy penalty," women without children face a potential penalty (from conservative voters) or potential advantage (from liberal voters).

The partisan identification of voters may also influence the evaluation of candidates based on gender and parental status. An experiment conducted by the Pew Research Center in 2008, weeks before Sarah Palin was selected as the vice presidential nominee, found that Republicans were significantly less likely to support a fictional female congressional candidate with two young children than a fictional male congressional candidate with two young children. Democrats, on the other hand, were significantly more likely to vote for a mother with small children than a father with small children. This difference was likely driven by Democratic women, as their relative support for the mother candidate was high. In contrast, among Democratic men, there was no difference in support for the mother and father candidates. These results suggest that party may moderate the impact of parenthood on voter candidate evaluations, such that Republicans may penalize mothers of young children who run for major office, while Democrats (particularly Democratic women) penalize fathers or reward mothers.

Of course, these results emerge from a study that took place before Sarah Palin's rise and the creation of her "Mama Grizzly" moniker in 2010. Republican support for her vice presidential candidacy may have shifted Republican voters' level of support for mothers running for office. Burrell (2014) suggested that GOP voters were more open to female candidates with young children based on her examination of women who ran for the House in 2010. In the more recent study by Bell and Kaufmann (2015), there was no difference between Democratic and Republican respondents in their support for candidates with or without children, and no evidence of a "mommy penalty." Thus, we do not know if partisan identification operates consistently as a moderating variable in the evaluation of candidates in the contemporary political environment. However, Bauer (2015b) found that individuals without partisan attachments were more likely to employ gender stereotypes when evaluating candidates and that this led to lower levels of support for female candidates. Perhaps intensity of partisan attachment, rather than the candidate's party label, shapes voters' reactions to mothers on the campaign trail.

Research also suggests that candidates make strategic decisions about whether to highlight or hide their status as a parent. Studies on the appearance of family in campaigns found that male candidates were more likely than female candidates to feature family in their ads and campaign websites. Bystrom et al. (2004) found that in gubernatorial and Senate candidate websites, women were less likely to display photos of their own children than were men, though these differences did not reach statistical significance.[1] Stalsburg and Kleinberg's (2015) examination of 324 House and Senate candidates in competitive races in 2008 and 2010 showed that compared to father candidates, mothers were less likely to showcase their children or highlight their status as a mother on their campaign websites. Thomas and Lambert (2015) examined the websites of members of the Canadian Parliament (MPs) in 2011 and came to similar conclusions, finding that male MPs were more likely to include photos of their families (about 14 percent of the male MPs) than were women (about 4 percent of female MPs).[2] Thomas and Lambert also found that party label may condition whether or not MPs display photos of their children; conservative men were more likely than men and women from other parties to display their children. While female MPs generally did not offer visuals of their children, those who did were from the Conservative Party (11–12).

Stalsburg and Kleinberg (2015) suggested that these gender differences in strategic presentation of family emerge from concerns over the activation of gender stereotypes. The presence of negative stereotypes of mothers in leadership could potentially hurt female candidates, which might motivate women to divert focus from their families. If one's status as a mother activates an association with traits that are seen as a mismatch with the "masculine" traits associated with leadership—as Bauer highlights in the previous chapter—voters may be less likely to support these women. Thus, women in the political arena may prefer to keep the spotlight off their children, while men may not be worried.

In contrast, Campbell, Childs, and Cowley (2015) found that in 2013, male and female members of Parliament in the UK were equally likely to mention their children in their campaign websites. Although these results do not comport with those of Stalsburg and Kleinberg (2015) and Thomas and Lambert (2015), important differences across the studies may explain the differential findings. First, Stalsburg and Kleinberg looked at campaign websites of both winners and losers of competitive congressional races, whereas Campbell and colleagues and Thomas and Lambert looked at the websites of candidates who ultimately won their elections and did not consider factors such as competitiveness of the race. Second, cross-national differences may compel women in the U.S. and Canada to hide their children, whereas women in the UK feel free to display them openly.[3] Finally, Stalsburg and Kleinberg's analyses included regression models with controls while the other studies offer descriptive analyses. Thus, although these three studies ask similar questions, it is difficult to assess what factors are responsible for their differing conclusions: national context, inclusion criteria, method of analysis, or other factors.

Summary: Women and Parental Status

Do voters evaluate mothers who run for office more favorably than women without children? The research discussed here suggests that the answer is yes. Mothers do not appear to face a penalty from would-be voters when running for office, but women *without* children may be penalized. Future research might determine the source, but it may be because childless women violate expectations of what a woman "should be"—or it may be due to the perception that women without children lack the policy expertise on family and child-related issues that mothers are assumed to have.

As Bauer points out in the prior chapter, not all individuals will utilize gender stereotypes when evaluating candidates. Similarly, not all individuals are equally likely to penalize childless women who run for office (e.g., Bell and Kauffman 2015). While it is unclear if partisan identification plays a role in determining how voters view female candidates with and without children, to the extent that support for traditional motherhood overlaps with party identification or political ideology, Republican or conservative women who run for office might be more vulnerable to the not-a-mommy penalty.

The Impact of a Maternal Appeal

Another line of research has conceptualized a broader, more diffuse "maternal appeal"; verbal statements or visual images that indicate a candidate's commitment to maternal values or highlight a candidate's maternal traits (Deason 2011, 2014a). Research in psychology indicates that compared to women in general, mothers are stereotyped as particularly warm, loving, and selfless (Deason 2014b; Ganong and Coleman 1995). Deason (2011) makes the argument that when candidates invoke these stereotypical qualities, they knowingly or unknowingly reference motherhood. Maternal appeals may also call attention to a candidate's personal experiences with family, drawing on notions of the moral sphere of the private home that date back to late 1700s (Kerber 1980, 1995). Twenty-first-century mothers are associated with a set of practical skills assumed to come from mothering activities, such as multi-tasking, mediating conflicts, and managing a family budget (Warner 2010). Thus, candidates can use maternal appeals to make an argument that skills and qualities associated with mothers in the private sphere are applicable and desirable.

Maternal appeals are linked to stereotypes of mothers, but they are distinct from one's status as a mother, and can be used by both male and female candidates. For example, in the 2008 presidential campaign, Barack Obama and Joe Biden emphasized their emotional connection to their children and the active role they play in caregiving. In a debate, Biden disputed the implicit belief that, "because I'm a man, I don't know what it's like to raise two kids alone" (Vice Presidential Debate 2 October 2008). Charlie Baker, during his Massachusetts gubernatorial campaign, similarly showcased his active involvement in intimate forms of childcare closely associated with mothers—bathing, feeding, and bedtime rituals (Levenson 2014). Although it might seem more natural to refer to maternal appeals by male candidates as *paternal* appeals, the term "maternal appeal" refers to the stereotypical qualities associated with mothers—warmth, nurturance, and selflessness. In contrast, stereotypical qualities associated with the father's traditional breadwinner role carry a distinct set of meanings.

Candidates who are not parents can also claim the benefits of motherhood using a maternal appeal. After Sarah Palin's "Mama Grizzly" ad went viral in 2008,[4] she bestowed the title "Mama Grizzly" on a handful of candidates to indicate their commitment to "commonsense conservative values." Capitalizing on the popular idea that mothers have special skills that can be useful in the political domain, Palin claims in the video that conservative women are coming together as a force for change because "moms just kind of know when something's wrong." The video does present a gender-specific version of a maternal appeal, with its references to women as a "herd of pink elephants," but notably, some women included did not have children.

The impact of maternal appeals has been examined directly in an experimental study in which Deason (2011) varied the gender, partisan identification, and maternal content of a candidate's message in a fictional campaign ad. The maternal appeal included two elements: The candidate appeared with his or her children and was endorsed by a mother and her children. In the maternal condition, the candidate also discussed issues in terms of family and children and used family to justify his or her political positions. In contrast, in the control conditions, the candidate appeared with other adults, was endorsed by a woman who appeared alone rather than with her children, and used neutral language. Results indicated that maternal appeals offered benefits to male candidates, improving perceptions of their competence to handle feminine issues such as education and health care. By contrast, maternal appeals were detrimental for female candidates, perhaps because they made female candidates seem a particularly poor fit for the masculine role of a political leader (see Eagly and Karau 2002).

In another experimental study, Bauer (2015a) did not focus directly on motherhood but used a similar method, manipulating "feminine traits" in a description of a fictional candidate's campaign. The study was administered via Amazon's Mechanical Turk. In the experimental conditions, Bauer (2015a) described a male or female candidate as "nurturing" and "compassionate"—key feminine qualities, but also consistent with the notion of a maternal appeal. As in Deason's (2011) work, results of the study indicated that a campaign that highlights stereotypical feminine traits can reduce voter support for women candidates. Bauer (2015a) reasoned that campaign ads that highlight traits that activate gender stereotypes "may lead voters to see women as weak, emotional, and more fit for motherhood than the rigors of serving in Congress" (704).

Bauer (2015a) and Deason (2011) also examined the impact of maternal appeals in real campaigns. Using data from the Wisconsin Advertising Project, each study selected different subsets of the campaign ads for coding: Bauer (2015a) included positive ads sponsored by incumbent candidates that appeared in the last eight weeks of the 2000 and 2004 U.S. House elections, whereas Deason (2011) analyzed data from the 2003 and 2004 U.S. House, U.S. Senate, and gubernatorial elections. The studies also diverged in their method of coding. Consistent with Deason's (2011) broader definition of maternal appeals, ads were coded as maternal when they focused on family and/or family roles (e.g., "as a wife, mother, and sister"), used family experiences as a justification for policy positions, or portrayed the candidates as having maternal traits such as "understanding," "empathetic," and "helpful." Bauer (2015a) coded the ads for a narrower set of feminine traits: "caring," "family-oriented," "honest," and "focused on values." Despite differences, both studies replicated the experimental results in real election contexts. In each study, ads with a maternal emphasis harmed women's chances of winning the election, and provided an advantage for men.

Based on these studies, placing emphasis on feminine qualities like motherhood appears to offer a greater benefit to male than to female candidates. However, Deason's (2011) research also indicated that the relationship between maternal appeals and candidate evaluation is dependent on a candidate's partisan identification. In particular, maternal appeals were uniquely damaging to evaluations of female Republican candidates. When the candidate was portrayed as a female Republican who used maternal appeals, voters from both parties rated her less competent and were less likely to vote for her, relative to her non-maternal counterpart. In contrast, the female Democrat was rated equally competent, and was equally likely to receive votes, regardless of whether she used maternal appeals. Meanwhile, male Republicans were able to benefit from maternal appeals on only one dimension of evaluation: perceptions of their competence on such feminine issues as education, health care, and social programs. Party-based differences in the effects of maternal appeals may reflect differences in how the parties approach gender and family. Maternal messages may be consistent with the expectations that voters already have for Democratic candidates. In contrast, female Republicans who make maternal appeals may be evaluated particularly harshly due to their party's more conservative views on the gendered division of social roles.

The results of this study also raise questions about why female Republicans would choose to emphasize motherhood in their campaigns. In her vice presidential campaign and her Mama Grizzly endorsements, Palin used maternal language to frame traditionally Republican issues such as small government, and to advance an image of conservative women as tough and sensible. Although the results of the studies above suggest that maternal appeals by Republican women will be ineffective, another possibility is that maternal appeals can be an effective tool for female Republicans, if they are balanced with messages about toughness and an emphasis on Republican issues.

Deason (2014a) tested the possibility that Mama Grizzly-style themes of strength and common sense would mitigate the negative impact of maternal appeals for female Republicans. Undergraduate student participants watched a campaign ad featuring a female Republican candidate in which the presence of maternal themes was experimentally manipulated. The ad was modeled after the campaigns of female Republican candidates endorsed by Sarah Palin in the 2010 midterm elections. When balanced with Republican themes of strength and toughness, a maternal appeal did not produce the same negative evaluation of the female Republican candidate shown in the studies described above. Thus, the way that motherhood is highlighted in a campaign message, and whether the maternal appeal is accompanied by references to other personal traits or party-linked issues, is also likely to influence levels of electoral support.

Psychological characteristics of the audience are also likely to moderate the relationship between a maternal appeal and voters' response. Deason (2014a) examined authoritarianism, a general preference for social conformity and deference to authority that is associated with gender traditionalism (Altemeyer 1996; Duncan, Peterson, and Winter 1997; Stenner 2005), and gender schematicity, a tendency to assimilate incoming information into masculine and feminine categories (Bem 1981). Results of an experiment indicated that individuals *low* in authoritarianism and those who were *gender-aschematic* evaluated a female candidate more positively when her campaign ad did not include a maternal appeal. Such voters appear to prefer a message from a female candidate that does not feed into gender stereotypes.

Bauer's (2015b) study of "stereotype reliance," described in the previous chapter, found that in the context of a political campaign, attention to politics, degree of partisan commitment, and other demographic factors influenced the degree to which a given voter will rely on stereotypes to evaluate an individual female candidate. Because maternal appeals draw on stereotypes of mothers, maternal appeals may also be more impactful among voters who are less informed and attentive and thus, more likely to use other, nonpolitical cues to form an evaluation of a candidate. More broadly, both Bauer (2015b) and Deason (2014a) found that individual-level characteristics influence the public's response to candidates.

Summary: Impact of a Maternal Appeal

Research on maternal appeals indicates that an emphasis on the traits and qualities associated with mothers offers a greater benefit to male than to female candidates. Female candidates who made maternal appeals—particularly Republicans—were evaluated more negatively than their non-maternal counterparts, whereas male candidates—Republican men in particular—were seen as more competent to handle feminine issues when they made a maternal appeal. Notably, these results diverge from the findings of research on the effects of parental status described in the previous section: Women with children did not face a penalty at the polls relative to their childless counterparts, and men without children were seen as stronger candidates than those who were fathers. In order to untangle the impact of parental status from that of a maternal appeal, the psychological processes that underlie these effects must be further investigated. They may well defy the common wisdom that guides female candidates' hesitation to appear with their families: Perhaps *being a mother* is a safe and even advantageous electoral position, but *running as a mother* is a risk women should avoid.

Yet, this body of work also shows there are few hard and fast guidelines for campaign strategy. In addition to a candidate's gender and partisan affiliation, the style of the maternal message and psychological characteristics of the audience are also likely to shape the effect of maternal appeals on candidate evaluation. By carefully considering the balance of the maternal with other themes, and targeting the right voters, candidates of both genders may be able to use maternal appeals to their advantage.

Fighting for Families

A third way in which candidates invoke motherhood in a campaign is via a claim of advocacy on behalf of families. In 2012, Democratic Senate candidate Elizabeth Warren launched her campaign with an internet video stating that she wanted "Massachusetts families to have a level playing field" ("Who I Am") and went on to air TV ads in which she promised to "work her heart out" for families ("For All Our Families"). Indeed, one of the hallmarks of Warren's campaign was her promise to fight for middle-class families (Criss 2015).

Warren's emphasis on families is notable, but not unique. Family-based political appeals have been ubiquitous in American politics in recent decades (Elder and Greene 2013; Greenlee 2014). The divergence of the two major political parties on women's issues, coupled with an increased emphasis on female voters, has contributed to both parties' strategy of focusing on motherhood in order to attract women's votes (Greenlee 2014). Less is known about how family-based appeals—particularly a woman placing herself in a maternal advocacy role—shape voters' responses. It is possible that gender stereotypes lead voters to perceive female candidates as more competent advocates for families.

Greenlee and Langner (2013) examined whether references to gender-related and parent-related advocacy offered female candidates an advantage among female voters. In an experimental study, they examined the effect of fictional male and female candidates using "fighting for parents," "fighting for women," or "fighting for citizens" (control group) advocacy claims. Four hundred female voters from Ohio read a short fictional online newspaper article about the election of a candidate, Jennifer or John Hull, to the Senate. The penultimate paragraph of the newspaper article stated that he/she would pay attention to the needs of members of a particular group (women, parents, or citizens). The gender (male/female) and the partisan affiliation (Republican/Democrat) of the candidate were also manipulated in the article. Participants were randomly assigned to one of 12 conditions and rated how likable, competent, empathetic, and "like me" the candidate appeared.

Female candidates were perceived as more likable and more competent when they claimed to fight for parents, but there was no difference on these measures

TABLE 11.1 Candidate Evaluations by Candidate Gender and Group Prime

	Likability Female Candidate	Likability Male Candidate	Competence Female Candidate	Competence Male Candidate	Like Me Female Candidate	Like Me Male Candidate	Empathetic Female Candidate	Empathetic Male Candidate
Parent	.10**	−.06	.08**	−.08**	.08*	−.07	.09*	−.07
Prime	(.04)	(.04)	(.04)	(.04)	(.05)	(.05)	(.04)	(.05)
Woman	.06	−.06	.06	−.08★★	.02	−.07	.10**	−.06
Prime	(.04)	(.04)	(.04)	(.04)	(.05)	(.05)	(.05)	(.05)
PID	.08**	.04	.10**	.06*	.12**	.12**	.08**	.07*
Match	(.03)	(.03)	(.03)	(.03)	(.05)	(.04)	(.04)	(.04)
Constant	.61	.74	.51	.61	.46	.51	.53	.62
R2	.074	.022	.068	.049	.069	.058	.046	.037
S.E.	.203	.213	.205	.202	.249	.263	.247	.240
N	183	178	183	176	183	177	183	178

Source: Greenlee and Langner 2013, Community Sample of Female Respondents from Ohio

between when they advocated for women or citizens. In contrast, male candidates did not receive a boost in likeability when mentioning fighting for parents and were perceived as less competent when mentioning fighting for parents or women (see Table 11.1). Interestingly, female respondents were favorable towards female candidates who advocated for parents, regardless of their own parental status. They did not, however, respond positively to male candidates who did the same.

These findings suggest that parent and family-linked issues are "female" issues, and that male candidates are unable to successfully trespass in that policy territory. In particular, there are benefits for female candidates who advocate for parents. However, although female candidates are seen as more empathetic when they advocate for women, they do not reap benefits in the other dimensions of candidate evaluation. In contrast, male candidates who advocate for parents do not reap the same benefits as their female counterparts, and may in fact harm their candidacies—at least among female voters.

Summary: The Meanings of Motherhood

In this chapter we asked if the increased focus on motherhood in American politics marks a shift in how women with children are evaluated when they run for office. Are they viewed favorably? What role does the gender of the candidate play in this? And how do voters evaluate candidates who claim to act as advocates for families, but who do not overtly emphasize feminine or maternal traits?

The answers to these questions paint a complicated picture. First, there is a mismatch between what candidates do and what voters think when it comes to presenting one's parental status (and children) publically. Although it appears that voters look more kindly on women who have children versus women who do not, research that focuses on whether candidates and officeholders mention or showcase their children suggests that women across the board do not do this.

Second, voters may be more supportive of mothers than non-mothers who run for office, but maternal appeals do not appear to help female candidates. These appeals—characterized as statements or visual images that emphasize a candidate's warmth, loving nature, and selflessness—appear to activate gender stereotypes and highlight a perceived mismatch between motherhood and leadership. The negative impact of maternal appeals is seen for Republican women in particular, though when paired with an emphasis on strength and toughness, these negative effects wash away. Maternal appeals benefit men, however, likely because there is no perceived mismatch between masculine leadership traits and the maternal traits that men exhibit in these appeals.

Finally, a third disjuncture is seen in how maternal appeals versus family advocacy messages resonate with would-be voters. While maternal appeals can benefit men and harm women, candidate claims to "fight for parents" appear to benefit female candidates and harm male candidates. Why the disconnect? There are substantial differences between the concepts of maternal appeal and family advocacy. Maternal appeals are based on feminine traits and likely prime gender stereotypes, while family advocacy messages do not tap into gender stereotypes about traits (though they may tap into stereotypes about policy expertise). Moreover, the samples used in these two studies (a student sample of men and women vs. a community sample of women) might also contribute to the conflicting results, as age and parental status—two factors that differ across samples—may be moderating variables.

Based on the results presented here, our advice to women currently on the campaign trail would be: If you have children, make it clear that you are a mother, but do not include maternal appeals in your campaign. Rather, say that you will fight for families, and leave it at that.

Unanswered Questions and New Directions

We, along with others, suggest that the impact of motherhood is complex and nuanced. Moreover, the findings in this small, yet growing, body of research diverge in many respects. Three factors—methodological approaches, women's political status, and the politicization of motherhood—contribute to the divergent nature of these findings. These three factors are highly variable, which means that differences in findings could be the result of variation in just one area or all three. How can we navigate these complicating factors?

One solution is to more fully understand how gender stereotypes—and specifically stereotypes of female politicians—look in the contemporary era. Schneider and Bos (2014) begin to do this, showing that stereotypes of female politicians are not clearly or fully defined in the minds of voters. We must explicitly ask how voters see motherhood as a part of—or perhaps as a counter to—stereotypes of female politicians. Motherhood might highlight feminine characteristics that are seen counter to masculine views of leadership. Or, they may give women a socially acceptable space in which to present themselves as "tough." Issues of intersectionality should be addressed as part of this research agenda. Does motherhood invoke the same characteristics for women of different racial groups who run for office? By answering all of these questions, we will better understand how voters see women.

A second solution is to replicate existing studies in this contemporary period, across different political domains, and with comparable methods. After developing a firmer hold on the nature of gender stereotypes, we need studies that allow for comparisons of how these stereotypes work across different levels of government and different political cultures. Research has shown in the past that women are seen as better equipped to serve in some elected roles than others (Fox and Oxley 2003; Kahn 1996). How do gender stereotypes that account for motherhood function differently across elected offices? Are female candidates who emphasize their role as a mother seen as more suitable for some offices over others? For example, might a mother be seen as a stronger candidate in a gubernatorial race that focused on domestic policies, such as education and health care, than in a U.S. Senate race where the economy might be a more salient issue? Future research agendas should pursue questions in multiple (replicating) studies in order to establish clear patterns.

Third, we must think carefully about how motherhood, parenthood, and maternal cues are conceptualized in this collection of research, and the implications of these conceptualizations for the findings produced by these studies. Some concepts, such as maternal appeals, may be more likely to activate gender stereotypes than other concepts (such as simply mentioning that a candidate is a parent), thus we might expect stereotypes to play a greater role in ultimately shaping voter responses. Indeed, a study that compared the effects of these different conceptualizations could be useful.

As Bauer (2015b) and Deason (2014a) note, not all voters are the same. Research that examines how individual differences shape responses to political appeals that highlight motherhood or maternal roles—both established constructs like authoritarianism and gender schematicity as well as new constructs like stereotype reliance (Bauer 2015b) and separate spheres ideology[5] (Miller and Borgida 2016). These investigations would extend prior work by specifically examining whether candidate emphasis on motherhood or maternal messages exacerbates the impact of stereotypes on evaluations. Moreover, looking at the role of separate spheres ideology might help us better understand when and why highlighting maternal roles might backfire for female candidates, particularly those from conservative parties.

Other important questions remain unanswered. How does the politicization of motherhood affect perceptions of male candidates who highlight parental roles and family themes? Though we have some insights into how voters respond to men who make maternal appeals (Deason 2011) or vow to advocate for families (Greenlee and Langner 2013), it is unclear how fatherhood fits in with stereotypes of male political leadership. Future research might attempt to define and investigate a "paternal appeal" in which candidates emphasize traditional characteristics of fathers. Such an appeal may include fathers' role as provider and protector, and possibly more nuanced aspects of fathering, such as support in competitive areas like athletics (Coakley 2006). A more systematic investigation into these questions would shed light upon how the contemporary politicization of family (Elder and Greene 2012; Greenlee 2014) might be shaping voter responses to male candidates who highlight their familial role.

Finally, as we begin to understand the implications of motherhood on the campaign trail, we also must consider other gendered familial roles. For example, is grandmotherhood the same as motherhood when it comes to understanding voter responses? Can women (and men) highlight other family roles in their campaigns to convey to voters positive aspects of their candidacies? Or is motherhood (or fatherhood) distinct in what it communicates to voters? Certainly the public discourse around highly visible political figures like Hillary Clinton and her role as a grandmother (and a presidential candidate) can and should be informed by scholarly research (Beinert 2015).

To fully understand women's political experiences, we must understand how motherhood affects both perceptions of candidates and leaders, but also how these women present themselves. As we have shown in this chapter, the tremendous variation in current research is due to the lack of a clear theoretical framework on what motherhood means and why it matters in the political arena. We call on scholars to engage in theory building exercises in order to clarify and better organize our understanding of motherhood, gender stereotypes, and political campaigns. In engaging in this important work, we should draw on the rich scholarship on motherhood from other disciplines, including sociology, history, and women's and gender studies. In doing so, we will advance our knowledge of gender and politics in a productive and cohesive way.

Notes

1. A possible confounding factor is that women at this level of politics are less likely to have children who they might feature in their ads. Bystrom et al. (2004) found that women were more likely to feature children who were unrelated to them in their ads, possibly to compensate for childlessness.
2. Thomas and Lambert (2015) also found that over 70 percent of male MPs were parents, compared to 55 percent of female MPs. Fewer than 12 percent of all Canadian MPs displayed photographs of families on their official websites, though such photos are more common in official constituent communications such as holiday cards.
3. Of note, men in Canada are also reluctant to offer photos of their children (Thomas and Lambert 2015).
4. Available at www.youtube.com/watch?v=fsUVL6ciK-c.

5. The separate spheres ideology (SSI) is a new psychological construct that captures beliefs that gender differences are innate, and not culturally or situationally created; that innate differences lead men and women to participate willingly in different spheres in life; and that gender differences in public and private spheres is natural and desirable (Miller and Borgida 2016, 3).

References

Altemeyer, Bob. 1996. *The Authoritarian Specter.* Cambridge, MA: Harvard University Press.

Bauer, Nichole M. 2015a. "Emotional, Sensitive, and Unfit for Office? Gender Stereotype Activation and Support Female Candidates." *Political Psychology* 36: 691–708.

Bauer, Nichole M. 2015b. "Who Stereotypes Female Candidates? Identifying Individual Differences in Feminine Stereotype Reliance." *Politics, Groups, and Identities* 3: 94–110.

Beinart, Peter. 2015. "Hillary Clinton: Grandmother in Chief." *The Atlantic.* Accessed March 15, 2016. http://www.theatlantic.com/politics/archive/2015/02/grandmother-in-chief/385238/.

Bell, Melissa A., and Karen M. Kaufmann. 2015. "The Electoral Consequences of Marriage and Motherhood: How Gender Traits Influence Voter Evaluations of Female Candidates." *Journal of Women, Politics & Policy* 36: 1–21.

Bem, Sandra. 1981. "Gender Schema Theory: A Cognitive Account of Sex-Typing." *Psychological Review* 88: 354–364.

Burrell, Barbara. 2014. *Gender in Campaigns for the U.S. House of Representatives.* Ann Arbor: University of Michigan Press.

Bystrom, Dianne G., Terry Robertson, Mary Christine Banwart, and Lynda Lee Kaid. 2004. *Gender and Candidate Communication.* New York: Routledge.

Campbell, Rosie, Sarah Childs, and Philip Cowley. 2015. "The Impact of Parental Status on Parliamentary Candidate Behaviour and Evaluations." Working Paper, London, UK. www.revolts.co.uk.

Carroll, Susan J. 1989. "The Personal Is Political: The Intersection of Private Lives and Public Roles among Women and Men in Elective and Appointive Office." *Women & Politics* 9: 51–67.

Coakley, Jay. 2006. "The Good Father: Parental Expectations and Youth Sports." *Leisure Studies* 25: 153–163.

Criss, Doug. 2015. "Elizabeth Warren: My 2016 Dream Candidate Fights for Middle-Class Families." *CNN Politics.* Accessed April 10, 2015. http://www.cnn.com/2015/04/10/politics/elizabeth-warren-interview/.

Deason, Grace. 2011. *Maternal Appeals in Politics: Their Effectiveness and Consequences.* Ph.D. Dissertation, University of Minnesota-Twin Cities.

Deason, Grace. 2014a. "Maternal Appeals in Political Campaigns: An Asset or a Liability for Female Candidates?" Paper Presented at the New Research on Gender in Political Psychology Conference, Wooster, OH, October 9–12.

Deason, Grace. 2014b. "With Child in Tow: Comparing Stereotypes of Women and Mothers." Paper Presented at the Society for the Psychological Study of Social Issues 10th Biennial Convention, Portland, OR, June 28–30.

Deason, Grace, Jill S. Greenlee, and Carrie A. Langner. 2015. "Mothers on the Campaign Trail: Implications of Politicized Motherhood for Women in Politics." *Politics, Groups, and Identities* 3: 133–148.

Dodson, Debra L. 1997. "Change and Continuity in the Relationship between Private Responsibilities and Public Officeholding: The More Things Change, the More They Stay the Same." *Policy Studies Journal* 25: 569–584.

Duncan, Lauren, Bill Peterson, and David Winter. 1997. "Authoritarianism and Gender Roles: Toward a Psychological Analysis of Hegemonic Relationships." *Personality and Social Psychology Bulletin* 23: 41–49.

Eagly, Alice H., and Steven Karau. 2002. "Role Congruity Theory of Prejudice toward Female Leaders." *Psychological Review* 109: 573–598.

Elder, Laurel, and Steven Greene. 2013. *The Politics of Parenthood: Causes and Consequences of the Politicization and Polarization of the American Family.* New York: SUNY Press.

Ferraro, Geraldine. 1984. "Ferraro's Acceptance Speech." *CNN Interactive.* Accessed March 15, 2016. http://www.cnn.com/ALLPOLITICS/1996/conventions/chicago/facts/famous. speeches/ferraro.84.shtml.

Fox, R. L., and Z. M. Oxley. 2003. "Gender Stereotyping in State Executive Elections: Candidate Selection and Success." *Journal of Politics* 65: 833–850.

Ganong, Lawrence H., and Marilyn Coleman. 1995. "The Content of Mother Stereotypes." *Sex Roles* 32: 495–512.

Greenlee, Jill S. 2014. *The Political Consequences of Motherhood.* Ann Arbor, MI: University of Michigan Press.

Greenlee, Jill S., and Carrie Langner. 2013. "Fighting for Families: Gender Stereotypes and Candidate Evaluations." Paper Presented at the Northeastern Political Science Association Annual Meeting, Philadelphia, PA, November 15–17.

Herrnson, Paul S., J. Celeste Lay, and Atiya Kai Stokes. 2003. "Women Running 'as Women': Candidate Gender, Campaign Issues, and Voter-Targeting Strategies." *The Journal of Politics* 65: 244–255.

Kahn, Kim Fridkin. 1996. *The Political Consequences of Being a Woman: How Stereotypes Influence the Conduct and Consequences of Political Campaigns.* New York: Columbia University Press.

Kerber, Linda. 1980. *Women of the Republic: Intellect and Ideology in Revolutionary America.* Chapel Hill, NC: University of North Carolina Press.

Kerber, Linda. 1995. "A Constitutional Right to be Treated Like American Ladies: Women and the Obligations of Citizenship." In *U.S. History as Women's History: New Feminist Essays,* edited by Linda Kerber, Alice Kessler-Harris, and Kathryn Kish Sklar. Chapel Hill: University of North Carolina Press, 17–35.

Levenson, Michael. 2014. "This Time Around, Baker's Wife Steps into Foreground." *The Boston Globe.* Accessed October 17, 2014. https://www.bostonglobe.com/metro/2014/ 10/26/out-front-and-behind-scenes-lauren-baker-key-part-her-husband-campaign-for-governor/XKYDmQ8RfMLGI6wA4YqTWJ/story.html.

McMorris-Rodgers, Cathy. 2014. "State of the Union GOP Response: Cathy McMorris Rodgers." *Politico.* Accessed January 28, 2014. http://www.politico.com/story/2014/01/ state-of-the-union-2014-cathy-mcmorris-gop-response-102772.

Miller, Andrea L., and Eugene Borgida. 2016. "The Separate Spheres Model of Gendered Inequality." *PLoS ONE* 11(1): e0147315. doi:10.1371/journal.pone.0147315.

Palin, Sarah. 2008. "Palin's Speech at the Republican National Convention." *The New York Times.* Accessed September 3, 2008. http://elections.nytimes.com/2008/president/ conventions/videos/transcripts/20080903_PALIN_SPEECH.html.

Pew Research Center. 2008. "Revisiting the Mommy Wars." Accessed March 15, 2016. http://www.pewsocialtrends.org/2008/09/15/revisiting-the-mommy-wars/.

Plutzer, Eric, and John F. Zipp. 1996. "Identity Politics, Partisanship, and Voting for Women Candidates." *Public Opinion Quarterly* 60: 30–57.

Schneider, Monica C., and Angela L. Bos. 2014. "Measuring Stereotypes of Female Politicians." *Political Psychology* 35: 245–266.

Stalsburg, Brittany L. 2010. "Voting for Mom: The Political Consequences of Being a Parent for Male and Female Candidates." *Politics & Gender* 6: 373–404.

Stalsburg, Brittany L., and Mona S. Kleinberg. 2015. "'A Mom First and a Candidate Second': Gender Differences in Candidates' Self-Presentation of Family." *Journal of Political Marketing*: 1–26.

Stenner, Karen. 2005. *The Authoritarian Dynamic.* Cambridge: Cambridge University Press.

Terkel, Amanda. 2015. "Paul Ryan Demands Family Time in His New Job: Many Americans Aren't So Lucky." *Huffington Post*. Accessed October 20, 2015. http://www.huffingtonpost.com/entry/paul-ryan-family-leave_us_5626efeae4b08589ef49a940.

Thomas, Melanee, and Lisa Lambert. 2015. "Private Mom vs. Political Dad? Communications of Parental Status in the 41st Canadian Parliament." Working Paper, University of Calgary, Calgary, Alberta, Canada.

Thomas, Sue. 2002. "The Personal Is Political: Antecedents of Gendered Choices of Elected Representatives." *Sex Roles* 47: 343–353.

Van Meter, Jonathan. 2010. "In Hillary's Footsteps: Kirsten Gillibrand." *Vogue Magazine*. Accessed March 15, 2016. http://www.vogue.com/865477/in-hillarys-footsteps-kirsten-gillibrand/.

Vice Presidential Debate. 2008. http://elections.nytimes.com/2008/president/debates/transcripts/vice-presidential-debate.html.

Warner, Judith. 2010. "The New Momism." *New York Times Magazine*, MM11.

Warren, Elizabeth, Elizabeth Warren for Senate. 2012a. "For All Our Families." Accessed March 15, 2016. http://elizabethwarren.com/video/for-all-our-families.

Warren, Elizabeth, Elizabeth Warren for Senate. 2012b. "Who I Am." Accessed March 15, 2016. http://elizabethwarren.com/video/elizabeth-warren-first-ad-who-i-am.

PART III

Women in Political Leadership

12

THE IMPACT OF GENDER IN THE LEGISLATIVE PROCESS

Brian Frederick and Shannon Jenkins

There are numerous examples of women attaining positions of power and influence in the legislative process over the last generation. Most notable among them is the ascent of U.S. Representative Nancy Pelosi to the position of Speaker of the U.S. House of Representatives in 2007. Following massive Democratic victories in the 2008 elections that strengthened the party's majority control of the U.S. House of Representatives, Speaker Pelosi announced one of her top legislative priorities: to expedite passage of the Lilly Ledbetter Fair Pay Act (Peters and Rosenthal 2010). This legislation overturned a Supreme Court decision[1] limiting the ability of victims of pay discrimination from filing claims against their employers (Sorok 2010). Enacting this law was a top priority of women's groups and leading female members of Congress. With her ability to control the agenda of the legislative process, Pelosi helped shepherd this legislation swiftly through the House. After receiving final passage in the U.S. Senate, the Lilly Ledbetter Fair Pay Act became the first major piece of legislation signed by President Barack Obama during his first term.

Considering there was unified government, it was likely the law would have been enacted at some point during President Obama's first two years. However, what also seems clear is that it would not have occupied such a prominent place on the legislative agenda so early without the concerned efforts of Pelosi and other female members of Congress (Peters and Rosenthal 2010). This example illustrates that the presence of female legislators can bring about tangible gains for the substantive representation of women; the question is whether this case is atypical or indicative of a larger pattern of women's impact.

In this chapter we outline theories accounting for gender differences in the behavior of male and female lawmakers with particular emphasis on psychology as a source for providing explanations for why they exist. Next we explore the general state of the research on gender differences in legislative bodies including surveys of the literature covering the U.S. House of Representatives, the U.S. Senate, and state legislatures with an eye toward identifying where such differences have manifested themselves and where they have not. We then turn to a discussion of recent studies successfully utilizing a psychological understanding of behavior to illuminate the gendered dimensions of legislative activity. While the barriers to studying elite behavior from a psychological perspective are many—including gaining the cooperation of elites, persuading scholars that the external validity of experimental research can apply to legislators, and the limited number of female legislators—we delineate future avenues for overcoming these hurdles and building on this scholarship to contribute to a greater understanding of the differences between male and female legislators and the reasons why those differences might exist.

Theories Explaining Gender Differences in Legislative Behavior

Prior to examining the empirical evidence on gender differences in legislative institutions, theoretical insights of psychology are useful in explaining why they exist in the first place. Differences in the way women and men act in legislatures may be attributable to gender role socialization, which leads women to focus on relations to others and on contextual factors when problem-solving (Jenkins 2012). As Lizotte notes in her chapter in this volume, Social Role Theory may help explain gender differences in the political behavior of women in the mass public *and* female elites; because women are socialized to inhabit different roles, they adopt traits, such as being compassionate and helpful, associated with these roles. These differences may spill over into the behavior of elected officeholders where "men tend to prioritize and think along the lines of rights, and the regulation or freedom of those rights, while women tend to be motivated by need for help and by their perceived ties others and to approach the world with empathy" (Karpowitz and Mendelberg 2015, 65).

However, as Swers (2002) notes, these differences may arise because voters anticipate that female legislators will act this way. As Bauer's chapter points out, voters have stereotypes that female candidates will be helpful and kind, and these perceptions may turn into expectations about how women ought to behave when they are in office; for example, voters might expect greater levels of constituency service from female legislators and this expectation might result in greater contact with those legislators, leading to observed differences between male and female lawmakers in time spent on casework.

Both of these explanations are consistent with observed difference between men and women on a variety of types of legislative behavior. For instance, female legislators are more prone to focus on social welfare issues where they are viewed as more capable than men (Fridkin and Kenney 2014). They might also work proactively to counter negative gender stereotypes by carving out reputations on national security policy in order to address the concerns of the voters—as well as their male colleagues—that they are not as well equipped to deal with military issues (Swers 2013).

Legislative leadership is another area where female legislators act differently than their male counterparts, paralleling findings in organizational and psychology research. For instance, Eagly and Carli (2007) identify numerous personality traits associated with enhanced leadership; they find that men and women are very similar when it comes to the traits commonly recognized as enhancing leadership, but that women score higher on other traits like compassion and ethics that are not typically included in leadership studies. Despite this apparent advantage for female leaders, people prefer male leaders to female leaders (Eagly 2007) and rate those leaders who share their social identity more highly (van Knippenberg 2011), which may disadvantage female leaders when it comes to achieving their goals in settings that are dominated by males, a situation that describes all U.S. legislatures. The challenges associated with incongruent social identity may be even greater for female leaders of color (Sanchez-Hucles and Davis 2010) or they may not (Livingston, Rosette, and Washington 2012), again highlighting the importance of intersectionality in studying female politicians.

The backlash effect against female leadership has been confirmed in other studies, stemming perhaps from a perceived conflict between perceptions about leadership roles and women's gender roles (Bos, Schneider, and Utz ND; Rudman et al. 2012), and has also been found in legislative settings. Leadership is typically seen as masculine, so rank and file legislators may find it difficult to assimilate their expectations for the behavior of women serving in these roles. Given that Wittmer and Bouche (2013) find a backlash effect against women's leadership on human trafficking, an issue that is typically seen as a women's issue, it is worth exploring whether there may be greater backlash effects when women assume leadership roles on issues that are not traditionally seen as women's issues.

Informational asymmetries between male and female legislators and their constituents can also provide explanatory leverage in understanding the role of gender in the legislative process (Butler 2014). Since male legislators are not as familiar with the problems of their female constituents, they may be less responsive and active on behalf of their concerns. Under this conceptualization of the legislative process, the higher priority female legislators assign to women's issues is a function of their personal knowledge about the experiences of their female constituents. Hence, the gender differences we observe in the legislative process are a reflection of informational disparities about women's issues that male legislators are less motivated to overcome. Male legislators are unwilling to invest the cognitive resources required to learn about and act upon issues of specific concern to women.

Gender socialization, gender stereotypes, backlash effects, and informational asymmetries offer compelling accounts of why gender differences emerge in legislative institutions. In most cases these theories complement rather than contradict one another. The challenge to assessing their explanatory power is designing an appropriate study that can capture the motivations of legislators in ways that go beyond traditional observational research. Thus, much of the research that we discuss focuses on documenting the differences between men and women rather than on explaining why these differences may emerge.

Gender in the U.S. House

While there are a variety of theoretical accounts of why male and female lawmakers may behave differently, in order to answer the subsequent question of whether the empirical evidence supports the proposition that such differences actually exist, scholars have turned to the U.S. House of Representatives. The primary reason for this disproportionate focus is based on the fact that the overwhelming majority of women who have served in the U.S. Congress have served in the House rather than the Senate (Frederick 2015) combined with the ease of data collection at the national level.

The extant research has sought to determine to what extent the gains in the descriptive representation of women have translated into the substantive representation of women's policy interests (Lawless 2015), concluding that female members of the House were more likely to reflect the interests of women in their roll call voting records (e.g., Swers and Rouse 2011). Whether looking at a variety of metrics indicating how liberal the representative is on the ideological spectrum or a specific set of issues substantively related to the concerns of women, a large body of scholarly inquiry documented that women tended to be more liberal than their male colleagues in each policy domain (Burrell 2014; Dodson 2006; Dolan 1997; Swers 2002). While this evidence buttresses the claim that male and female lawmakers in the House have meaningful differences on policy that are observable in their voting records, a handful of recent studies found that women were not significantly more liberal than their male colleagues (Frederick 2009, 2013, 2015; Schwindt-Bayer and Corbetta 2004; Simon and Palmer 2010).

Two major explanations account for these conflicting findings. Much of the earlier research focused on an era when the House was not as polarized as it is today. Frederick's (2009) analysis of the 99–109th Congresses indicated that women were consistently more liberal than their male counterparts in previous eras but this relationship began to diminish with an influx of conservative women elected to the House in the late 1990s. By the 108th and 109th Congresses the voting records of male and female representatives became virtually indistinguishable, a finding that has been confirmed in subsequent analyses. The second reason for the discrepancy is the quasi-experimental methodological approaches applied in some of the recent studies. Frederick (2015), Schwindt-Bayer and Corbetta (2004), and Simon and Palmer (2010) employed variations of the turnover model, which compared male and female House members representing the same district to determine whether differences in voting records exist. Essentially this approach provides for a "natural experiment," which holds constituency constant to determine the impact of party and gender on roll call voting patterns. This research found no differences in the voting records of House members with the exceptions of votes related to women's issues where male representatives were slightly less supportive of women's issues compared to the female representatives they replaced (Frederick 2015).

Of course, legislative behavior encompasses a wider range of activities than just voting on legislation; scholars have detailed a number of activities where gender differences manifest themselves in the House. Compared to roll call voting, many of these areas more consistently reveal patterns of gendered behavior because these activities are proactive rather than reactive, allowing for differences based on personal characteristics to be more readily discerned (Pearson and Dancey 2011a). For example, an examination of bill sponsorship activity in the 103rd and 104th Congresses revealed that both Republican and Democratic women were more likely to sponsor feminist and social welfare legislation than their male colleagues (Swers 2002). This relationship was confirmed when comparing representatives of the same party representing the same district in successive congresses (Gerrity, Osborn, and Mendez 2007). McDonald and O'Brien (2011) employed the quasi-experimental design examining pairs of House members representing districts in successive terms across a longer time span and found women are more likely to sponsor feminist legislation. Moreover, they find that this likelihood increases as the percentage of women in the House increases.

Pearson and Dancey (2011a) found that women spoke with greater frequency on the House floor overall and that the content of their speeches focused on issues of importance to women (Gerrity, Osborn, and Mendez 2007; Pearson and Dancey 2011b). Schulze (2013) documented that female House members were more likely to make spending requests related to women's issues, specifically related to violence against women and women's economic initiatives (Schulze and Hurvitz 2016), than their male colleagues.

Gender matters in the House as it applies to the substantive representation of women's concerns but also in the quality of the representation male and female representatives provide. Overall, women demonstrate more legislative effectiveness than men (Volden and Wiseman 2014). Anzia and Berry (2011) documented that female House members secured 9 percent more federal discretionary spending on average than their male colleagues in addition to sponsoring and cosponsoring bills at higher rates. These scholars suggested this relationship is a function of an election process that is more difficult for female candidates running for the House. Women running for the House tend to face more competitors in general (Lawless and Pearson 2008; Palmer and Simon 2012) and more high quality, experienced challengers (Milyo and Schosberg 2000). The end result is a selection effect where the female candidates that successfully navigate the electoral process turn out to be, on average, superior legislators to their male colleagues who get elected under less challenging circumstances. Volden, Wiseman, and Wittmer (2013) also confirmed that women are generally more successful legislators in the House but argued this relationship is conditioned by majority or minority party status. Examining the fate of House bills from the 93rd through 110th Congresses, minority women saw the legislation they sponsored get further than men while women in the majority did not.

Gender in the U.S. Senate

Scholarly inquiry into the role of gender in the legislative process has been more limited in the U.S. Senate, principally because of the small number of women elected or appointed to the Senate (Frederick 2010; Swers 2013). Historically, women have comprised approximately 1 percent of the senators who have ever served in the body. However, with the contingent of female senators climbing to 20 percent in the 113th and 114th Congresses, studies examining gender in the Senate's legislative process have begun to steadily proliferate. Overall, the evidence indicates that gender is a significant variable in many aspects of senatorial behavior but this relationship is conditional on party, issue domain, and the political context in which legislative behavior occurs.

In the most comprehensive research to date, Michele Swers (2007, 2013) analyzed whether legislative behavior among U.S. senators is gendered. By examining bill sponsorship patterns on women's issues in the 107th and 108th Congresses, she found that depending on the political context, female senators in both parties were more likely than male senators to sponsor such bills. Qualitative interviews with Senate staffers indicated these patterns are linked to the unique personal experiences that female senators bring to their jobs (Swers 2013). However, gendered role expectations factor in as well. Swers argues the Senate remains an institution dominated by masculine values and when issues of concerns to women do arise on the agenda, male party leaders frequently pressure their female colleagues to take the lead on "women's issues" such as education, health care, reproductive rights, and gender pay equity because they believe that voters will view them as better able to handle these issues. At the same time, female senators felt the need to address negative gender stereotypes about the ability of women to handle national security by demonstrating greater legislative activity in this area than their male colleagues.

In the Senate judicial confirmation process, female senators were more keenly aware of the policy implications for women if certain nominees were confirmed (Swers and Kim 2013). Women in the Senate demonstrated slightly less support for Bush Supreme Court nominees John Roberts and Samuel Alito than male senators in a series of confirmation votes. Female Democratic senators were more likely than their male Democratic colleagues to make references to women's issues in their speeches during the debate over these nominees. However, there were no such differences in the speech patterns of Senate Republicans. When examining the percentage of speeches on a wider array of issues given by senators in the 106th Congress, female senators were more likely to speak on issues related to women's health care, crimes, and family concerns (Osborn and Mendez 2010).

Roll call voting on legislation also occupies a large share of the scholarly attention given to the relationship between gender and senatorial behavior. In a series of studies, Frederick (2010, 2011, 2013, 2015) applied scrutiny to this relationship from a number of angles. A pooled cross-sectional study of Senate roll call voting from the 101st–109th Congresses found only minor gender differences among Senate Democrats but a significant gap in voting behavior between Senate Republicans (Frederick 2010). Female Senate Republicans were both more liberal overall than their male colleagues but also more significantly liberal on women's issues.

A comparison of the voting records of all House members and Senators in the 109th–111th Congresses on a standardized scale[2] found that male and female Democrats in the House and Senate were indistinguishable once constituency factors were accounted for (Frederick 2013). Similar patterns emerged among male and female House Republicans and male Senate Republicans. However, it appears that female Senate Republicans were the ideological outlier with voting records well to the left of their other GOP colleagues. It is still an open question whether this finding is merely a function of a small unrepresentative group of female senators like Snowe and Collins of Maine or a more systematic trend that will be confirmed with additional data points.

Frederick (2011, 2015) applied a quasi-experimental turnover model comparing the voting records of senators who have replaced one another representing the same state. Holding constituency constant revealed that female senators were more supportive of women's issues than the male senators they replaced and male senators were less supportive of women's issues than the female senators they replaced. While there were not sufficient cases of gender turnover within the parties to conduct meaningful analysis, this evidence does suggest that greater descriptive representation of women in the Senate does lead to greater substantive representation of women they serve.

Senators are also acutely aware of how gender stereotypes influence the public's views about the relative strengths and weaknesses of male and female officeholders, and in response, they consciously develop communications strategies that play up their advantages and neutralize their disadvantages with the public (Fridkin and Kenney 2014, 2015). While male senators tend to focus more on traditional male issues like national security policy, both male and female senators seek to counteract negative gendered trait stereotypes held by voters, with male senators emphasizing caring and empathy and female senators being more likely to send messages highlighting their experience and decisiveness.

While this recent uptick of scholarship dedicated to gender differences in senatorial behavior has expanded knowledge far beyond where it was even a decade ago, any effort to go further will continue to be plagued by the small sample of women serving the body, particularly Republican women. However, the key takeaway from this evidence indicates that female senators do provide greater substantive representation on average than their male colleagues.

Gender in State Legislatures

Research at the state level examining the differences between male and female legislators generally confirms what has been found at the national level. Scholars of state legislative behavior have confirmed that the policy preferences and legislative behaviors of female state legislators were different than their male counterparts. Female state legislators tended to be more liberal than their male counterparts (Carey, Neimi, and Powell 1998; Poggione 2004, 2006; Thomas 1994) and placed a greater priority on women's issues both in their beliefs and in their sponsorship of bills (Berkman and O'Connor 1993; Osborn 2012; Poggione 2006; Thomas 1994). They also had different views of their legislative role; they were more likely to see representing women's interests as an important part of their job (Reingold 1992; Thomas 1994) and saw themselves as working harder and being more attuned to constituency needs (Dolan and Ford 1998). Female state legislators spent more time in their districts and on constituency service, as compared to the male counterparts (Carey, Neimi, and Powell 1998).

While there are clear differences between male and female state legislators in some aspects of their work, there are fewer differences in other areas. Research found the roll call voting records of female state legislators were no different than those of their male counterparts when controlling for other factors such as ideology, party identification, and constituency (Jenkins 2012; Osborn 2012; Reingold 2000), although some found that differences in roll call voting emerged in certain circumstances in state legislatures, for Democrats or on issues that create cross-pressures within parties (Hogan 2008). Female state legislators were also as successful in securing passage of the legislation they sponsor as their male counterparts, when controlling for other factors (Jenkins 2016). Thus, as at the Congressional level, research at the state level has identified numerous ways in which the legislative behavior of female legislators is different than their male counterparts and other ways in which it is more similar.

The lack of uniformity across states in terms of data collection and reporting can make it difficult to study the legislative behavior of women in the states. However, there are two key advantages. First, because there are more women serving in state legislatures, research has examined how the behavior of different groups of female legislators varies. For instance, in 2016, there were 104 women serving in the U.S. Congress, and only 30 of them were Republicans.[3] At the state level though, there were just over 1,800 women serving in 2016, and 704 of these women were Republican. In comparing these different types of female legislators, scholars found that while Republican female state legislators were more conservative than male and female Democratic state legislators, they were more liberal than Republican male state legislators (Carey, Neimi, and Powell 1998). Despite this, Republican women did not prioritize women's issues in their legislative activities, as they sponsored fewer bills on specific women's issues (Osborn 2012).

There are also far more female legislators of color in the states. There are just 19 female representatives of color in the U.S. Congress, but there are 398 female legislators of color in the states. African American female legislators report difficulties in working both with African American male legislators and White female legislators, highlighting the importance of intersectionality to understanding the legislative behavior of female minority legislators (Darling 1998). The importance of intersectionality is highlighted by research that suggests female legislators of color have legislative agendas that are distinct from male legislators of color and female legislators (Barrett 1995; Bratton and Haynie 1999; Brown 2014; Fraga et al. 2007). However, some research suggests that these female legislators were less successful in securing passage of their legislative priorities, leading to perceptions amongst their colleagues that female legislators of color were not influential (Bratton and Haynie 1999; Smooth 2001). These findings highlight the need to examine whether conclusions about the differences (or lack thereof) between male and female legislators extends to all female legislators and to understand the particular challenges that female legislators of color face in these raced-gendered institutions (Hawkesworth 2003).

There are also far more female legislative leaders in the states, as compared to Congress. There has only been one female party leader to run a chamber in Congress—Nancy Pelosi—but in 2016 alone, 21 women serve as either presiding officers of a state legislative chamber. Because there are more women in leadership roles (both party leaders and committee chairs) in these institutions, research has been able to examine the leadership styles of female state legislators, confirming these styles were different from their male counterparts (Jewell and Whicker 1994; Kathlene 1998; Rosenthal 1998; Whicker and Jewell 1998). For instance, female committee chairs emphasized interpersonal skills and working as a group to accomplish policy goals; they also spoke less, took fewer turns speaking, and made fewer interruptions than their male counterparts (Kathlene 1998; Rosenthal 1998). Across the board, research has confirmed that female state legislative leaders have a different way of leading. They tended to focus more on working together, building consensus, and seeking input from a broader array of voices (Kathlene 1998; Whicker and Jewell 1998). Whicker and Jewell labeled this the "feminization" of state legislative leadership. However, the motivations for these different leadership styles have not been thoroughly examined; psychological and organizational theories explaining these questions should serve as an inspiration for future study of female legislative leaders.

The second advantage to using state legislatures to study the behavior of female legislators is that there is greater variation in the political conditions, institutional rules, and institutional resources across the states. Research has demonstrated that the context in which legislators serve shapes their legislative behavior (Jenkins 2016), but it is difficult to study how institutional context may affect the behavior of female legislators in Congress because the institutional rules and resources vary so infrequently there. But there is tremendous variation in the context of state legislatures, so research has examined how factors like committee autonomy, political parties, the proportion of female legislators, and gender stereotypes in an institution affects the work of female legislators and the outputs of the institutions they serve in.

For instance, critical mass theory (Kanter 1977) argues that women will transform the institutions in which they work or serve once they reach some critical number in these institutions. But where exactly this critical mass kicks in is not entirely clear. It is difficult to test where this number may lie using Congress as the percent of women serving has never passed 20 percent. The percent of women at the state level varies considerably by state though, ranging from a high of 42 percent in Colorado to a low of 13.3 percent in Wyoming in 2016. Research has shown that as the presence of women grew in these institutions, they were more likely to advocate and lead on behalf of women's interests (Berkman and O'Connor 1993; Bratton 2005; Thomas 1994).

And research also suggests there is some potential for backlash effects, with male legislators reacting negatively to the increase in women in these state leg-islatures (Kanthak and Krause 2012; Kathlene 1994; Rosenthal 1998). Indeed, female leadership on women's issues can have its costs; states were more likely to invest resources in combatting human trafficking when there were more women in the legislature and when more of these women signed on to sponsor these bills, but states were less likely to do so when the majority of the sponsors on a bill were female (Wittmer and Boucher 2013). As Wittmer and Boucher (2013, 271) note, gendered sponsorship may "entrench traditional gender roles within the institution by sending the message that men care about guns and women care about butter."

Other contextual factors can shape the legislative behavior and ultimately success of female legislators. Political parties play a key role in shaping both the election and success of female state legislators, and the effects are different for Democrats and Republicans (Osborn 2012; Sanbonmatsu 2002). Women's par-ticipation on welfare committees leads to more generous state welfare policy, and that this relationship is enhanced when committees have a greater degree of autonomy (Poggione 2006). As Poggione notes (195), "women legislators' opportunities for influence are mediated by the institutions in which they serve."

Future research ought to continue to use the advantages offered by state legislatures to further explore the legislative behavior of female legislators. While progress has been made in this respect, more work remains to be done, so scholars would be well advised to examine how different contexts may be more or less hospitable to different types of female legislators and whether female legislators in different context have different motivations for their behavior.

Testing Psychological Theory on Gender and Legislative Behavior

As the previous sections of this chapter indicate, scholars have made great strides in understanding gender dynamics in the legislative process. But while this research has done a good job in establishing differences in the behavior of male and female legislators, more needs to be done to understand why these differences have emerged. Are female legislators socialized to adopt different roles in the legislative process? Are they responding to differing constituent demands? Experimental methods can help us answer these questions, but there is little of this research because legislators at any level of government are not inclined to subject themselves to that process. However, some studies have incorporated experimental methodology using subjects who are not in fact legislators. These studies attempt to understand why female legislators act differently as compared to their male counterparts in the context of institutional rules and features.

For instance, Kennedy (2003) conducted a game theoretic experiment with 90 undergraduates to simulate an allocative decision-making process similar to a legislative committee setting and found that women were more likely than men to report being motivated by altruistic concerns and expressed a preference for universalistic solutions. Male participants were more likely than women to report being motivated by self-interest and to have a preference for a competitive solution, demonstrating that women have different motivations for their behavior, which points to social role theory as a potential explanation for gender differences in legislative behavior.

Experimental research can also help us understand how institutional features such as the number of women and institutional rules influence the behavior of female legislators. For example, Hannigan and Larimer (2010) conducted a laboratory experiment where undergraduates were asked to divvy up a small amount of money with another player to see whether the distributional patterns of participants varied by gender depending on the composition of the group. Female preferences tracked closer to the mean of the group, while male preferences exhibited far more variance, particularly in all male groups, suggesting that "increasing gender equity within decision making bodies is likely to result in more democratic decision making and produce outcomes closer to universal median preferences" (63).

Decision rules can also shape the nature of the deliberative process, as Karpowitz and Mendelberg (2015) demonstrated in a deliberative justice experiment with 470 participants including students and community members. In general, women were often disadvantaged in debate participation under multiple decision rule settings while the men in their study never were. Speech participation rates of women in the numerical minority tended to reach equality with men when decisions were made through unanimous rule as opposed to majority rule. In contrast, when men were in the minority, the speech participation rates of men tended to exceed the rates of women in unanimous rule situations. The authors concluded that "minority women leverage unanimous rule to reach equality while minority men leverage it to exacerbate inequality" (138). Based on their findings, Karpowitz and Mendelberg maintained that political institutions should adopt unanimous decision rules as a means of facilitating greater gender equality in the deliberative process. Such conditions support the more cooperative mindset female legislators have been socialized to bring to the process.

A few emerging studies have started to unearth motivations for differing behavior. Broockman (2013) examined how legislators reacted to constituent requests when they have no electoral connection to the requester by contacting legislators via email and randomizing whether the sender lived in the legislator's district or not. However, he did not examine how gender conditioned these responses, which is unfortunate as it would help determine whether differences in casework behavior are due to female legislators responding to different demands from constituents. Butler (2014) examined how gender shapes responses to constituent requests, and found that female legislators were about equally as likely to respond to concerns over women's issues compared with other issues. In contrast, male legislators were far less likely to respond to issues concerning women compared to all issues they were contacted about. Butler attributed this differential outcome to informational asymmetries that are linked to male legislators' lack of knowledge and interest in the concerns of their female constituents.

Opportunities and Obstacles for Future Research

Each of these studies has laid a foundation that should serve as catalysts for political scientists and scholars of other disciplines to investigate motivations for gender differences in legislative behavior. Given the unanswered questions identified in the existing body of research, the benefits for better teasing out motivations and causal relationships should not be ignored (Hannigan and Larimer 2010; Kennedy 2003). Yet as they develop plans to build on this emerging body of scholarship, experts on the relationship between gender and legislative behavior must take note of the multiple issues raised throughout this chapter including: difficulty in getting cooperation from legislators, external validity concerns, and the limited sample size of female legislators in many legislative bodies. These challenges will not be resolved overnight but researchers must think creatively to overcome them. If they do so then a more complete understanding of gender in the legislative process will be achieved.

Notes

1. Ledbetter v. Goodyear Tire & Rubber Co., 550 U.S. 618 (2007).
2. For more information about the process of scaling legislator ideology across institutions see Poole (2005).
3. Data on the number of women serving in U.S. legislatures comes from the Center for American Women and Politics.

References

Anzia, Sarah F., and Christopher R. Berry. 2011. "The Jackie (and Jill) Robinson Effect: Why Do Congresswomen Outperform Congressmen?" *American Journal of Political Science* 55: 478–493.

Barrett, Edith J. 1995. "The Policy Priorities of African American Women in State Legislatures." *Legislative Studies Quarterly* 20: 223–247.

Berkman, Michael B., and Robert E. O'Connor. 1993. "Do Women Legislators Matter? Female Legislators and State Abortion Policy." *American Politics Quarterly* 21: 102–124.

Bos, Angela L., Monica C. Schneider, and Brittany L. Utz. ND. "Gender Stereotypes and Prejudice in US Elections." Unpublished manuscript.

Bratton, Kathleen A. 2005. "Critical Mass Theory Revisited: The Behavior and Success of Token Women in State Legislatures." *Politics & Gender* 1: 97–125.

Bratton, Kathleen A., and Kerry L. Haynie. 1999. "Agenda Setting and Legislative Success in State Legislatures: The Effects of Gender and Race." *The Journal of Politics* 61: 658–679.

Broockman, David E. 2013. "Black Politicians Are More Intrinsically Motivated to Advance Blacks' Interests: A Field Experiment Manipulating Political Incentives." *American Journal of Political Science* 57: 521–536.

Brown, Nadia. 2014. *Sisters in the Statehouse: Black Women and Legislative Decision Making.* Oxford: Oxford University Press.

Burrell, Barbara. 2014. *Gender in Campaigns for the U.S. House of Representatives.* Ann Arbor, MI: University of Michigan Press.

Butler, Daniel M. 2014. *Representing the Advantaged: How Politicians Reinforce Inequality.* Cambridge: Cambridge University Press.

Carey, John M., Richard G. Neimi, and Lynd W. Powell. 1998. "Are Women State Legislators Different?" In *Women and Elective Office: Past, Present, and Future*, edited by Sue Thomas and Clyde Wilcox, 87–102. New York: Oxford University Press.

Darling, Marsha J. 1998. "African-American Women in State Elective Office in the South." In *Women and Elective Office: Past, Present, and Future*, edited by Sue Thomas and Clyde Wilcox, 150–162. New York: Oxford University Press.

Dodson, Debra L. 2006. *The Impact of Women in Congress.* Oxford: Oxford University Press.

Dolan, Julie. 1997. "Support for Women's Interests in the 103rd Congress: The Distinct Impact of Congressional Women." *Women and Politics* 18: 81–94.

Dolan, Kathleen, and Lynne E. Ford. 1998. "Are All Women State Legislators Alike?" In *Women and Elective Office: Past, Present, and Future*, edited by Sue Thomas and Clyde Wilcox, 73–86. New York: Oxford University Press.

Eagly, Alice H. 2007. "Female Leadership Advantage and Disadvantage: Resolving the Contradictions." *Psychology of Women Quarterly* 31: 1–12.

Eagly, Alice H., and Linda L. Carli. 2007. *Through the Labyrinth: The Truth about How Women Become Leaders.* Cambridge, MA: Harvard Business School Press.

Fraga, Luis Ricardo, Valerie Martinez-Ebers, Ricardo Ramirez, and Linda Lopez. 2007. "Gender and Ethnicity: Patterns of Electoral Success and Advocacy among Latina and Latino State Officials in Four States." *Journal of Women, Politics, and Policy* 28: 121–145.

Frederick, Brian. 2009. "Are Women Still More Liberal in a Polarized Era? The Conditional Nature of the Relationship between the Descriptive and Substantive Representation." *Congress and the Presidency* 36: 181–202.

Frederick, Brian. 2010. "Gender and Patterns of Roll Call Voting in the U.S. Senate." *Congress and Presidency* 37: 103–124.

Frederick, Brian. 2011. "Gender Turnover and Roll Call Voting in the U.S. Senate." *Journal of Women Politics and Policy* 32: 193–210.

Frederick, Brian. 2013. "Gender and Roll Call Voting Behavior in Congress: A Cross-Chamber Analysis." *American Review of Politics* 34: 1–20.

Frederick, Brian. 2015. "A Longitudinal Test of the Gender Turnover Model among U.S. House and Senate Members." *Social Science Journal* 52: 102–111.

Fridkin, Kim L., and Patrick J. Kenney. 2014. "How the Gender of U.S. Senators Influences People's Understanding and Engagement in Politics." *Journal of Politics* 76: 1017–1031.

Fridkin, Kim L., and Patrick J. Kenney. 2015. *The Gender of U.S. Senators and Constituent Communications: The Changing Face of Representation.* Ann Arbor, MI: University of Michigan Press.

Gerrity, Jessica C., Tracy Osborn, and Jeanette M. Mendez. 2007. "Women and Representation: A Different View of the District?" *Politics & Gender* 39: 179–200.

Hannigan, Rebecca J., and Christopher Larimer. 2010. "Does Gender Composition Affect Group Decision Outcomes? Evidence from a Laboratory Experiment." *Political Behavior* 32: 51–67.

Hawkesworth, Mary. 2003. "Congressional Enactments of Race-Gender: Toward a Theory of Raced-Gendered Institutions." *American Political Science Review* 97: 529–550.

Hogan, Robert E. 2008. "Sex and the Statehouse: The Effects of Gender on Legislative Roll Call Voting." *Social Science Quarterly* 89: 955–968.

Jenkins, Shannon. 2012. "How Gender Influences Roll Call Voting." *Social Science Quarterly* 93: 415–433.

Jenkins, Shannon. 2016. *The Context of Legislating: Constraints on the Legislative Process.* New York: Routledge.

Jewell, Malcolm E., and Marcia Lynn Whicker. 1994. *Legislative Leadership in the American States.* Ann Arbor, MI: University of Michigan Press.

Kanter, Rosabeth. 1977. "Some Effects of Proportions on Group-Life: Skewed Sex Ratios and Responses to Token Women." *American Journal of Sociology* 82: 965–990.

Kanthak, Kristin, and George A. Krause. 2012. *The Diversity Paradox: Political Parties, Legislatures and the Organizational Foundations of Representation in America.* Oxford: Oxford University Press.

Karpowitz, Christopher F., and Tali Mendelberg. 2015. *The Silent Sex: Gender, Deliberation and Institutions.* Princeton, NJ: Princeton University Press.

Kathlene, Lyn. 1994. "Power and Influence in State Legislative Policymaking: The Interaction of Gender and Position in Committee Hearing Debates." *American Political Science Review* 88 (3): 560–576.

Kathlene, Lyn. 1998. "In a Different Voice: Women and the Policy Process." In *Women and Elective Office: Past, Present, and Future,* edited by Sue Thomas and Clyde Wilcox, 188–202. New York: Oxford University Press.

Kennedy, Carole. 2003. "Gender Differences in Committee Decision Making." *Women and Politics* 25: 27–45.

Lawless, Jennifer L. 2015. "Female Candidates and Legislators." *Annual Review of Political Science* 18: 349–366.

Lawless, Jennifer L., and Kathryn Pearson. 2008. "The Primary Reason for Women's Underrepresentation? Re-Evaluating the Conventional Wisdom." *Journal of Politics* 70: 67–82.

Livingston, Robert W., Ashleigh Shelby Rosette, and Ella F. Washington. 2012. "Can An Agentic Black Woman Get Ahead? The Impact of Race and Interpersonal Dominance on Perceptions of Female Leaders." *Psychological Science* 23: 354–358.

McDonald, Jason, and Erin E. O'Brien. 2011. "Quasi-Experimental Design, Constituency, and Advancing Women's Interests: 'Critically' Reexamining the Influence of Gender on Substantive Representation." *Political Research Quarterly* 64: 472–486.

Milyo, Jeffrey, and Samantha Schosberg. 2000. "Gender Bias and Selection Bias in House Elections." *Public Choice* 105: 41–59.

Osborn, Tracy. 2012. *How Women Represent Women: Political Parties, Gender, and Representation in the State Legislatures.* New York: Oxford University Press.

Osborn, Tracy, and Jeanette Morehouse Mendez. 2010. "Speaking as Women: Women and Floor Speeches in the Senate." *Journal of Women Politics and Policy* 31: 1–20.

Palmer, Barbara, and Dennis Simon. 2012. *Women in Congressional Elections: A Century of Change.* New York: Lynne Rienner Publishers.

Pearson, Kathryn L., and Logan Dancey. 2011a. "Elevating Women's Voices in Congress: Speech Participation in the House of Representatives." *Political Research Quarterly* 64: 910–923.

Pearson, Kathryn L., and Logan Dancey. 2011b. "Speaking for the Underrepresented in the House of Representatives: Voicing Women's Interests in a Partisan Era." *Politics and Gender* 7: 493–519.

Peters, Ronald M., and Cindy Simon Rosenthal. 2010. *Speaker Nancy Pelosi and the New American Politics.* Oxford: Oxford University Press.

Poggione, Sarah. 2004. "Exploring State Legislators' Policy Preferences." *Political Research Quarterly* 57: 305–314.

Poggione, Sarah. 2006. "Women State Legislators: Descriptive and Substantive Representation." In *Women in Politics*, edited by Lois Duke Whitaker, 182–198. Upper Saddle River, NJ: Pearson/Prentice Hall.

Poole, Keith T. 2005. *Spatial Models of Parliamentary Voting.* New York: Cambridge University Press.

Reingold, Beth. 1992. "Concepts of Representation among Female and Male State Legislators." *Legislative Studies Quarterly* 17: 509–537.

Reingold, Beth. 2000. *Representing Women: Sex, Gender, and Legislative Behavior in the American States.* Chapel Hill, NC: University of North Carolina Press.

Rosenthal, Cindy Simon. 1998. "Getting Things Done: Women Committee Chairpersons in State Legislatures." In *Women and Elective Office: Past, Present, and Future*, edited by Sue Thomas and Clyde Wilcox, 175–187. New York: Oxford University Press.

Rudman, Laurie A., Corinne A. Moss-Racusin, Julie E. Phelan, and Sanne Nauts. 2012. "Status Incongruity and Backlash Effects: Defending the Gender Hierarchy Motivates Prejudice against Female Leaders." *Journal of Experimental Social Psychology* 48: 165–179.

Sanbonmatsu, Kira. 2002. "Political Parties and the Recruitment of Women to State Legislatures." *Journal of Politics* 64: 791–809.

Sanchez-Hucles, Janis V., and Donald D. Davis. 2010. "Women and Women of Color in Leadership." *American Psychologist* 65: 171–181.

Schulze, Carol. 2013. "Women, Earmarks and Substantive Representation." *Journal of Women Politics and Policy* 34: 138–158.

Schulze, Corina, and Jared Hurvitz. 2016. "The Dynamics of Earmark Requests for the Women and Men of the US House of Representatives." *Journal of Women Politics and Policy* 37: 68–86.

Schwindt-Bayer, Leslie A., and Renato Corbetta. 2004. "Gender Turnover and Roll-Call Voting in the U.S. House of Representatives." *Legislative Studies Quarterly* 29: 215–229.

Simon, Dennis M., and Barbara Palmer. 2010. "The Roll Call Voting Behavior of Men and Women in the U.S. House of Representatives, 1937–2008." *Politics and Gender* 6: 225–246.

Smooth, Wendy G. 2001. *African American Women State Legislators: The Impact of Gender and Race on Legislative Influence*. Ph.D. Dissertation, Department of Government and Politics, University of Maryland.

Sorok, Carolyn. 2010. "Closing the Gap Legislatively: Consequences of the Lilly Ledbetter Fair Pay Act." *Chicago Kent Law Review* 85: 1199–1216.

Swers, Michele L. 2002. *The Difference Women Make: The Policy Impact of Women in Congress*. Chicago, IL: University of Chicago Press.

Swers, Michele L. 2007. "Building a Reputation on National Security: The Impact of Stereotypes Related to Gender and Military Experience." *Legislative Studies Quarterly* 32: 559–596.

Swers, Michele L. 2013. *Women in the Club: Gender and Policy Making in the Senate*. Chicago: University of Chicago Press.

Swers, Michele L., and Christine C. Kim. 2013. "Replacing Sandra Day O'Connor: Gender and the Politics of Supreme Court Nominations." *Journal of Women Politics and Policy* 13: 23–48.

Swers, Michele L., and Stella Rouse. 2011. "Descriptive Representation: Understanding the Impact of Identity on the Substantive Representation of Groups." In *The Oxford Handbook of the American Congress*, edited by Eric Schickler and Frances Lee, 241–272. Oxford: Oxford University Press.

Thomas, Sue. 1994. *How Women Legislate*. New York: Oxford University Press.

van Knippenberg, Daan. 2011. "Embodying Who We Are: Leader Group Prototypicality and Leadership Effectiveness." *The Leadership Quarterly* 22: 1078–1091.

Volden, Craig, and Alan E. Wiseman. 2014. *Legislative Effectiveness in the United States Congress: The Lawmakers*. Cambridge: Cambridge University Press.

Volden, Craig, Alan E. Wiseman, and Diana Wittmer. 2013. "When Are Women More Effective Lawmakers than Men?" *American Journal of Political Science* 57: 326–341.

Whicker, Marcia Lynn, and Malcolm Jewell. 1998. "The Feminization of Leadership in State Legislatures." In *Women and Elective Office: Past, Present, and Future*, edited by Sue Thomas and Clyde Wilcox, 163–174. New York: Oxford University Press.

Wittmer, Dana E., and Vanessa Bouche. 2013. "The Limits of Gendered Leadership: Policy Implications of Female Leadership on 'Women's Issues'." *Politics and Gender* 9: 245–275.

13

GENDER AND THE BENCH

Does Judge Sex Influence Citizens?

Kjersten Nelson

The issue of gender balance on the courts took center stage in 2005 when Justice Sandra Day O'Connor, the first woman to be confirmed to the Supreme Court, announced her intention to retire. Because Justice O'Connor's departure would leave the Supreme Court with only one serving woman (Justice Ruth Bader Ginsburg), public debate raged as to the merits of a more gender-balanced court.[1] President Bush, who was responsible for nominating O'Connor's replacement, was focusing his search to find "an acceptable female or minority legal figure."[2] President Bush's initial nominee, Harriet Miers, reinforced these speculations. However, opposition to Miers was strong, given her lack of experience; concern from the right that she was not conservative enough; and concern from the left that she would not uphold progressive policies. During the Miers debate, President Bush gained another opportunity to nominate a woman when Chief Justice William Rehnquist died. Given the visibility of the debate about gender and racial minorities, it is notable that, after the Miers nomination hit hard times and Miers withdrew from consideration, Bush ultimately nominated, and the Senate confirmed, two male nominees (Chief Justice John Roberts and Justice Samuel Alito). In the process, the Supreme Court moved from 22 percent female justices to a mere 11 percent.

Despite attention and debate about increasing diversity on the bench, we have little empirical work that investigates how gender diversity influences the court, particularly in terms of how citizens assess it. Studies that have investigated gender dynamics have primarily focused on how female judges behave differently than their male colleagues—or, more accurately, how similar female judges' behavior is to their male colleagues (e.g., Boyd et al. 2010; Martin and Pyle 2005; Ostberg and Wetstein 2007; Segal et al. 2005). This chapter, then, addresses three key questions. First, does the sex of a judge affect the substance of a court's decisions? Second, do citizens use gender expectations and stereotypes to assess female and male judges differently? And, third, does judge sex affect citizens' orientations to the courts, as democratic institutions, and assessments of their own roles in democracy? I proceed with a review of what we do know about female judges and the courts. I then turn to a framework for an investigation of the judiciary: Specifically, the work on gender expectations and female candidates provides guidance on the kinds of stereotypes citizens may employ as they process the decisions of female and male judges. Finally, I present data that directly test when citizens assess female judges through a gendered lens and the extent to which these assessments affect overall assessments of judicial institutions and the citizen's place in democracy, more broadly.

For decades, there have been concerted calls to diversify political leadership, primarily focused on gender, race, and ethnicity. The arguments center on two justifications: First, that diverse leaders will bring different perspectives to policy debates and, ultimately, change policy outcomes to better-reflect the needs of underrepresented populations. This argument inspired lines of research that aimed to test, empirically, whether female judges actually decide differently than male judges. The second argument points to the symbolism of leadership. The lack of certain groups in leadership communicates to these groups a sort of second-class citizenship—in other words, that leadership positions are reserved for certain types of citizens. Empirical tests of these arguments are sparse, and have tended to look at elected leaders (e.g., members of Congress, governors, etc., though see Scherer and Curry 2010). If female judges can serve as role models for the next generation of leaders, it is vital to understand the gender expectations citizens use in assessing these judges. Future leaders exist in a context; it seems reasonable that they will not just see the presence of female judges as a signal of what is (and isn't) possible, but also assess the responses to those female judges, of those around them, for additional information as to how normal or fraught being a female judge is. Finally, a very small segment of the population will even aspire to a career in politics or the law, while a very large segment of the population are citizens. If we have a better sense of how political leaders—even less prominent political leaders, like judges—could inhibit or inspire political engagement, then we also have a better sense of how political role models could be leveraged to broaden and deepen political participation.

Female and Male Judges: More Alike Than Different

The primary question relating to the role of judge sex has aimed to test the theory that judge diversity is vital because women, based on their different life experiences, will decide differently than their male counterparts. Many of these inquiries rely on Gilligan's (1982) work, which posited that the "feminine perspective" or life experiences of women are so fundamentally different from men's that there will be significant differences in decisions (Boyd et al. 2010; Sherry

1986, 160). This general framework led to conflicting hypotheses, however. Compassion may lead the average female judge to be more lenient in sentencing than her male counterpart. At the same time, because women are more likely to experience sexual violence and to be more fearful of crime in general, they may be inclined to impose harsher sentences on defendants in these types of cases. Finally, it may be that women's experiences with gender discrimination would make them more empathetic towards all types of discrimination, including racial discrimination. This experience may lead female judges to be more equal in their sentencing decisions, across races and ethnicities, than male judges (Spohn 2009).

While there are many versions of the gender-difference expectations, they are countered by the organizational model. This model proposes that, while male and female judges have undoubtedly experienced different paths and backgrounds in their journeys to judgeships, the acculturation process will have evened out most gender-based differences (e.g., Boyd et al. 2010; Steffensmeier and Hebert 1999). In this model, the primary identification of judges—male and female—is *judge*. The empirical evidence has not emphatically supported any of these hypotheses. Sociological and criminological studies have found support for the hypothesis that differences between male and female judges will be minimal or nonexistent (Gruhl, Spohn, and Welch 1981; Johnson 2006; Kritzer and Uhlman 1977); *and* support for the hypothesis that female judges sentence more harshly than male judges (Spohn 1990; Steffensmeier and Hebert 1999).

Political science has trained its inquiry of judge sex on the outcome of whether male and female judges tend to render different decisions. These studies have focused on two broad questions: Whether individual judges decide differently based on their sex and whether female judges might inspire "panel effects"—that is, that female judges might influence their fellow (male) judges to decide differently than if the female judge was not there. Like the sentencing literature, quantitative findings are inconsistent. Sometimes there were differences between male and female judges (e.g., Ostberg and Wetstein 2007; Peresie 2005); sometimes there were panel effects (e.g., Martin and Pyle 2005; Peresie 2005); but oftentimes there were neither (e.g., Segal, Spaeth, and Benesh 2005; Westergren 2004). Qualitative analyses typically reinforced the no-difference findings (Aliotta 1995; Davis 1993; Maveety 2010).[3] Boyd et al. (2010) appear to have settled the question by using propensity matching scores to match judges that, but for their gender, are otherwise very similar. They found that female judges tended to find for the plaintiff more often in sex discrimination cases than male judges and tended to influence their male colleagues (i.e., there are panel effects). Beyond this small sliver of cases, however, they did not find any sex-based decision differences.[4]

Most recently, Boyd (2013, 2015) has begun investigating whether there may be sex differences that emerge somewhere other than final decisions. For example, she found that female judges successfully fostered settlements in their cases more quickly and more often than their male counterparts (2013) and, in motions throughout a trial, were more likely to decide in favor of parties alleging gender discrimination (2015). The presence of female judges may affect other aspects of the courtroom experience, such as intolerance for sexist behaviors; increased self-monitoring of sexist behavior from other court actors in the presence of a female judge; a focus on hiring female law clerks; or, perhaps, more attention to women's issues. However, many of these effects are highly contingent upon the individual judge or justice studied and are likely prone to lurking variable effects (i.e., different generations of judges and justices experience sexism differently, leading to different behaviors; the women being studied were all nominated by Democratic presidents; or that presidents use different criteria when vetting female nominees than male nominees) (Beiner 2003; Dixon 2010; Kenney 2013; Martin 1989).

Finally, we have the least insight on the role judge sex plays from a psychological or political psychological approach. We do have the rare interview to point to—for example, (at the time, future) Justice Sotomayor's statement regarding the value of including the viewpoint of a "wise Latina,"[5] to hold in contrast with Justice O'Connor's repeated statements that "wise men and wise women make the same decisions,"[6] At this point, we lack a systematic understanding of lower court judges' perspectives on the role of sex and gender consciousness (though see Martin 1989) and, particularly, how judges may navigate gender and professional stereotypes in ways that are similar to and different from regular citizens and other political leaders. This gap is due to many factors, including a small-n problem, the tendency of judges on all matters to be guarded, and the legal norms of objectivity that would lead judges, either consciously or not, to downplay the roles of non-legal factors in decision-making.

Citizens' Use of Gender Expectations to Evaluate Judges and the Courts

Perhaps, though, scholars' near-obsession with finding differences between female and male judges should clue us in to another aspect of this issue—citizens might *expect* male and female judges to behave differently, regardless of whether male and female judges actually do behave differently. And, if citizens expect men and women to behave differently, then it is possible that citizens' assessments of court decisions, the judges, and the courts more broadly may be contingent on judge/justice sex.

The effects of citizens' gender expectations of leaders has undoubtedly focused on elected leaders due to the central role citizens play in choosing elected leaders (i.e., voting). However, citizens' gender expectations are consequential for judges, justices, and courts, as well. First, 87 percent of state court judges in the U.S. are elected to those positions; 39 states have at least some elected judicial positions (Liptak 2008). While the nature of these elections are different than

Congressional elections, many judges will be navigating the gender expectations of voters. Second, even if not elected, judges and justices contend with public opinion, if only indirectly. They carefully tend to the maintenance of public support of their institutions when addressing legal questions (e.g., Caldeira and Gibson 1992; Clark 2009; Segal, Westerland, and Lindquist 2011). If citizens use individual characteristics of the authoring judge to assess the decision—and ultimately the court—then judge gender has consequential effects for the way the judiciary conducts its business.

While direct study of the courts in this regard has been sparse, we have ample guidance from the study of gender's role in citizen evaluations of other political actors. On the one hand, it is possible that the expectations attached to the role of "judge" are so powerful—and, perhaps relatedly, citizens are becoming accustomed to seeing women in political leadership positions, making gender a less salient evaluation cue—that citizens do not rely on judge sex as they form evaluations. In other words, the role of "judge" may have its own stereotype connected to it, which complicates the straightforward application of gender stereotypes (Deaux and Lewis 1984; Kunda and Spencer 2003). Similarly, as Nichole Bauer points out in her chapter in this volume, it is possible to possess stereotypes of women and not automatically ascribe them to women in all circumstances (see also Bauer 2013; Dolan 2014). Indeed, while voters continued to hold gender expectations of female political leaders, these expectations did not ultimately affect voting decisions (Dolan 2014). Experimental designs that manipulated candidate sex revealed that, when male and female candidates express emotion, the responses were less gendered than might be expected (Brooks 2011). Schneider and Bos (2013) found that while gender stereotypes are enduring, stereotypes of female politicians were distinct from the stereotypes individuals hold of women in general. These works provide a baseline level of evidence for us to expect a minimal role for judge sex in citizen evaluations.

Yet the broader literature on gender stereotypes provides reason to believe gender expectations could be a powerful cue. Gender expectations play a larger role in low-information environments (Dolan 1998; McDermott 1997). Citizens pay little attention to the courts and, consequently, know little about them, qualifying this area as a low-information environment.[7] In addition, those studies that showed less reliance on gender expectations demonstrated that partisan identity overwhelms candidate sex (Dolan 2014; Schneider and Bos 2013). In the case of judges, evaluators generally do not have a partisan cue. Discussing judges in the context of court decisions where gender is a salient aspect of the case itself may also increase evaluators' likelihood to depend on sex-based expectations (Nelson 2015).

As Nichole Bauer explains in her chapter, gender expectations tend to come through in three areas: ideology, expertise, and traits. In particular, citizens expected female political leaders to be more liberal than their male counterparts (e.g., Alexander and Andersen 1993; Dolan 1998; Koch 2000; McDermott 1997), and more competent on "compassion issues" and "women's issues" (Dolan 2010, 2012; Huddy and Terkildsen 1993; Sanbonmatsu and Dolan 2009; Shapiro and Mahajan 1986). In terms of traits, Jamieson (1995) articulated the idea of the "double-bind": while female leaders enjoyed an empathy (or "compassion") advantage over their male counterparts (Dolan 2010; Schneider and Bos 2013), this empathy advantage was balanced by an expectation that the same female leader will be less competent in general (Eagly and Karau 2002; Koenig et al. 2011; Schneider and Bos 2013). The extent to which these gender expectations are applied to female judges could affect support for those judges, their opinions, and decisions.

Implications for Political Efficacy

Gender representation may also have broader implications for democracy if citizens' assessments of judges and the courts had implications for their own feelings of efficacy or an individual's perception that government institutions and actors are responsive to citizen influence (Balch 1974; Converse 1972). In non-courts literature, external efficacy is usually included in studies as an independent variable, owing to its broad conceptualization as a relatively stable trait (Ainsworth 2000; Atkeson and Carillo 2007; Valentino et al. 2009). A small but growing literature investigated the impact elected officials might have on individuals' levels of external efficacy, particularly as it relates to the descriptive representation of women.[8] For example, women in U.S. congressional districts that sent women to the U.S. House of Representatives had higher political efficacy and perceived confidence (High Pippert and Comer 1998). Women also reported higher levels of external efficacy as the percentage of women in their state legislatures increased (Atkeson and Carrillo 2007). Men exhibited similar increases when represented by a female governor. However, Lawless (2004) found no relationship between being represented by a woman and higher levels of efficacy—at least for women. Men who were represented by a female member of Congress do report higher levels of efficacy than men who were represented by a male.

It certainly seems reasonable that citizens might base some portion of their external efficacy on whether or not the people elected to represent their interests *look like them* in certain key ways—such as gender. But how might the dynamics change if a female judge authors a decision that is supportive of women's rights (i.e., substantively representative) versus authoring a decision that fundamentally alters the basis for women's workplace protections? If descriptive representation is sufficient, the presence of a female judge—pro- or anti-woman—should not affect levels of external efficacy. However, if substantive representation is a necessary component of increasing external efficacy, a female judge who issues an anti-woman decision could depress external efficacy. The lack of substantive representation, by the person most likely to provide it, may significantly alter individuals' hopes that these government actors would be responsive to citizen influence.

Methods and Data

To begin answering these questions, I undertook two experimental surveys where participants read an article, purportedly from the *New York Times*, which reported on a decision rendered by the 7th Circuit Court of Appeals. The decision, which was closely modeled after an actual decision released by the Supreme Court in 2007, held that women who want to sue for sex-based pay discrimination must do so within 180 days of receipt of the first paycheck.[9] (Previous practice, established by the Equal Employment Opportunity Commission, restarted the 180-day clock with the receipt of *each* paycheck.) The decision significantly narrowed women's access to legal remedies in the case of gender-based pay discrimination.

The article included excerpts from the majority judge and the dissenting judge, though the decision author's sex was manipulated to create the experimental conditions. In the first condition (Male Majority), a male judge authored the decision that restricts women's ability to sue and a female judge wrote the dissenting opinion.[10] In the second condition, it was a female judge who was attributed with writing the majority opinion, greatly restricting women's right to sue (Female Majority), while a male judge penned the dissent. For the first experiment, after reading one of the two articles, respondents were asked a range of questions regarding their assessments of the judges; the decisions; and the court overall. Specifically, respondents were asked to report on the ideology of the opinions and the authoring judges; the judges' knowledge; and the judges' empathy. This first experiment was conducted with a nationally representative sample through a grant from Time-Sharing Experiments for the Social Sciences (TESS) in April 2013. See Nelson (2015) for a more thorough description of the methodology and sample.

I undertook the second survey through Mechnical Turk (MTurk), Amazon's online workplace, on November 18–19, 2015.[11] The survey experiment proceeded in the same way as the first one; however, these respondents also rated their feelings of external efficacy on a two-item scale, which asked them to agree or disagree with the statements, "Public officials don't care much what people like me think," and "People like me don't have any say about what the government does." These are standard external efficacy items used by the National Elections Study, and verified by Niemi et al. (1991) and Valentino et al. (2009).

Findings: Gender Expectations

I turn first to reporting the results from the first experiment, which asked respondents to report their assessments of the ideology of the decision, the ideologies of each judge, and assessments of the judges' competence and empathy. As Table 13.1 shows, some assessments of the authoring judges are gendered but the context of the decision is key. Judge sex matters only in the dissenting opinions (i.e., the decision that is supportive of an expanded interpretation of

TABLE 13.1 Difference in Assessments, by Majority and Minority Opinions

	Comparison between the Male Majority and Female Majority Conditions	
	Majority Decision	Dissenting Decision
(a) Support for the decision	M = F	F = M
(b) Decision ideology	M = F	F = M
(c) Judge ideology	M = F	F = M
(d) Specific knowledge	M = F	F < M
(e) General knowledge	M = F	F < M
(f) Specific empathy	M = F	F > M
(g) General empathy	M = F	F > M

M = Male author, F = Female author. Noted differences between the male and female author are statistically significant, $p < .05$. More information on these analyses can be found in Nelson (2015, 256).

the anti-discrimination policy) (Nelson 2015). Respondents rated the male and female majority judges (and the decisions they authored) equal in terms of how liberal or conservative they are; how knowledgeable they are; and how empathetic they are. Overall, too, the gender of the majority judge did not sway support of the decision—support for the majority decision remained low regardless of whether a male or female judge penned it (Row a), and was significantly lower than support for the dissenting opinion.[12] In sum, the substance of the majority opinion "appears to reinforce the identity of judge above gender, manifest in the complete absence of gender-based assessments for the majority opinion and majority-authoring judge" (Nelson 2015, 255).

However, the gender of the authoring judge does matter for assessments of the dissenting judge. Recall that the dissenting opinion is the opinion that would be interpreted as the substantively representative decision on behalf of women—it argues to uphold a more flexible standard that would maintain women's ability to sue for gender-based pay discrimination. When a female judge authors this substantively representative decision, it appears to emphasize the judge's identity as a woman, triggering gender expectations in those assessing the judge. For example, when a female judge authors the substantively representative dissent, she is assessed as being more empathetic to women who experience discrimination and more empathetic to women in general than when a male judge writes the exact same dissent. At the same time, respondents assess that same female dissenting judge as being less knowledgeable in this area of the law and less knowledgeable about the law in general.

These findings begin to sketch a picture of just how complex the interplay of judge sex, genderless judge roles, and decision-substance is. It would be more parsimonious to be able to say that citizens either do or do not use gender expectations when assessing judges and their associated decisions. These findings prove it is more complicated than one way or the other. On the one hand, in the case where a female judge didn't emphasize her identity as "woman," (i.e., when she writes a decision that undermines the right of women to sue for gender-based pay discrimination), she gets assessed just like the male judge who writes the same decision.[13] Such a finding might lead to the conclusion that gender expectations don't matter; particularly given that most decisions a judge authors in any given term are likely not related to issues that emphasize the judge's identity as a woman. In other words, while citizens may typically be assessing judges in a low-information environment—which would predict increased reliance on stereotypes—the substance of the decision itself may serve as additional information, reinforcing and undercutting various stereotypes in different circumstances (Kunda and Spencer 2003).

However, it is key to note that the substance of the decisions that *do* inspire respondents to invoke gender expectations in their assessments of judges are the very types of decisions that proponents of increased diversity on the bench were hoping to achieve—that is, decisions that will protect and expand the rights of marginalized groups. Here, then, we see another manifestation of Jamieson's (1995) "double-bind"—the judges who come on the court as a conduit for underrepresented interests to gain more voice on the court will be penalized, at least in terms of their competence ratings, when they carry out that role. This might be a particularly difficult line to walk for a judge who faces re-election (as they do in many states). But it also raises the question whether a reputation of protecting women's rights might lead a potential nominator (say, a president or a governor) or potential questioners (such as members of the Senate Judiciary Committee) to presume female nominees with this history are less knowledge-able (and more empathetic), which could influence their odds of success in the nomination and confirmation process.

External Efficacy

Finally, I ask whether there are any different effects on external efficacy for respondents based on which condition they participated in. The data I report here were collected through MTurk, in the second iteration of the survey experiment.

Again, a simple look at the data suggests few statistically significant results. Column a of Table 13.2 shows there is no statistically significant difference in levels of external efficacy between the two conditions for the full sample. How-ever, it is reasonable to expect there to be effects based on the gender of the respondent—a woman who sees a female judge circumscribing her legal remedies may be particularly deflated, providing one (more) example of a time that gov-ernment institutions and actors were *not* responsive to citizen influence, particularly in a situation where a female respondent might expect a female judge to be *especially* responsive (Balch 1974; Converse 1972). Columns b and c of Table 13.2

TABLE 13.2 Alternative Regression Models Predicting External Efficacy

	(a) Baseline (Full sample)	(b) Women Only	(c) Men Only	(d) Male Majority Condition	(e) Female Majority Condition
Constant	5.01*	5.62*	4.53*	4.53*	4.86*
	(.22)	(.32)	(.29)	(.29)	(.28)
Condition	.10	−.20	.33		
(0 = Male Majority,	(.31)	(.44)	(.41)		
1 = Female Majority)					
Respondent Sex				1.08*	.56
(Male = 0,				(.44)	(.42)
Female = 1)					
n	156	70	86	77	79

*: $p < .05$

break the sample out by respondent gender. Again, however, there are no statistically significant results, although the coefficients suggest that men and women are moving in opposite directions as we move from the male majority condition to the female majority condition. Men's external efficacy is perhaps reinforced as they see a female judge write in support of more limited means to sue, while women's external efficacy is perhaps diminished by the same condition.

Table 13.2 (columns d and e) takes one more look at the data and shows that, within each condition, there *are* statistically significant differences in external efficacy between the male and female respondents. Of the respondents who read a female dissent, women report higher levels of external efficacy than men ($p = .02$, two-tailed). However, men and women in the female majority condition report equivalent levels of external efficacy ($p = .18$). The models also show that the movement appears to come from women responding positively to a female judge writing the substantively representative minority opinion. Men in the male majority condition report, on average, an external efficacy of 4.5, similar to men in the female majority condition (on average, 4.9) and women in the female majority condition (on average, 5.4). Women in the male majority condition, however, report an average level of external efficacy of 5.6.

Discussion and Future Directions for this Research

This is just the beginning in our quest to understand whether and how citizens use gender expectations as they assess judges and the decisions they render, as well as extrapolate these to assessments of citizens' effectiveness in the larger system. From a normative perspective, the findings in this chapter are mixed. On the one hand, under certain circumstances—specifically, when judges are writing decisions that do not emphasize their identities as women—respondents do not differentiate between male and female judges (though see endnote 15). Moreover, the primary effect on external efficacy is to increase women's external efficacy in cases where a female judge writes a substantively representative dissent. Given the strong association between external efficacy and participation (e.g., Verba et al. 1995), the potential for a substantively representative judge to inspire women to political participation—perhaps even insofar as considering participation as a leader herself (e.g., Atkeson and Carillo 2007)—is profound. Given that cases of gender discrimination are one of the few issue areas where female judges appear to decide differently than men—in a pro-woman direction—the real-world potential for increased external efficacy among female citizens is real.[14]

All the same, many of these findings give us pause. Female judges who write a substantively representative decision are subject to gendered assessments. She may be assessed as more empathetic than her male counterpart but, simultaneously, is seen as less knowledgeable than her male counterpart. In addition, while substantively representative female judges boost the external efficacy of women, there is suggestive evidence that a substantively *non*-representative female judge might actually boost men's external efficacy. These competing effects would be similar to those found in the scholarship on descriptive representation, race, and court legitimacy. Specifically, for African American respondents, as the perceived percentage of African American judges increases, their legitimacy assessments increase. *At the same time,* as the perceived percentage of African American judges increases, Whites decrease their legitimacy assessments (Scherer and Curry 2010). While these are about two different dependent variables (external efficacy versus legitimacy), the backlash effect looks similar and is cause for normative concern.

This particular approach to measuring the use of gender expectations in the assessment of judges and courts can contribute to a larger understanding of the importance of descriptive and substantive representation, beyond what we can understand by looking at elected officials. For example, in this experimental survey, I measure the effect of two specific judges' actions on individuals' assessments. Much previous work on descriptive representation has measured responses to aggregate descriptive representation (e.g., Atkeson and Carillo 2007; Scherer and Curry 2010; Tate 2003). This study rounds out that knowledge by taking a different perspective—do the descriptive characteristics of *specific political leaders* have ramifications for those leaders and their decisions, but also for larger measures of democratic health, such as external efficacy?[15] Second, this method has one central advantage over studies that look at democratically elected leaders: lack of party affiliation. Certainly, judges themselves have partisan proclivities, but the vast majority of citizens will be unfamiliar with the partisan or ideological leanings of a given judge (or even justice). Given the important effects of party affiliation on the use of gender expectations, judges can serve as a party-less control group of sorts.

Third, using judges as the objects of interest in trying to assess how citizens use gender expectations maintains a level of external validity that can be lost when including democratically elected leaders in experiments. Certainly, experiments that convey information about candidates and elected officials have yielded significant knowledge; the difficulty is that citizens do not usually make decisions and assessments of candidates/leaders in such an information-poor environment. Citizens rely on repeated news items, party cues, and the opinions of peers as they develop complex attitudes towards leaders and candidates. On the other hand, citizens—if they even have opinions about judicial actions—typically develop those opinions in very information-poor environments. It is feasible that an individual may consult a newspaper, read about a decision that was authored by a judge that individual has never heard of before, then adjust various attitudes about policy or the court accordingly. The parsimony of this experimental manipulation may actually approximate the real-world acquisition of news about the courts and their decisions.

Finally, this particular experimental design allowed us to investigate the intersection of descriptive *and substantive* representation. The work that examines the extent to which a diversity of representation influences citizens, on all sorts of dependent variables, measures that increased representation as an increase in descriptive representation (e.g., being represented by a woman, versus not; believing there are more African American judges versus fewer, etc.). Again, the effects of descriptive representation are important to understand, but only begin to unearth the complexities of representation. Once again, it is easier to manipulate this variable in the context of judges, where we can realistically argue that the substance of this one decision could serve as the sole basis for evaluation of a given judge.

Returning to those initial key questions, this chapter addresses them through a mix of existing and new analyses. The chapter began by reviewing extensive and conflicting work that, ultimately, suggests that the sex of a judge can affect the substance of a court's decision, but only in a limited range of case types. Second, experimental findings support the idea that citizens use gender expectations and stereotypes to assess female and male judges differently, but that these gender effects are conditioned by the substance of the opinion itself. Finally, and in a similarly nuanced way, experimental findings suggest that judge gender affects citizens' assessments of external efficacy, though the effects are contingent upon the substance of the decision, the gender of the judge, *and* the gender of the citizen.

The area of gender and the courts offers many exciting directions for further research. For example, as the number of retired female judges increases, the opportunity to qualitatively explore their experiences with gender on the court is growing. Certainly, we have the perspective of some key female justices—for example, Justices Sandra Day O'Connor, Ruth Bader Ginsburg, and Sonia Sotomayor have been particularly candid about the role of gender and judging (and, interestingly, have very different perspectives on it). Our knowledge can only expand if these inquiries can be taken to different levels of the court (e.g., interviews with circuit court retirees) and with an increasing sample size. The sample may be approaching the point where a survey could yield data that can be quantitatively analyzed, and could even include measures of individual difference that might illuminate the ways that different judges navigate gender. For example, how might variations in judges' gender consciousness influence decision-making or perspectives on the role of judge gender? Or how might differences in judges' endorsements of gender stereotypes help explain the times where judge sex predicts different opinions or judicial behavior?

The second venue for extension would be to pursue inquiries in other issue areas. Gender effects should become less central as inquiry moves on to issue areas that are less-explicitly related to gender identity; however, we also know that supposedly "genderless" issues tend to get ascribed to men or women more often when it comes to candidates. For example, Huddy and Terkildsen (1993) find that respondents tend to think female candidates are more competent on issues like health care and education, while they presume male candidates are more competent on issues like defense and national security. These competency expectations could play a role in gendered assessments of judges in issue areas besides work-based gender discrimination. Moreover, if the results here prove anything, it is that these effects are complex and subtle; it would be premature to presume that they would not be operating similarly in other issue areas.

A third promising line of inquiry is investigating not just how gender expectations play out at this final stage of judging—that is, drawing conclusions from final opinions—but how gender expectations might play out throughout the course of a case *and* a judge's (or potential judge's) lifetime. First, as Boyd (2013, 2015) has begun investigating, there are other key decisions in the life of a case that come well before a final decision. Identifying how gender—of the judge and, perhaps, of the litigants—might factor in at these stages is vital to understanding the larger picture. Backing up even further, investigating how gender expectations might funnel certain legal professionals into, or away from, a career of judging will even further illuminate behavior at these later stages. For example, Dancey et al. (2011, 2014) have found few gender differences in the kinds of questions that Article III court nominees get asked by the Senate Judiciary Committee; it is tempting to conclude that gender does not matter in this process. However, if *getting nominated* is considered an outcome, scholars can investigate how gender shapes the path from lawyer to nominee, potentially weeding out certain lawyers/judges along the way and contributing to the appearance of gender-neutrality in that nomination hearing.

Finally, the study of gender and judging opens a host of possibilities for examining how individual differences in citizens might influence gendered perspectives of the court. Measures of gender consciousness is the most obvious construct to include. In fact, incorporating individual differences—for both citizens and judges themselves—would be a potential solution for grappling with the critique of the judging and gender literature that the concept of judge sex is too essentialized (e.g., see Kenney 2013). Instead of simply including judge sex as an individual difference, additional measures—such as gender consciousness or stereotype endorsement—could serve as more precise measures of how gender influences attitudes and decision-making.

In sum, the study of gender in the judiciary branch provides a great opportunity for scholars to take what we have learned from other lines of inquiry and apply them. This new context can provide insight to the gender and politics literature, but also new ways of understanding how justice is carried out in the United States. The growing number of female judges and justices—both serving and retired—will continue to enrich these opportunities, and provide scholars with ever-improving data to address key questions of justice, democracy, and gender.

Notes

1. e.g., Argetsinger, Amy and Elizabeth Williamson. 2005. "O'Connor Successor Debated; Views Differ on Whether a Female Replacement Is Needed." *Washington Post*, July 3; Liptak, Adam. 2005. "O'Connor Leap Moved Women Up the Bench." *New York Times*, July 5.
2. Baker, Peter. 2005. "Court Search Focuses on Women, Minorities." *Washington Post*, July 16.
3. See Boyd et al.'s (2010) online appendix for a full listing of relevant studies.
4. These findings mesh well with Kenney's (2013) critique that researchers appear to be intent on finding sex difference even when the data do not bear that out. She writes, "It is thus astonishing that observers are so determined to find that distinct female essence of judging, when, instead, they could be asking how the experiences of particular judges, shaped by gender, have affected their perspectives" (34).
5. Sotomayor, Sonia. 2002. "A Latina Judge's Voice." *Berkeley La Raza Law Journal* 13 (1): 87–93.
6. e.g., 2008. "A Conversation with Justice Sandra Day O'Connor." *Vanderbilt Lawyer* 37 (2). https://law.vanderbilt.edu/alumni/lawyer-vol37num2/news-oconnor.html; McFeatters, Ann Carey. 2005. *Sandra Day O'Connor: Justice in the Balance*. Albuquerque, NM: University of New Mexico Press.
7. For example, one poll showed that only 49 percent of respondents could identify a single case heard by the Supreme Court (CSPAN 2009) and more than half of respondents in another survey could not name a single Supreme Court Justice (Ford 2006).
8. Descriptive representation posits that representation takes place (or at least can take place) when "representatives are in their own persons and lives in some sense typical of the larger class of persons whom they represent" (Mansbridge 1999, 629). In the case of gender and representation, this typically means that women are represented by female elected representatives.
9. Greenhouse, Linda. 2007. "Justices' Ruling Limits Lawsuits on Pay Disparity." *New York Times,* May 30. http://query.nytimes.com/gst/fullpage.html?res=9505E4D81430 F933A05756C0A9619C8B63&scp=6&sq=ledbetter&st=nyt. The article the participants read was based very closely on this particular account of the decision. This case has come to be known as the Lilly Ledbetter case.

10. This is the condition that most closely mirrors reality, as it was Justice Samuel Alito (a man) who wrote the majority decision in the Lilly Ledbetter case, significantly restricting the time limit for suing. Justice Ruth Bader Ginsburg wrote the dissent.

11. MTurk is gaining legitimacy as a means of accessing relatively representative samples (Berinsky, Huber, and Lenz 2012). As such, my MTurk sample compared favorably to the nationally representative TESS sample on many key characteristics, if a bit more Democratic and slightly younger.

12. The sample's opinion regarding the majority and dissenting opinions mirrored public opinion following the actual Supreme Court decision. Congress and President Obama quickly acted to pass legislation that overturned the decision. Stolberg, Sheryl Gay. 2009. "Obama Signs Equal-Pay Legislation." *New York Times,* January 29. www. nytimes.com/2009/01/30/us/politics/30ledbetter-web.html?ref=lillymledbetter .

13. Even this is more complex than it seems, given that, in multiple regression models, different criteria predict support for the opinion based on whether it is the majority or minority opinion and, within each type of opinion, whether it is written by a male or female judge (Nelson 2015, 256–258).

14. Though, to be fair, probably with less potential as a source than the potential for female elected leaders to generate similar positive feelings, simply given the limited attention most individuals give to the court and its decisions. However, the potential for all these positive role models and influences to converge should not be understated.

15. This would be closer to previous studies that account for "dyadic descriptive representation," meaning that individuals are actually represented by someone who resembles them on key characteristics (e.g., Banducci, Donovan, and Karp 2004; Box-Steffensmeier et al. 2003; but see Tate 2003). Though, given the non-democratic nature of judges, the relationship between citizens and judges is distinct from that measured in these studies.

References

Ainsworth, Scott H. 2000. "Modeling Political Efficacy and Interest Group Membership." *Political Behavior* 22: 89–108.

Alexander, Deborah, and Kristi Andersen. 1993. "Gender as a Factor in the Attribution of Leadership Traits." *Political Research Quarterly* 46: 527–545.

Aliotta, Jilda M. 1995. "Justice O'Connor and the Equal Protection Clause: A Feminine Voice?" *Judicature* 78: 232–235.

Argetsinger, Amy, and Elizabeth Williamson. 2005. "O'Connor Successor Debated; Views Differ on Whether a Female Replacement Is Needed." *Washington Post*, July 3.

Atkeson, Lonna Rae, and Nancy Carrillo. 2007. "More Is Better: The Influence of Collective Female Descriptive Representation on External Efficacy." *Politics & Gender* 3: 79–101.

Baker, Peter. 2005. "Court Search Focuses on Women, Minorities." *Washington Post*, July 16.

Balch, George I. 1974. "Multiple Indicators in Survey Research: The Concept 'Sense of Political Efficacy'." *Political Methodology* 1: 1–43.

Banducci, Susan A., Todd Donovan, and Jeffrey A. Karp. 2004. "Minority Representation, Empowerment, and Participation." *Journal of Politics* 66: 534–556.

Bauer, Nichole. 2013. "Rethinking Stereotype Reliance: Understanding the Connection between Female Candidates and Gender Stereotypes." *Politics and the Life Sciences* 32: 22–42.

Beiner, Theresa M. 2003. "The Elusive (but Worthwhile) Quest for a Diverse Bench in the New Millennium." *University of California Davis Law Review* 36: 597–617.

Berinsky, Adam J., Gregory A. Huber, and Gabriel S. Lenz. 2012. "Evaluating Online Labor Markets for Experimental Research: Amazon.com's Mechanical Turk." *Political Analysis* 20: 351–368.

Box-Steffensmeier, Janet M., David C. Kimball, Scott R. Meinke, and Katherine Tate. 2003. "The Effects of Political Representation on the Electoral Advantages of House Incumbents." *Political Research Quarterly* 56: 259–270.

Boyd, Christina L. 2013. "She'll Settle It?" *Journal of Law and Courts* 1: 193–219.

———. 2015. "Representation on the Courts? The Effects of Trial Judges' Sex and Race." Paper Presented at the 2015 Midwest Political Science Association Annual Meeting, Chicago, IL.

Boyd, Christina L., Lee Epstein, and Andrew D. Martin. 2010. "Untangling the Causal Effects of Sex on Judging." *American Journal of Political Science* 54: 389–411.

Brooks, Deborah Jordan. 2011. "Testing the Double Standard for Candidate Emotionality: Voter Reactions to the Tears and Anger of Male and Female Politicians." *Journal of Politics* 73: 597–615.

Caldeira, Gregory A., and James L. Gibson. 1992. "The Etiology of Public Support for the Supreme Court." *American Journal of Political Science* 36: 635–664.

Clark, Tom S. 2009. "The Separation of Powers, Court Curbing, and Judicial Legitimacy." *American Journal of Political Science* 53: 971–989.

Converse, Philip E. 1972. "Change in the American Electorate." In *The Human Meaning of Social Change*, edited by Angus Campbell and Philip E. Converse, 263–337. New York: Russell Sage Foundation.

C-SPAN. 2009. "New C-SPAN/Penn, Schoen and Berland Associates Poll: What Americans Know about the U.S. Supreme Court and Want Changed about the Court." Accessed March 3, 2015. http://supremecourt.c-span.org/assets/pdf/CSPANSupremeCourtPollSept242009.pdf.

Dancey, Logan, Kjersten Nelson, and Eve Ringsmuth. 2011. "'Strict Scrutiny?' The Content of Senate Judicial Confirmation Hearings during the George W. Bush Administration." *Judicature* 95 (3): 126–135.

———. 2014. "Individual Scrutiny or Politics as Usual? Senatorial Assessment of US District Court Nominees." *American Politics Research* 42: 784–814.

Davis, Susan. 1993. "The Voice of Sandra Day O'Connor." *Judicature* 77: 134–139.

Deaux, Kay, and Laurie Lewis. 1984. "Structure of Gender Stereotypes: Interrelationships among Components and Gender Label." *Journal of Personality and Social Psychology* 46: 991–1004.

Dixon, Rosalind. 2010. "Female Justices, Feminism, and the Politics of Judicial Appointment: A Re-Examination." *Yale Journal of Law and Feminism* 21: 297–338.

Dolan, Kathleen A. 1998. "Voting for Women in the 'Year of the Woman'." *American Journal of Political Science* 42: 272–293.

———. 2010. "The Impact of Gender Stereotyped Evaluations on Support for Women Candidates." *Political Behavior* 32: 69–88.

———. 2012. "Political Gender Stereotypes and Voting for Women Candidates in 2010." Presented at the Annual Meeting of the Southern Political Science Association, New Orleans, LA.

———. 2014. *When Does Gender Matter? Women Candidates and Gender Stereotypes in American Elections*. Oxford: Oxford University Press.

Eagly, Alice H., and Steven J. Karau. 2002. "Role Congruity Theory of Prejudice toward Female Leaders." *Psychological Review* 109: 573–598.

Ford, William. 2006. "The Polls—Supreme Court Awareness." Accessed March 3, 2015. http://www.elsblog.org/the_empirical_legal_studi/2006/02/supreme_court_a.html.

Gilligan, Carol. 1982. *In a Different Voice: Psychological Theory and Women's Development.* Cambridge, MA: Harvard University Press.

Greenhouse, Linda. 2007. "Justices' Ruling Limits Lawsuits on Pay Disparity." *New York Times,* May 30.

Gruhl, John, Cassia Spohn, and Susan Welch. 1981. "Women as Policymakers: The Case of Trial Judges." *American Journal of Political Science* 25: 308–322.

High Pippert, Angela, and John Comer. 1998. "Female Empowerment: The Influence of Women Representing Women." *Women & Politics* 19: 53–67.

Huddy, Leonie, and Nayda Terkildsen. 1993. "Gender Stereotypes and the Perception of Male and Female Candidates." *American Journal of Political Science* 37: 119–147.

Jamieson, Kathleen Hall. 1995. *Beyond the Double Bind.* New York: Oxford University Press.

Johnson, Brian D. 2006. "The Multilevel Context of Criminal Sentencing: Integrating Judge- and County-Level Influences." *Criminology* 44: 259–298.

Kenney, Sally J. 2013. *Gender & Justice.* New York: Routledge.

Koch, Jeffrey W. 2000. "Do Citizens Apply Gender Stereotypes to Infer Candidates' Ideological Orientations?" *Journal of Politics* 62: 414–429.

Koenig, Anne M., Alice H. Eagly, Abigail A. Mitchell, and Tiina Ristikari. 2011. "Are Leader Stereotypes Masculine? A Meta-Analysis of Three Research Paradigms." *Psychological Bulletin* 137: 616–642.

Kritzer, Herbert M., and Thomas M. Uhlman. 1977. "Sisterhood in the Courtroom: Sex of Judge and Defendant in Criminal Case Disposition." *Social Science Journal* 14: 77–88.

Kunda, Ziva, and Steven Spencer. 2003. "When Do Stereotypes Come to Mind and When Do They Color Judgment? A Goal-Based Theoretical Framework for Stereotype Activation and Application." *Psychological Bulletin* 129: 522–544.

Lawless, Jennifer L. 2004. "Politics of Presence? Congresswomen and Symbolic Representation." *Political Research Quarterly* 57: 81–99.

Liptak, Adam. 2005. "O'Connor Leap Moved Women Up the Bench." *New York Times,* July 5.

Liptak, Adam. 2008. "Rendering Justice, With One Eye on Re-election." *New York Times.* Accessed March 15, 2016. http://www.nytimes.com/2008/05/25/us/25exception.html?_r=0.

Mansbridge, Jane. 1999. "Should Blacks Represent Blacks and Women Represent Women? A Contingent 'Yes'." *Journal of Politics* 61: 628–657.

Martin, Elaine. 1989. "Differences in Men and Women Judges: Perspectives on Gender." *Journal of Political Science* 17: 74–85.

Martin, Elaine, and Barry Pyle. 2005. "State High Courts and Divorce: The Impact of Judicial Gender." *University of Toledo Law Review* 36: 923–948.

Maveety, Nancy. 2010. "Difference in Judicial Discourse." *Politics & Gender* 6: 452–465.

McDermott, Monika L. 1997. "Voting Cues in Low-Information Elections: Candidate Gender as a Social Information Variable in Contemporary United States Elections." *American Journal of Political Science* 41: 270–283.

McFeatters, Ann Carey. 2005. *Sandra Day O'Connor: Justice in the Balance.* Albuquerque, NM: University of New Mexico Press.

Nelson, Kjersten. 2015. "Double-Bind on the Bench: Citizen Perceptions of Judge Gender and the Court." *Politics & Gender* 11: 235–264.

Niemi, Richard G., Stephen C. Craig, and Franco Mattei. 1991. "Measuring Internal Efficacy in the 1988 National Election Study." *American Political Science Review* 85: 1407–1413.

Ostberg, C. L., and Matthew Wetstein. 2007. *Attitudinal Decision Making in the Supreme Court of Canada.* Vancouver: University of British Columbia Press.

Peresie, Jennifer L. 2005. "Female Judges Matter: Gender and Collegial Decisionmaking in the Federal Appellate Courts." *Yale Law Journal* 114: 1759–1790.

Sanbonmatsu, Kira, and Kathleen Dolan. 2009. "Do Gender Stereotypes Transcend Party?" *Political Research Quarterly* 62: 485–494.

Scherer, Nancy, and Brett Curry. 2010. "Does Descriptive Race Representation Enhance Institutional Legitimacy? The Case of the U.S. Courts." *Journal of Politics* 72: 90–104.

Schneider, Monica C., and Angela L. Bos. 2013. "Measuring Stereotypes of Female Politicians." *Political Psychology* 35: 245–266.

Segal, Jeffrey A., Harold J. Spaeth, and Sara C. Benesh. 2005. *The Supreme Court in the American Legal System.* New York: Cambridge University Press.

Segal, Jeffrey A., Chad Westerland, and Stefanie A. Lindquist. 2011. "Congress, the Supreme Court, and Judicial Review: Testing a Constitutional Separation of Powers Model." *American Journal of Political Science* 55: 89–104.

Shapiro, Robert Y., and Harpreet Mahajan. 1986. "Gender Differences in Policy Preferences: A Summary of Trends from the 1960s to the 1980s." *Public Opinion Quarterly* 50: 42–61.

Sherry, Suzanne. 1986. "Civic Virtue and the Feminine Voice in Constitutional Adjudication." *Virginia Law Review* 72: 543–616.

Sotomayor, Sonia. 2002. "A Latina Judge's Voice." *Berkeley La Raza Law Journal* 13 (1): 87–93.

Spohn, Cassia. 1990. "Decision Making in Sexual Assault Cases: Do Black and Female Judges Make a Difference?" *Women & Criminal Justice* 2: 83–105.

Spohn, Cassia. 2009. *How Do Judges Decide? The Search for Fairness and Justice in Punishment.* Thousand Oaks, CA: Sage.

Steffensmeier, Darrell, and Chris Hebert. 1999. "Women and Men Policymakers: Does the Judge's Gender Affect the Sentencing of Criminal Defendants?" *Social Forces* 77: 1163–1196.

Stolberg, Sheryl Gay. 2009. "Obama Signs Equal-Pay Legislation." *New York Times,* January 29.

Tate, Katherine. 2003. *Black Faces in the Mirror: African Americans and Their Representatives in the U.S. Congress.* Princeton, NJ: Princeton University Press.

Valentino, Nicholas A., Krysha Gregorowicz, and Eric W. Groenendyk. 2009. "Efficacy, Emotions and the Habit of Participation." *Political Behavior* 31: 307–330.

Verba, Sidney, Kay Lehman Schlozman, and Henry Brady. 1995. *Voice and Equality: Civic Voluntarism in American Politics.* Cambridge, MA: Harvard University Press.

Westergren, Sarah. 2004. "Gender Effects in the Courts of Appeals Revisited: The Data since 1994." *Georgetown Law Journal* 92: 689–708.

14

CONCLUSION

Angela L. Bos and Monica C. Schneider

In the introduction, we argued that the interdisciplinary field of political psychology is uniquely positioned to help us understand the various gaps in attitudes and behavior between men and women, as well as how gender shapes political experiences in the U.S. more broadly. This volume fulfills this promise by providing syntheses of interdisciplinary research that can serve as a primer to new scholars and interested practitioners, while also laying out cutting-edge future research frontiers for scholars already versed in this research. Through studying a broad range of political outcomes—for example, party identification, activism and participation, attitudes towards policies, political ambition, candidate evaluations, efficacy, and perceptions of legitimacy—the authors underscored the ways in which political psychologists can contribute both theoretically and methodologically to our understanding of gender politics. To conclude, we discuss the broad implications across chapters.

One conclusion is that gender matters, but its effects vary based on context. For instance, in political campaigns, as Bauer shows, gender stereotypes do not matter unless activated, a conclusion that can be useful as we think forward to the 2016 presidential campaign. Similarly, the evaluations of judges may not differ by the gender of the judge unless they write an opinion that has a pro-female conclusion, in which case gender stereotypes will be invoked (Nelson). Women's behavior changes as a result of women's sensitivity to contextual factors. For instance, women's lack of political participation seems to be exacerbated by a context of self-objectification (Calogero) but improved by intervention attempts to socialize girls into activist traditions (Brinkman). Women's attention to close, personal relationships means that when they are asked by someone in their network, they will be more likely to consider a run for office (Sanbonmatsu and Carroll). In a final example, female legislators seem to behave differently than males in office, but these effects are contingent on the type of office, the legislator's party, the rules of the body, and whether or not their party is in the majority (Frederick and Jenkins). In short, gender matters, but scholars must pay attention to the particular contexts and circumstances in which it matters.

Moreover, future researchers should think carefully about the conceptualization and measurement of constructs and how they might affect their results. Multiple chapters challenge us to problematize political concepts such as political ambition (Kanthak, Sanbonmatsu, and Carroll) or political engagement (Brinkman) when they are defined by a male norm, as this renders the constructs insufficient for understanding women's actions. For example, Sanbonmatsu and Carroll argue that traditional theories of nascent political ambition based on education, occupation, self-interest, and opportunity do little to explain women's choices to run for office; instead, their Relationally Embedded Model re-conceptualizes the decision calculus to account for the ways in which women make decisions. In another chapter, Greenlee, Deason, and Langner outline a new construct—politicized motherhood—that captures the many ways that motherhood affects perceptions of candidates as well as candidates' strategies throughout political campaigns. Interdisciplinary research provides important opportunities to communicate with other scholars about how concepts are—or should be—conceptualized, measured, and experimentally manipulated.

This volume also demonstrates the many ways in which women are not a monolithic group. For instance, their status as mothers matters—not just for their political attitudes (Lizotte) but also for their campaign strategies and how those strategies are perceived (Greenlee, Deason, and Langner). Bejarano's chapter lays out a strong case for conceptualizing the intersection, rather than the sum, of two identities to better understand the unique combination of gender with other identities. Intersectionality is noted as a promising approach for future research in virtually all areas of study, but particularly important when thinking about stereotyping (Bauer), the gender gap in political issue positions (Lizotte), and youth socialization and girls' activism (Brinkman).

Related, we must also consider whether our observations occur at the appropriate point in the life cycle to understand the origins of gender gaps. Specifically, studying the early political and gender socialization process can help understand gender gaps in adults, yet not enough attention is paid to these processes. The Oxley and Brinkman chapters highlight the importance of examining these early years with regard to how children are socialized to politics—and how gender shapes that process. Kanthak highlights how longitudinal studies of children could help to get at the root of gender differences in political ambition while Calogero notes that we know little about how early socialization of self-objectification diminishes girls' political capacity.

Beyond explaining why we observe gender differences, this volume also illustrates how we might fruitfully explore gender differences by using multiple methodologies. In this volume, authors use precise laboratory experiments to observe causal mechanisms (e.g., Kanthak, Nelson), large-N representative samples to test psychological theories (e.g., Lizotte, Oxley), and pre-post designs that provide good external validity (e.g., Brinkman). By demonstrating the unique value of each of these methods, this volume can inspire future researchers to consider a broad range of methodologies to study gender.

Through methodological pluralism, combined with increased theoretical cross-fertilization with *other* fields such as economics and communication studies, we can build even stronger theories of human behavior. Kanthak's examination of political ambition illustrates this as it draws heavily on behavioral economic and psychological theory and methods, illustrating the promise in integrating the social sciences to understand gender differences in politics. Other chapters discuss the impact of media and campaign communication (e.g., Bauer, Greenlee et al.), underscoring the value of broader synthesis of political and psychological approaches with the field of communication.

Finally, this volume underscores how human psychology poses challenges to the creation of positive change for women. This is illustrated by the dire political consequences of sexual objectification in demotivating women's political participation (Calogero) and that women are unlikely to support redistributive policies that would be especially beneficial for them (Bullock and Reppond). Indeed, system justification and hierarchy-enhancing theories in psychology suggest that people, even those without power, are motivated to support the current societal structure, despite its many inequalities. Because women and other minorities are especially likely to demonstrate this tendency, it is all the more difficult to change women's subordinate status. In short, there are many psychological obstacles to effecting positive change for women that deserve further study.

Conclusion

As we began with the unique questions of gender in the 2016 presidential primaries, it seems fitting to end with a brief consideration of how this volume can help make sense of the gender dynamics in the race and the potential implications of electing the first woman president. Throughout the campaign, if feminine gender stereotypes are activated, for example through media coverage highlighting how Clinton is caring and sensitive, stereotypes might then negatively impact voter reactions to Clinton (Bauer). Greenlee, Langner, and Deason suggest that one way Clinton could boost evaluations would be to emphasize her role as a mother; it is speculative, but perhaps appearing with her grandchildren would have the same positive effect. The gender gap in political attitudes is likely to continue throughout the campaign; Clinton might see some success from appealing to women who are also mothers by emphasizing policies these women support, such as government spending on childcare and public schools as well as general government provisions of services (Lizotte).

If Clinton is elected as the first female president, this may affect children being socialized to politics. Perhaps mothers will be more likely to discuss politics with their children, thus increasing their impact on their children's political attitudes (Oxley). Moreover, role models can help young girls build social capital to participate in politics (Brinkman). Citizens may view Clinton's actions in a gendered light; for instance, if she issues an executive order on an issue linked to gender, female citizens might experience higher levels of efficacy, but voters in general might be more likely to use negative gender stereotypes in their evaluations of her (Nelson). Based on studies of legislators (Frederick and Jenkins), we might expect that the issues Clinton emphasizes might differ from her male predecessors, perhaps stemming from her life experiences and role as a woman. As such, women might gain in terms of both descriptive and substantive representation.

We believe this volume has illuminated the value of political psychology research to improve our understanding of the political experiences of women in the U.S. It is our hope that students and scholars of political science and psychology, as well as campaign strategists and journalists, can gain new understanding from this approach. Through building on the strengths of political science and psychology—both theoretically and methodologically—the chapters here offer promising results and future research avenues. In doing so, this volume provides a springboard for future research that can facilitate women's political representation in the United States.

INDEX

Note: Page numbers in *italics* indicate figures and tables.